Big Feelings

TRACKING POP

SERIES EDITORS: JOCELYN NEAL, JOHN COVACH, ROBERT FINK, AND LOREN KAJIKAWA

RECENT TITLES IN THE SERIES:

Big Feelings: Queer and Feminist Indie Rock After Riot Grrrl
by Dan DiPiero

Prince, Musical Genre, and the Construction of Racial Identity
by Griffin Woodworth

Owning My Masters (Mastered): The Rhetorics of Rhymes & Revolutions [Online Resource]
by A.D. Carson

The Bastard Instrument: A Cultural History of the Electric Bass
by Brian F. Wright

Tracks on the Trail: Popular Music, Race, and the US Presidency
by Dana Gorzelany-Mostak

Here for the Hearing: Analyzing the Music in Musical Theater
by Michael Buchler and Gregory J. Decker, Editors

Queer Voices in Hip Hop: Cultures, Communities, and Contemporary Performance
by Lauron J. Kehrer

Critical Excess: *Watch the Throne* and the New Gilded Age
by J. Griffith Rollefson

Soda Goes Pop: Pepsi-Cola Advertising and Popular Music
by Joanna K. Love

The Beatles through a Glass Onion: Reconsidering the White Album
edited by Mark Osteen

The Pop Palimpsest: Intertextuality in Recorded Popular Music
edited by Lori Burns and Serge Lacasse

Uncharted: Creativity and the Expert Drummer
by Bill Bruford

Big Feelings

Queer and Feminist Indie Rock After Riot Grrrl

Dan DiPiero

University of Michigan Press

Ann Arbor

Published in the United States of America by the
University of Michigan Press
First published October 2025

A CIP catalog record for this book is available from the British Library.

Library of Congress Control Number: 2025017476

ISBN 978-0-472-07770-0 (hardcover : alk. paper)
ISBN 978-0-472-05770-2 (paper : alk. paper)
ISBN 978-0-472-22234-6 (e-book)

Cover image: Illustration by Dan DiPiero.

This book will be made open access within three years of publication thanks to Path to Open, a program developed in partnership between JSTOR, the American Council of Learned Societies (ACLS), University of Michigan Press, and The University of North Carolina Press to bring about equitable access and impact for the entire scholarly community, including authors, researchers, libraries, and university presses around the world. Learn more at https://about.jstor.org/path-to-open/

Authorized Representative: Easy Access System Europe, Mustamäe tee 50, 10621 Tallinn, Estonia, gpsr.requests@easproject.com

To Hannah

To Christine

Contents

Digital materials related to this title can be found on the Fulcrum platform via the following citable URL: https://doi.org/10.3998/mpub.12792008

Figures

Acknowledgments

I can remember the first time I tried to write about rock music. I was visiting my Nonna in Boardman, Ohio, in the condo development she had moved into after many decades in the same home. In the afternoon, I walked down to the little manmade pond, jotting observations with a pencil and legal pad, surprising myself. I remember being concerned with how bands like Linkin' Park and Limp Bizkit sounded different from bands like Soundgarden and Nirvana, which probably puts the memory between 1998 and 2000—I would have been between twelve and fourteen. I am confident that whatever I wrote was supremely uninspired; but I remember clearly how thrilling it felt in that moment to write it, how excited I was to see myself seeing, observing something (semi)coherent and articulable about what I had previously simply immersed myself in—the videos I watched late at night on MuchMusic, coming into our basement TV from up north. I held onto those pages for a long time, passively, stuffed into one of the many CD wallets I carried around through my high school and college years. I can't find them today, but those folded yellow squares have become so symbolic in my memory because they're one of those clues about my life that only makes sense in retrospect—after decades of playing music, professional flailing, and academic writing about genres other than rock, it feels appropriate, knowing what I know about myself, that it took me some twenty years to find my way back to where I started. This book feels like a homecoming for that reason, although I am grateful for how much I've changed in the interim.

I am extremely fortunate to have many people to thank for helping this book come into its own, colleagues and friends who have contributed to this project with their thoughts and feedback, both formal and informal, whether at conferences or one on one. These include Morgan Bimm, Amy Coddington, Sara Jo Cohen, Christine Capetola, Theo Cateforis, Jael Goldfine, Norm

Hirschy, Robin James, Raechel Anne Jolie, Jacob Kopcienski, Patrick Nickleson, Brad Osborn, Hannah Segrave, Barry Shank, Amy Skjerseth, and Alyx Vesey. Christine, Raechel, and Hannah were particularly involved in the beginning stages, helping me to understand what I was trying to say. Brad was critical at the end, graciously helping with a last-minute, music-theoretical panic, and greatly improving the second chapter. Barry, Christine, Raechel, and Eleanor Paynter read (and thought with, and talked with me about) entire drafts of this book, a true gift for which I thank them most sincerely. And on that note, my deepest gratitude goes to an absolute dream team of initially anonymous peer reviewers for this book: each of them has, along with my early readers, strengthened this project in deeply substantial, absolutely concrete ways, from proposal to final manuscript. What you are reading would not be here as such without their help, which was sharper and more generous than I could have dared hope of anyone.

Since 2021, several conferences and the communities that compose them have been critical in strengthening both my ideas and my overall spirit, including IASPM-US, American Musicological Society, American Studies Association, and Pop Con. Thanks to everyone I met and spoke with about Big Feelings, and to the broader pop music studies communities that have helped me feel so welcome. In addition to those mentioned above, Elizabeth Ault, Lydia Bangura, Varun Chandrasekhar, Jacob Cupps, Norma Coates, Kyle DeCoste, Stephanie Doktor, Emily Gale, Kaleb Goldschmitt, Paula Harper, Kwame Harrison, Eric Harvey, Jessica Holmes, Phoebe Hughes, Lauron Kehrer, AJ Kluth, Jonathan Leal, Danielle Fosler-Lussier, Matthew Jones, Lee Kimura Tyson, Andrew Mall, Elliott Powell, Antonia Randolph, Francesca Royster, Victor Szabo, Mikkel Vad, Steve Waksman, Eric Weisbard, Brian Wright, and many more people are incredibly inspiring colleagues with whom I am so happy to be connected. I must also express my boundless and warmest gratitude to the budding crush collective , who have done so much to make me feel like I belong in the place I want to, have made that place with me. I am perpetually crushing on your brilliance and your friendship.

Among this wonderful group of popular music scholars, readers will see Christine Capetola's name repeated again and again, reflecting the fact that, since we met in 2017, they were my first-call reader, a friend and fellow traveler whom I trusted completely with drafty work, experimental thoughts, and timid feelings. Around a month before I turned this book in, Christine passed suddenly and unexpectedly, shaking our little corner of the world. It was in Christine's 2020 article on Janet Jackson that I first read the phrase "feminist affect," which has become fundamental to this project; my thinking would simply not be what it is without them. Thank you, Christine. We miss you.

Many happy thank-yous go to the Ophelias—Mic Adams, Andrea Gutmann Fuentes, Spencer Peppet, and Jo Shaffer—for talking with me at length for this project, for their music, and for their spirit: generous, kind, anti-capitalist. Likewise, every listener who I spoke with for this project was tremendously helpful, and I thank them each for their earnest engagement with my questions: Abby, Alyssa, Beth, Cameron, Chris, Dan, Deanna, Destiny, Elysium, Izzy, Katie, Sam, Sara, Stephen, Tom, as well as many other listeners I talked to in more informal ways, including Jael, Jane, Maya, Varun and many more.

I have been thrilled to once again work with the folks at University of Michigan Press. In particular, Sara Cohen has again been an ideal collaborator, whose enthusiasm and vision for this book have made all the difference. Thanks also to Annie Carter, Danielle Coty-Fattal, Kianna Delly, Michael Hylton, Delilah McCrea, Matthew Somoroff, Amaranth Tupelo, Haley Winkle, as well as the Tracking Pop team, including Jocelyn Neal, lead editor for this project.

This book really found its footing while I was teaching at Ithaca College. I want to thank all my colleagues there—particularly Sara Haefeli, Alex Reed, Elizabeth Medina-Gray, and Peter Silberman—for their trust and support. Thanks especially to Sara, who taught me so much during that year, and spent a great deal of her own time doing so. I also want to thank my students at Ithaca, particularly those who volunteered their time to talk with me about indie bands. Your enthusiasm and brilliance enriched my short time upstate. Now at UMKC, I've landed on my feet only with the help of incredible new colleagues and friends. Stewart Duncan, Jane Sylvester, and Noel Torres-Rivera make coming to work joyful, and though I see them less regularly outside of our little hallway, I am also very grateful to Andrew Granade and Alison DeSimone for their continued friendship and support. Here too, I have been blessed with fantastic students, and I thank them all for helping me feel welcome in this community—with particular thanks again to those who agreed to be interviewed for this book.

My Ohio communities continue to be a central source of family, strength, and inspiration. Thanks to Philip Armstrong for unflagging, constant support, and for dramatically altering my life trajectory by introducing me to the Ophelias. Additional cheers to John Brooks, Danielle Fosler-Lussier, Gene Holland, Erica Levin, Danny Marcus, Ryan Skinner, Lucy Zimmerman, and my now/again colleague Deja Beamon. Through everything, Barry Shank has remained a most constant friend and mentor, a total role model, fellow Scorpio, and source of my most weightily regarded opinions—I'm so grateful to continue thinking with you, so proud to have been your student.

The porch swing at 2915, Dottie the cat, Alex Burgoyne, and Devin Copfer have all been critical for this book and for my life, collectively a second home without which I would be so much less of myself. As ever, Alex, Devin, Josh Bryant, Abhilasha Chebolu, Sydney McSweeny, Kayla Sadowy, Andrew Sais, and the Columbus music community fill my cup—likewise Dunkle (Gennaro Di Tosto and Eleanor Paynter), and my hometown heroes (Joseph Mastrantoni, Akshai Singh, Courtney Yergin, Tom Kychun). Thank you to Jeff Laser for the Indigo/Ophelias tickets, and for always nerding out with me. Thank you to Abhi for help with guitar voicings and for understanding what I mean about the Pumpkins. I also owe a lot to J. R. Jaffe, and in many ways. Perhaps most pertinently, they introduced me to Yuck, whose music helped set into motion the thinking that has resulted in this book.

Big thanks to my family—Darien, Frank, and Justin—for every manner of support, and lots of fun besides. Likewise to Segrave City, progenitors of all the good chaos in my life. Finally and always my deepest gratitude goes to Hannah, in part for the ways in which our partnership has helped me understand my changing self, more and differently every year. So much of what I care about in this world has come into my life because of her, and I am just tremendously proud of how far we've come just since the last time I wrote in this genre, both professionally and personally. So lucky / to be / the one you run to see.

This work has been supported by an American Musicological Society Career Development Grant in American Music, as well as travel support from the Dr. Elizabeth Noble fund at UMKC. An early version of Chapter Two appeared as Dan DiPiero, "'I Wanna Be That Cool': Soccer Mommy's Big Feelings," *Journal of Popular Music Studies* 35, no. 2 (2023): 39–65. Before that, a (very) early sketch of the introduction was published as Dan DiPiero, "Big Feelings: Feminist Affect in Indie Rock After 2000," *Journal of Popular Music Studies* 33, no. 4 (2021): 16–22. Thanks again to those everyone reviewed, selected, and improved my work throughout each of these stages.

This book is dedicated to my partner Hannah, so instrumental in helping me become the person who could write this book, and to Christine, my friend, who should be here to read it.

Introduction

The Unspeakable

Articulating the feeling is hard
When it's so dense and familiar
—Great Grandpa[1]

On a January night in 2014, I had just had the best first date of my life splitting spicy pig intestine at a Cleveland spot called Szechuan Gourmet. Afterward, as I was driving us back to the west side via Carnegie, the final track from Yuck's 2011 self-titled debut started filling up my 2007 Honda Fit, an enormous sound for such a small car, and too cold for the windows to come down. In my memory, we sat in complete silence while the guitars steadily dug in, over the course of seven long minutes, unearthing every feeling they could find buried in my chest and inflating them to the point of bursting. But then again, in my memory, I can also hear Hannah telling me how much she loves this song, so that one of those feelings getting amplified and unbearable was the one that would help me to know with a laughable certainty, some scant weeks later, that the person in my passenger seat was it for me.

I didn't feel quite *so* intensely every time I listened to "Rubber"—but almost. Part of what made the above listening experience so poignant has to do with how the music brought back into my life a sound I immediately recognized as formative. In other words, I heard something in both that song and in the album it closed that was different from other types of rock music, a sound that I associated closely with my childhood, with my most formative adolescent experiences, and with the music that got me through them. It wasn't the sound of just any rock, but a particular strain that I first heard as a kid growing up in the 1990s, a certain kind of indie or grunge that I associate with bands like Pavement, Hole, and Nirvana. It was exciting and meaning-

1. From "Human Condition," track 9 on *Four of Arrows* (2019).

ful to me that a band in 2011 was not only reviving those sounds but contributing to the development of that vocabulary by writing such a great record. I didn't know how to talk about what that sound was or why it mattered so much to me—but I kept thinking about it in the background while I went through grad school, finished my PhD, and started writing my first book. The "revival" of '90s rock that I heard in Yuck is one important moment in the development of this second project and its titular concept: Big Feelings.

Probably the first moment that matters in this trajectory happened much earlier, around 1995. I was playing at my friend Jimmy's house, where he had the radio tuned to "Cleveland's rock alternative: 107.9 'The End.'" At some point during an afternoon of video games, backyard exploration, and hanging out with Jimmy's two cats (Pie and Minski), what I today know as the Smashing Pumpkins' "1979" froze me in my tracks. In my head, I'm looking at the corner of the living room couch. This is a memory both incomplete and clear: what I have is basically a single frame, the room as it was set up, from the angle where I was standing in place, completely captivated by what I was hearing. As so often happened in those days, the song soon gave way to another, and another, lost in an unknowable succession. At nine years old, I was too young to know how to track it down. It wasn't until years later that I would find out what that song was called, and that the band who made it had lots of other music besides.

The Smashing Pumpkins are important to this story not only because they became a critical first step in my development as a rock fan, but also because their music in particular trained me to obsess about my feelings. It's true that, as a white boy in the suburbs, many of those feelings corresponded with the tropes of normative masculine adolescence. But the very idea that I imagined my own feelings as important—worth dwelling on, expressing, and sharing—that alone matters for how it started to put me at a certain kind of odds with heteronormative masculinity, or put differently, with the other boys around me. Listening to the Pumpkins rendered feeling deeply not just worthwhile but *heroic*. While the melodramatic, embarrassingly bald earnestness of Billy Corgan's lyrics contributes to a complicated (often problematic) set of implications (about which more later), for me, one of the ways the music succeeds is by effectively performing the interior life of adolescence, wherein feelings are experienced at the kind of high volume that the Pumpkins' baroque excess itself generates.

In my case, because of a variety of lucky factors in my life, taking my own feelings seriously opened up the potential for something I would only realize years later, helping me to eventually recognize and name the type of masculinity that tormented me throughout my youth, that caused kids I admired to bully me, that irrevocably marked my personality even as I belatedly endeavored to explore other ways of being. Touched by the culture in which I was raised, I continue at times to have difficulty expressing and managing my feelings. But the importance of doing so, and of caring for the feelings of others, has become central in my life in no small part because of music like this. It isn't that music caused this change in me, but that it functioned as a gateway—one of surely any number—toward valuing things that US patriarchal culture does not.[2] As much as the music, it is the status of feelings vis-à-vis patriarchy that forms the basis for this study.

The third moment that clicked this project into focus came in 2019, when I found a multimedia package *The New York Times* had published two years earlier. Titled "Women Are Making the Best Rock Music Today: Here Are The Bands That Prove It" (Coscarelli 2017), the print, audio, and visual project is given an impressive and almost epiphanic treatment—but, as writers Jenn and Liz Pelly later point out, its framing is also (predictably) problematic (in Caramanica 2017). By the time I discovered this package, I had finished my PhD, and had spent several years studying and teaching the aesthetics and politics of the riot grrrl movement—a movement that I had not known growing up, but which I found deeply compelling as an adult trying to, as Sara Ahmed puts it, live a feminist life (2017). Through feminist media scholarship, I had also learned how the "women in rock" trope here recuperated by the *Times* has an exhausting history, one that, despite how almost comically clichéd it has become, never loses its potential to temper the musical and social efficacy of the music it is ostensibly invested in praising (Coates 1997; Davies 2001; Fournier 2015). As many scholars have shown, to identify "women in rock" not only reduces diverse musical projects to the single commonality of gender identity, but also reinscribes their exclusion by positioning them as not belonging to rock in the first place—hence the perceived need to specifically identify when they do appear. The problem here is not the *Times*' identification of the fact that women and queer musicians are making a ton of amazing music right now; the problem is that there would never be a multimedia package celebrating "men" or "white dudes in rock." The suggestion is on its face preposterous.

Begrudgingly, I also noted at the time how much of the music included in the *Times*' package was music I found very compelling. Moreover, I was

2. Though ostensibly concerned with moods, affects, and emotions, what the contemporary vibes economy values is the ability to measure and modulate feeling, rather than the experience of feeling itself. It will not explore an emotion with you in order to help you better understand yourself and others; it will sell your own experience back to you, advertising products that correspond with a given genre.

admittedly struck by the fact that it seemed to be coming into the world all at once, and often enough with the same kind of captivatingly nostalgic lean that Yuck had revived some ten years earlier. I was loving Soccer Mommy's *Clean*, the Beths' *Future Me Hates Me*, and had been listening to Snail Mail for some time already. I started thinking about other groups as well: Girlpool, Fazerdaze, and Great Grandpa, as well as earlier precedents that the *Times* implicitly writes out of history, including P.S. Eliot, Wye Oak, Broken Social Scene, and Land of Talk.

The release of the *Times* package is significant for this project not because I endorse its framing, but because it signals that even mainstream news outlets understand that something is happening in indie rock,[3] a shift that has seen women, trans, gender-nonconforming, and otherwise queer musicians—basically everybody *but* cis white guys—move to the front of the cultural conversation about rock music. Importantly, I also hear these musicians *reformulating what rock means*. In this book, I suggest that this wave of new rock musicians *does* constitute an important intervention into indie history—and though this intervention often takes on consistent sonic characteristics (particularly around the revival of a certain '90s rock sound), it is also multifaceted, approached in unique ways by each artist I discuss. From this hypothesis comes a series of associated questions: is there something about this shift to a '90s rock sound that has to do with the fact that so many bands performing it this time around are not straight dudes? What exactly is *that sound* that I find so affecting across so many of these bands? Finally, in the years since the mainstream press widely understood the riot grrrl movement to have given way to postfeminist "girl power" pop music, what happened to feminism in indie rock *after* riot grrrl?

Big Feelings grapples with such questions by exploring a certain kind of indie rock and the ways that it matters to people. I start with such personal narratives because I want to be clear that I am not exempted from the "people" about whom I am writing. In other words, I do not approach this topic from the measured distance of a dispassionate analyst, but rather from a position of certain intimacy. In my own listening journey, the older I got and the more I understood about my own revulsion toward normative/aggressive masculinity, the more alienated I felt from the sounds that I had grown up loving. For this millennial listener, then, the artists that I write about in this book have allowed me to love rock music again. The revised revival of these sounds and the reappropriations that artists are consciously exercising brings

3. "Indie" and "indie rock" are both contested categories whose boundaries can't necessarily be assumed and which I take up further in the following chapter.

aesthetics and politics into alignment in ways that matter to me, that make indie rock feel *for me* in a way that it hadn't since I was young and different from how I understand myself today. Curious about other listeners—particularly the young fans who share a generational cohort with the artists themselves—I started working on this project in earnest.

My personal investment in the music also matters insofar as the work I discuss throughout this book is both feminist and queer: it is axiomatic in feminist scholarship, queer theory, critical race theory, and adjacent cultural-studies disciplines that epistemologies are socially situated, that claims of objectivity do less to illuminate than they do obscure how sociopolitical categories shape what counts as knowledge in a particular milieu. Beyond aligning with my values, then, queer-feminist and intersectional methodologies are also necessary in my attempt to do the music—as well as those who make and listen to it—some justice.

Slightly less than case studies, this book explores key thematics performed by artists and bands like Land of Talk, Soccer Mommy, Indigo De Souza, Mitski, Jay Som, SASAMI, the Ophelias, Vagabon, boygenius, and more. Throughout, the argument I present is that their music produces powerful queer-feminist affects that draw in and foster certain political orientations,[4] but that a critical aspect of this dynamic is that it happens indirectly, primarily through a focus on the ostensibly abstract/personal subject of *feelings*. Put another way, while it is easy to read this music as apolitical on the surface, listeners and musicians alike nevertheless recognize its affective pull, its capacity to foster community and consciousness around issues disproportionately affecting minoritized subjects, and the ways that musical affects perform the kind of social catharsis that writers like Sara Ahmed (2014), Lauren Berlant (2008) and Ann Cvetkovich (2003) have variously theorized as a kind of "public feeling." Following this work suggests that part of the reason this music resonates in the ways that it does has to do with the social context in which it sounds, a political backdrop of normal, unceasing crisis for young people globally, and in the United States, uniquely. Like feelings themselves, the issues with which this music grapples may be more easily felt than articulated.

4. In using terms like "orientation," and "obliqueness," I'm invoking Sara Ahmed's work, particularly in *Queer Phenomenology* (2006), where she expands the notion of sexual orientation almost literally, theorizing subjectivity in part as a matter of how one moves through the world.

Big Feelings as Concept

I am not the only one to have noticed an increasing turn toward feelings in American popular culture, nor even the only one to name it as I have; for example, in February 2021, as I was sitting on an early draft of this work, journalist Laura Snapes published "Big Feelings and Nowhere to Go: How Gen Z Reinvented the Power Ballad" in *The Guardian*. The piece focuses much of its attention on Olivia Rodrigo's just-released smash, "Driver's License," reading it as broadly reflective of Generation Z's attempts to grapple with their experience of the world. Also citing Phoebe Bridgers, Jensen McRae, and Claud (among others), Snapes writes that "Rodrigo is the flag-bearer for a wave of predominantly young women, non-binary and queer songwriters penning power ballads that are as emotional as ever, but project that emotion inward, trading bombast for hush" (2021). This increased emphasis on emotional vulnerability in pop music, Snapes writes, has to a certain extent replaced (or at least supplemented) the previous emphasis on "empowerment"—what Robin James calls "resilience" (2015)—reflecting an overall cultural climate in which young people's mental-health struggles, in the face of successive sociopolitical crises, have become overdeterminative. Rather than limiting their emotional focus to matters of heartbreak, Emily Gale (2023), Kate Hamori (2023), and others have connected young people's introspection to larger structural issues, demonstrating how Rodrigo represents "a generation of fiercely soft youth who have chosen to speak forcefully and publicly about their experiences of violence, patriarchy, mental health, the climate crisis, global capitalism, and the connections between them" (Gale 2023). Honing in more specifically on experiences of depression, Jessica Holmes (2023) has also focused on negative affects in Billie Eilish's music, perhaps the artist most responsible for mainstreaming frank discussions of mental health struggles in the upper tiers of US popular music.

Relatedly, Big Feelings is also connected to "sad girl indie," understood as "female and femme indie rock artists who decline feminine performances of optimism, positivity, and confidence that girl power norms render compulsory for young women" (Goldfine 2017). Using Mitski and Frankie Cosmos as case studies, Jael Goldfine tracks negative affects across indie rock artists who predate those whom Snapes observes turning toward vulnerability and feeling across pop music writ large; these earlier artists set a kind of precedent or permission structure for more mainstream artists to tap into. But for Goldfine, popular culture's current, widespread adoption of vulnerability as valuable represents an appropriation of sad girl indie's insistence on sitting with negative feelings (2019). Indeed, as scholars have shown, popular feminist cultures value vulnerability only to the extent that it helps to shore up resilience narratives (Ciccone 2020; Orgad and Gill 2022; Thelandersson 2023).[5] Today these dynamics take place in a post-lockdown context where discussions of mental/emotional health and queer-feminist approaches to care have become more generalized, meeting up with pop-psychology treatments, therapy frameworks, and children's books that also index emotional literacy with the idea of "big feelings." Fellow '90s music obsessive Rob Harvilla's book, *60 Songs That Explain the '90s*, includes a final chapter titled "Big Feelings," again with a nod to children (but this time more from a parent's point of view). Finally, Willow Smith deploys a McFerrin-adjacent prog/soul backdrop for 2024's "b i g f e e l i n g s" to further demonstrate how the term has traveled, becoming a general cultural reference for any navigation of overwhelming experiences that refuses simple repression or denial.

Each of the above examples—as well as the general cultural mainstreaming of the language of mental health—deeply inform this project, even as my version of Big Feelings aims to describe something in some ways more limited and in others more expansive. On the one hand, this book focuses on how a turn to feeling manifests in indie rock particularly, rather than popular music writ large. On the other, I am interested in the ways that Big Feelings artists seem to dial up and center feelings in general, whether negative, positive, or in many cases, ambivalent. In other words, *Big Feelings* is concerned not just with negative affects or even emotional disclosure in indie rock, but rather with locating how the performance of public feeling resonates in nuanced ways with listeners,[6] particularly feminist and queer listeners who

5. This progression or cycle mandated by "confidence culture" (Orgad and Gill 2022)—from vulnerability to confidence—mirrors what Robin James has pointed out about "resilience" discourse (2015): in spite of its ostensible focus on empowerment, resilience first *requires* damage in order for women to performatively overcome obstacles. That there remain plentiful challenges thrown at women and other minoritized subjects under white supremacist patriarchies is not a point often interrogated by such empowerment discourses.

6. Recent scholarship has further developed "resonance" as a key heuristic for theorizing contingent connections across disparate spatio-temporal locations (Lordi 2013; Napolin 2020). A term based in acoustics, "resonance" references the kind of "sympathetic vibrations" that can occur when two sounding bodies are in proximity and share certain natural harmonics produced by their physical construction. The natural harmonics of one body will sound when they come into contact with corresponding vibrational forces from the another. (The clearest example from my own life happens every time I leave the wires engaged on my snare drum—they always buzz of their own accord when other instruments in the band play certain notes, automatically and often annoyingly responding to frequencies from other instruments.) Rich with theoretical possibility, resonance is essentially relational, the "physical, social, linguistic, and psychological fact of the more than one" (Napolin 2020, 4).

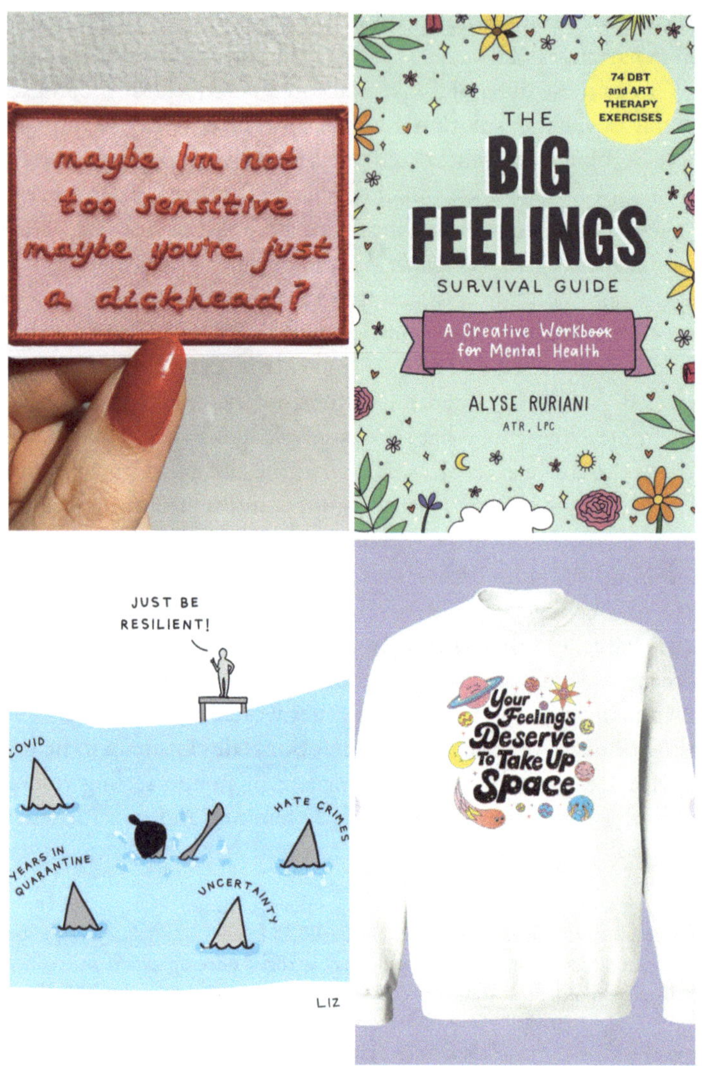

Figure 1. Clockwise from upper left: sticker by Sophie King; art therapy workbook by Alyse Ruriani; sweater from @selfcareisforeveryone; illustration from Liz Fosslien and Mollie West Duffy's *Big Feelings: How to Be Okay When Things Are Not Okay*

are exhausted by the world at the same time that they strive to build their own joyful spaces within it. This also matters insofar as previous "women in rock" discourses have flattened artistic contributions down to a single emotional affect (namely, "anger") as an extension of the effort to isolate the music as somehow aberrant in the genre.[7] In contrast to reductive readings of this kind of indie rock as sad girl music, I suggest that even loud, dramatic, and aggressive Big Feelings music has more in common with femme performances of "softness," which subsequent chapters will explore as "both a politically informed aesthetic and a code of conduct in femme Internet culture" (Schwartz 2020, 2). In soft femme cultures, all feelings are always already valid, worth exploring, and *important* as structuring experiences in the world. In response to capitalist patriarchy's diminishment and demeaning of emotions—particularly those felt by women and queer folks—Big Feelings expands whole aesthetic worlds around them, taking joy as seriously as pain, and tying that full spectrum of feeling to concrete understandings of the collective social experiences that inform it.

At the nexus of non-normative identification with the world and a certain indie-rock sound sits Big Feelings—not a genre, but an affect produced within a genre. As affect, it can't be boiled down to a particular musical gesture, lyrical subject, or any other one factor that is definitively identifiable. It instead emerges through the collective interplay of several elements I discuss further below, including the central role of women and queer musicians; subject matter that remains at first glance "abstract" or "personal"; a 1990s-inflected approach to rock musical vocabulary; tuneful, catchy melodies; and an affective overloading of sonic space that serves to physically manifest emotional experience. This "overloading" is often achieved through the presence of "excess" chord tones that I argue—particularly in combination with these other characteristics—carry a feminist political valence. Importantly, while the feelings being staged by Big Feelings bands *are* political, many musicians decline to discuss them as such, instead maintaining the possibility of reading such emotions as apolitical, or "merely personal."

The feelings conjured by Big Feelings artists are consistently performed in ways that evoke and often reify experiences of overwhelm. This is one of

---

7. On the overdetermination of women playing rock by discursive appeals to "anger," see Schilt (2003); Fisher (2013); Fournier (2015). Following Ahmed's reading of Audre Lorde (particularly in "The Uses of Anger"), the issue with the press' dismissal of women playing rock via the trope of anger is not the identification of anger per-se but the treatment of anger as trivial rather than justified, critically useful, and world-making. "Indeed, historically, the reading of feminism as a form of anger allows the dismissal of feminist claims, even when the anger is a reasonable response to social injustice" (Ahmed 2014, 177).

many factors that varies from artist to artist, given their unique approach: some, like Soccer Mommy, represent intensity of feeling through a kind of dissociated flatness, signaling a state in which feeling has become too much for the narrator to sustain. Bands like Bully, Mannequin Pussy, and Wednesday are more literal, performing the size of their emotions through walls of distorted sound, faders all in the red.[8] By slowing down and turning up, or by adding lush harmonic layers on top of one another, this kind of indie rock heightens and variously intensifies the experience of being inside of a given feeling, thus bringing listeners (back) into the quintessentially teenaged condition whereby one's own feelings seem to carry outsized weight—seem to be and thus effectively become the center of one's universe. In doing so, this music insists on the validity of those feelings well beyond adolescence, asserting the wisdom of young people who don't yet know to discount their own responses to the world. In the same way that adolescent feelings can become so intense as to take on physical force, this kind of indie rock creates sounds that threaten to do the same, to materially embody the experience of feeling fiercely. Hence: Big Feelings.

Methods

In this book I employ methods from the overlapping fields of affect theory, cultural studies, and popular music studies. I also supplement these frameworks with ethnographic conversations that have proven critical for both testing and nuancing my theses. I say "conversations" (rather than "interviews") in an effort to be transparent about how I approached this aspect of the work, which I positioned from the beginning as a dialogue among fellow fans. Rather than structure questions around more objective/neutral attempts at analysis, and rather than solicit all kinds of social-science data about the people I spoke with, my aim was to work collaboratively with respondents, to bounce ideas off one another in pursuit of a common excitement. Throughout, my questions were less concerned with diagnosing the nuts and bolts of what this music is, who listens to it (and so on) than they were with helping create a space where listeners could share with me how they experience the qualities of the music that I found compelling, that I suspected were relevant to their lives as mostly young and queer fans. To achieve this, interviews were approached explicitly as unstructured con-

8. For a provisional list of Big Feelings artists, see Appendix A. For two playlists, see Appendix C.

versations where my own fandom was self-evident and a part of how I engaged respondents.[9]

My understanding of affect is indebted to scholarship emerging from queer theory, music and sound studies, as well as affect theory itself, including the work of Sara Ahmed (2006; 2014), Lauren Berlant (2008; 2011), Christine Capetola (2020), Ann Cvetkovich (2003), Greg Seigworth and Melissa Gregg (2010), Kara Keeling (2019), Brain Massumi (2002; 2015), Dylan Robinson and Patrick Nickleson (2023), Kathleen Stewart (2007), Chris Stover (2017), and Marie Thompson (2017; Thompson and Biddle 2013). I would characterize these uses, in spite of some differences, along a Deleuzean axis, which is to say that they are primarily concerned with thinking through the consequences of one body's capacity to affect another and to be affected in return, where "body" is understood as anything that exerts force. Fundamentally relational, affect attends to the singularity and indeterminacy of these forces as they are embodied in a particular situation, or more to the point, as they bring about the situation as such. In the order of that previous sentence, affect is concerned with singularity (because it is understood as the unique feeling, sense, or effect that distinguishes one situation from every other); indeterminacy (because, in spite of how we may study, participate in, or describe that situation, there is no perspective from which we could possibly "capture" or fully exhaust affect's complexity); and embodiment in a moment (because the "same" forces manifest differently in each situation that brings them into being, because the participants in a situation react to any force in their own unique ways). Because both affects and emotions have to do with what a body experiences, they are clearly caught up in each other; but beyond their similarities, the former is particularly useful when trying to identify a feeling of which we aren't (yet or explicitly) conscious. Like the bodily shock that results from a suddenly slamming door, we feel forces more quickly and less rationally than we might have time or space to fully cognize. In this way, affect is related to but not identical with sense and sensation, emotion(s) and feeling(s).

I find it most useful to distinguish affect from feeling and emotion insofar as that distinction helps me to trace what musicians are doing that might not be consciously enacted, or else which might hit listeners in ways that they can't necessarily pin down. Put differently, I believe that music affects us in ways that we can't always articulate or even consciously attend to, and this is as true for the artists who make it as for the listeners who feel it. Therefore, affect can be useful in talking about the unspoken feelings that music con-

9. See Appendix D for further information on respondents and methodology.

nects across bodies, even when they are not literally or obviously present in the lyrics, sounds, or artistic intentions involved. That being said, however, for the remainder of this book, I will largely decline to distinguish among "affect," "feeling," and "emotion," using whichever word feels most appropriate and sometimes interchanging them. I do this intentionally, because, for however helpful distinguishing these ideas might be *conceptually*, I follow Sara Ahmed in considering them to be caught up in one another as they are actually lived and experienced (Ahmed 2014). Like Ahmed, I'm uninterested in separating out affect from emotion precisely because "consciousness and intentionality, on the one hand, and physiological or bodily reactions on the other" (208) can't be so cleanly disentangled—and because emotions are not per-se reducible to subjective, internal reactions (but are rather, following Ahmed, scaffolded into socially constructed genres of feeling). My gamble is that the productive conflation of sense, feeling, emotion, and affect will allow for more resonance than would be possible through a fixation on definitions and strict adherence to analytical categories. In this I hope to follow not only Ahmed but also the feminist traditions upon which she draws, including the work of Arlie Hochschild, bell hooks, Audre Lorde, and more.

Affect's close links to and conflations with matters of feeling brings it into natural proximity with feminist studies, although not without some difficulty. As Brigitte Bargetz writes, on the one hand, "emotions and the body have always been of major interest within feminist theory and philosophy, challenging main- and malestream understandings of the subject, politics, critique, and knowledge production" (2015, 581). On the other hand, Bargetz explains, is a debate surrounding affect's potential as a political force, which in her view has been taken up by feminist theorists in ways that too often problematically celebrate what is at the end of the day a neutral concept. For Bargetz as for myself (and I believe, the authors mentioned above), affect is a particularly complicated theory to use in search of emancipatory politics, because affect simply concerns forces present in a situation. Instead of an inherent progressiveness, then, affect names whatever forces happen to be experienced by those present in a circumstance—positive, negative, or both.

Even so, as Ana Hofman writes, in a time characterized by "political exhaustion," music scholars have turned to affect as a promising framework for elaborating how politics is not reducible to a given "message" as well as to "fashion new readings of the political in which the commercial or trivial is not in opposition to the emancipatory or engaged" (2020, 308). While Hofman writes that such approaches clearly shed new light on the relationships between music and social experience, she also argues that "in the search for the political potentiality of aural experience," music scholars have paid less attention to the ways in which affect is mobilized as a technology of control, or in service of the maintenance of current power relations (309). These concerns resonate with Bargetz's qualified embrace of affect as contingent and relational rather than a kind of panacea or liberatory force.

Progressive or oppressive and all points in between, affect references every force that particularizes a given situation in a moment, producing its haecceity by tying things together in motion. As such, it is always built from the terms of a given sense distribution, such that even when it articulates a desire for freedom, it always does so in the language of what Jacques Rancière calls the "police."[10] Following these views, my efforts to describe Big Feelings through queer-feminist affects are not intended to valorize a particular articulation of politics through aesthetics, but rather to first detail and second think with dynamics that appear in this music.

It is critical for this book that "affect" and "resonance" become key methodological terms, because such indirect means of communication are central to the feminist and queer lives of those in contemporary indie scenes for myriad reasons. For an example that I found quite striking, I'll loop in here the voice of one respondent I spoke with. On the subject of boygenius, Beth described the way their music functions in exactly affective terms—before immediately connecting experiences of musical enjoyment to experiences of close friendship, equally vital for this book. In her words,

> It's just really nice that they don't have to say in every song "by the way we're liberal and we're also kinda gay and . . . you are OK being depressed"; they don't have to say it outright in every song. . . . It feels the same way that . . . each of my friends that I think are my closest in the world . . . they're all on the autism spectrum and they're all queer . . . and I'm also in that group . . . and the four of us didn't know that about each other when we became friends. But we gravitated towards each other as people and then as the months went on we're like, "By the way you know I'm bi right?" And they're like, "Yeah we know, we figured that out." We kind of discovered that about each other as we went along. It wasn't the reason that we came together but there's

10. The police is Rancière's (1999) term for the already-established criteria by which a social order has determined what counts as "common sense," intellectually and aesthetically (through the senses).

> something about the people that I felt drawn to. I think the default being "acceptance" is something that you can sense in a room and you can sense in the music and I don't really know exactly how but you can just kinda tell if you're in the same space. (Beth C. 2023)

Beth struggles in this quote to articulate *how* matters of queerness, neurodivergence, and trusting acceptance can be perceived in the performances of both music and friendship, suggesting to my ear that that any serious understanding of either must take into account the role that affect plays in helping those who might have very good reasons to not be super overt about their positionalities nevertheless find one another. Instead of clear statements, Big Feelings artists more often deploy a variety of affective strategies to cohere a sense of community, including the use of shared languages and consistent cultural touchpoints. "An aspiration for a narrative about something shared," constructing a world in common becomes a key means of cultivating intimacy across queer-feminist spaces (Berlant 1998, 281). As we will see throughout this book, common themes in the Big Feelings world include references to contemporary witchcraft practices such as tarot and astrology; a focus on quotidian life (rendered exceptional, rare, and magical in its own right under conditions of chronic precarity, underemployment, and climate collapse); transportation (whether public or private); Salome, Ophelia, Artemisia Gentileschi (see Hana Vu's *Romanticism*) and other figures recuperated as feminist icons; as well as a series of images that may or may not link up directly with such often-circulating themes, including dogs, flowers, teeth, Hello Kitty, and more.

I discuss this imagery further in chapter 5. In the meantime, affect and resonance are also crucial for this project inasmuch as they prevent a reductive or clinical perspective from grouping diverse artists together under a rubric of definable criteria that would, in its efforts to explain, simply break understanding. If we insist that music is a "multiply mediated" phenomenon, "privileging affect over taxonomy allows us to find resonance between our lives and the lives of others without having to take up the position of the other" (Grover 2023, 6) at the same time that it prevents a kind of top-down, distanced perspective from taking hold.[11] To feel out connections in sound, we have to dive into the middle of everything.

11. For music as "multiply-mediated," see Born 2005; Born and Barry 2018. For more on the need to read music's separate elements as interdependent and co-emergent, see Eidsheim 2015; Stover 2017; DiPiero 2022.

Big Feelings as Aesthetic

Below, I outline the five characteristics that seem to me essential for identifying Big Feelings as an indie rock orientation. It may be helpful to note that removing any one of these five points from the equation collapses the entire *conceptual* framework as I mean to define it—it is their collective interplay that interests me, rather than any one particular point. Additionally, though, once the idea of Big Feelings has been established, I don't mean to suggest that it constitutes some kind of unitary, yes-or-no phenomenon; I think about these characteristics as overlapping tendencies rather than rigid categories as they are actually performed in the world. In other words, the purpose of the concept is not to sort and categorize, much less label; rather, it is a term that aspires to help us trace tendencies any band will approach differently, fully embracing some where others might not factor as prominently. This is again why I turn to affect theory and its insistence on singularity and interrelationality. Following this view, Big Feelings' main features should be read as co-constitutive, producing its effects through a synthesis that is both nonlinear and unique across each example. In describing the following characteristics, then, I often move across all five points, indicating the ways in which each of them is related to the others—that is, in trying to understand one point, it is often helpful to think with another.

1. Women and Queer Musicians Are Leading the Way.

Identifying this aspect of the music is not an attempt to reduce its significance to the fact of one's identity, but simply to emphasize that the music in question is not possible as such without the people who made it. Furthermore, as many scholars have argued, the embodied nature of both musical production and perception strongly suggests that our bodies not only make our musical performances possible but also leave perceptible traces of our subjectivities in sound (Iyer 2002; Wong and Eidsheim 2016). In this way, who we are matters to the sounds we make, or put in reverse, music is utterly dependent on our bodies, their capacities, and the accumulated life experiences that shape those capacities. The embodied nature of music performance in this case is one of the ways that this music produces feminist affects irreducible but related to the gender performance of its producers. Furthermore, one reason Big Feelings sounds distinct as a musical orientation has to do with how it reimagines older styles of indie rock through the perspectives of people who weren't widely associated with them the first time around—and this is a comprehensive project. It's not as simple as saying that '90s indie rock sounds different when women play it, or that everyone who plays in these bands belongs to the same demographic groups, which is rarely the case; rather than such rigid understandings of identity, Big Feelings artists use their situated perspectives to perform sounds and sentiments that cut against straight/cis-masculine cultural and musical norms. In the process, they reformulate what the sound of the past means today, changing the music as they go.

An effective example of this dynamic can be observed through the work of UK-based artist beabadoobee (Beatrice Kristi Ilejay Laus), who has talked openly about the influence of music from the 1990s on her own sound, even going so far as to pen a song titled "I Wish I Was Stephen Malkmus." Malkmus is one of the primary singer/songwriter/guitarists in the band Pavement, whose albums *Slanted and Enchanted* (1992) and *Wowee Zowee* (1995) have been described as some of the most influential of the decade (Goodman 2017; Browne et al. 2022). Beabadoobee's music, including her ode to Malkmus, freely partakes of—and often foregrounds—the musical vocabulary of this kind of '90s rock. But Laus doesn't just cite '90s indie rock in this tune; she also reworks it to reflect her subject position. This reworking is perhaps most easily grasped through the music video, which portrays Laus's character in a quintessentially feminized narrative: playing with dolls in her bedroom. From the title screen—stylized in multicolor crayon—to scenes in which Laus is institutionalized for drawing on her bedroom walls, "I Wish I Was Stephen Malkmus" picks up classic themes from angsty '90s alt-rock videos (Green Day's "Basket Case" comes to mind) while at the same time placing them within the universe of Laus's adolescent search for identity, rendering sight and sound alike decidedly *girly*. This girlishness isn't (just) about the fact that Laus is herself a young woman in this video (nineteen at the time), but rather how she performatively stages girlhood through references to prototypical feminized activities, spaces, and sonics. The performance of girlhood taking place through the lyrical perspective ("Got this new blue-haired phase / I think I kinda like it"; "You're up your butt / You never really ask me how I am") combines with visual cues in the music video to reinforce an unmistakably feminized perspective while at the same remaining irreducible to a strict question of the performer's identity.

In this creative reworking, we can hear a quick example of how the transformation of '90s alternative into Big Feelings takes place by virtue of people other than cis men productively reappropriating (that is, taking back) a rock subgenre in which, during its initial peak, women were overwhelmingly sidelined (Strong 2011). If, in other words, a variety of discursive and industry pressures kept women who play rock out of grunge and sequestered in the riot grrrl or "angry woman" categories throughout the '90s, Big Feelings becomes possible in a moment where mainstream culture doesn't care enough about rock to police women out of genres where they are perceived not to belong. But beyond the fact that women are taking up sounds that had previously been the purview of men, Big Feelings artists are also transforming those sounds, updating them, blending them with other influences, and incorporating them into novel articulations.

Lastly (on this point), I want to emphasize the ways in which Big Feelings artists amplify their queer-feminist affects while downplaying any neoliberal-inflected emphasis on a given individual and their personal, subjective journey by briefly considering the band-oriented nature of Big Feelings musicians: whether formal groups (Mannequin Pussy, Bully, Alvvays, et al.) or individual artists (Snail Mail, Indigo De Souza, Japanese Breakfast, et al.), the lack of obvious differences between the two categories strikes me as important and indicative of this moment in indie rock history. Like many individual artists, single Big Feelings musicians play in bands when they tour, or when they make a special appearance at an event. But it feels notable to me that in such contexts, the bands being formed tend to have consistent members in them, that they often have wider/deeper relationships with one another than simply musicians who happened to find themselves on the same gig. Most importantly, whether in examples central to this book (Indigo De Souza, Vagabon, Jay Som) or more peripheral (yeule, Bartees Strange, Tanukichan), these bands nearly invariably comprise folks of diverse gender expressions, sexual orientations, and racial backgrounds. Even if a single musician is responsible for most of the songwriting, any one individual subject position or narrative perspective is never in and of itself the point, is always softened, downplayed, refracted by a diverse group of musicians who come together to articulate something bigger. The importance of a group, and the relative lack of individual artists touring under their own individual names, feels to me a subtle but critical feature of the Big Feelings moment in indie rock, an indirect yet fundamental method of foregrounding of diversity, community, and non-normative politics as praxis—simply how things are done.

2. Lyrical Content Most Often Concerns Feelings, Sentiments, and Other "Abstract" Subject Matter.

Despite the centrality of political contexts to both the music and to the fan communities that consume it, Big Feelings tends to exclude overt political content in its lyrical address, which corresponds with the ways in which neither the artists nor the press coverage about them tend to center political questions. I suggest that this is one of the key ways in which Big Feelings builds on and in some ways departs from a kind of riot grrrl orientation, for while these movements are clearly connected, and while riot grrrl groups effectively reflected the actual inseparability of any as-such distinction between the "personal" and the "political," it is still important to note how Big Feelings bands downplay or evade certain political questions. The contrast between Big Feelings' indirect political orientation and the riot grrrl movement is further reinforced by the fact that, as many scholars have established, riot grrrl was not just about music; rather, it comprised a series of sociopolitical and artistic activities, including zine circulation, community meetings, fashion sense, and more (Dunn and Farnsworth 2012; Keenan and Darms 2013; Marcus 2010; Siegfried 2019). Thus, while I maintain that Big Feelings lyrics *are* actually political, they are not political in the way that riot grrrl lyrics often were, where topics well-recognized as such were denotatively named and concretely tied to extramusical activities.

For example, L7's 1992 track "Wargasm" takes up perpetual US imperialism and its public fetishization with lines like, "Wargasm, wargasm, one, two, three / Tie a yellow ribbon around the amputee / Masturbate, watch it on TV / Crocodile tears for the refugee." A later track from the same album, "Diet Pill," names not only the diet culture that disproportionately harms women, but also narrates a story wherein a woman flees her repressive domestic life, leaving "Victor" "sewn in the sheets with thread" and in a hurry—while "the frying pan is red." This is an obviously gendered scene, not only for who's singing it but also for the tropes of domesticity articulated throughout, which speak to women's suffocation in the home, while leaving ambiguous the nature (easily assumed) of the violence causing the narrator to escape. This gendered reading is further reinforced by another name-check: "Calgon can't take me away" Donita Sparks sings, referring to a line of bath products whose advertisements suggest that women exhausted by "having it all" can escape by relaxing in the tub.[12] Here, crass marketing toward perceived feminine desires—and by extension, capitalism's tone-deafness toward and facilitation of women's oppression in the home—are also invoked.

Though L7 and Bikini Kill differ in terms of their musical approach, Bikini Kill's famous track "White Boy" (discussed further below) provides another illustrative example of the kinds of more or less explicit lyrics that

12. See "Calgon Bath Powder Commercial—'Calgon, Take Me Away!,'" 1978 (available as of this writing on YouTube: https://www.youtube.com/watch?v=8yjGPgs0_S0).

characterized the riot grrrl movement, here tackling misogyny and toxic masculinity directly by calling out their practitioners in demographic terms: "I'm so sorry if I'm alienating some of you" Kathleen Hanna sings to her male listeners, "Your whole fucking culture alienates me / I cannot scream from pain down here on my knees / I'm so sorry that I think!" In these lines, Hanna invokes a sexual posture that also functions metonymically for both normative gender roles and the power imbalances that structure them. I suggest that this roughly mirrors L7's approach, where, while not all details are explicitly illustrated, the subjects of the narrator's critique are both clear and understood as political issues across wider popular culture.

Certainly, not all riot grrrl bands were so direct in their lyrical orientations, and it is also critical not to limit the discussion to the riot grrrl movement itself; by 1995, artists like Tori Amos and Alanis Morissette were singing about personal relationships in ways that can be read as "purely personal," but which resonated with women who recognized themselves and their gendered experiences in the artists' disclosures. This type of indirect resonance moves us more in the direction of the kind of orientation I hear in Big Feelings artists, though on the whole the latter is even more abstract. In the Big Feelings camp, Snail Mail's Lindsey Jordan, for example, sings in "Heat Wave" to an unidentified love interest with a longing ache that reads to me as both obviously feminine and perhaps less obviously sapphic: "And I hope whoever it is / Holds their breath around you / 'Cause I know I did," Jordan sings, both pining for her object and demonstrating that they are somehow beyond reach. Jordan's character hopes "the love that you find / Swallows you wholly / Like you said it might," the implication being that the subject of address is finding their (overwhelming) love with someone else almost as a foregone conclusion or assumption, though we have no lyrical evidence for why this might be so—there is something ultimately withheld about the admission of love, a kind of confession that's over before it begins.

Similarly, in "Hair to the Ferris Wheel," Lady Lamb's Aly Spaltro sings an abstract mixture of sentiments that range from nameless desire ("It's a zoo in your room when you part your lips / And you long to kiss like you won't exist") to a (possible) critique of the institution of marriage ("Take me by the arm to the altar / take me by the collar to the cliff"). Through its deferral of any one story or message, this song provides a particularly compelling example of the ways in which music can resonate indirectly with listeners—less *despite* lyrical vagueness and more *because* of the evocative possibilities ambiguity itself generates. In this case, we can see how this works through the reflections of Samantha Panepinto, who writes in *GO Magazine*:

> That winter break of my sophomore year, I was driving my dad's Toyota Rav4 when a sample of Lady Lamb's "Hair to the Ferris Wheel" came on the radio, and something inside me broke open. . . . Looking back now, I think it was the *yearning* in her songwriting, possibly the gayest of all emotions. Lines that fixated on the nape of the neck (what a queer body part!) hit me over the head with images of the cute butch from my Psych 1 class who I was too nervous to talk to. . . . *There weren't any names or pronouns in the [song], but somehow I knew she was singing to another woman.* (2021, my emphasis)[13]

I read Panepinto's line about the queerness of a nape and think of Berlant, who writes that

> queer work is skeptical about ordinary modes of attachment, repair, survival, and good objects. It describes the ambivalent position of being in desire while being unsure of what to do with what's overwhelming or threatening in it, and it opens the floodgates about what can be an object of desire: persons, objects, ways of life, a landscape, an angle, pets, ideas, and so on. (2022, 16)

The queer object to which it is directed clues Panepinto into something about the nature of Spaltro's desire. We can feel a similar kind of (queer) yearning in Jordan's lyrics above, I think, a reading that may be bolstered by the music video for "Heat Wave" (where she has fun with lesbian stereotypes) or by any number of examples from Snail Mail's media appearances and the discourse around them: Jordan is openly queer, knowledge of which obviously affects how we understand her music. At the time she released "Hair to the Ferris Wheel," Spaltro on the other hand was not out, at least not in her music; yet

13. Sharing a screenshot of Panepinto's article, Spaltro responds in the caption: "I am beside myself to wake up to this article today in @gomagazineny by @samrosefromthedead. I cannot stress enough the deep paranoia I felt starting out in my career that I would be 'outed' or 'pigeonholed' or 'cornered.' I was mortified at the thought that my queerness would be put on display and any light shining on Lady Lamb would be solely about it. That terrified me and even though I was fully out in my life, and had been for years, I was pretty unhappy for a long time because I felt that my queer expression needed to be a secret that I stashed away in my songs. / Except you found it. And I'm glad you did. And I'm sorry that I didn't make it a little easier to find back then—for those of you who yearned for understanding and to feel seen. I made you dig a little, huh? / Now I *live* to see my queerness and yours celebrated, elevated, validated. What a beautiful thing. Thank you, Sam and thanks to those of you who see me in my songs, and most importantly, see yourself. I see you in them too. 🌈🧡" (@ladylambjams 2021). My thanks go to Katie M. for pointing me toward this interaction.

this didn't prevent fans from perceiving queerness there. Thus, the broader point I am trying to make here is that Big Feelings doesn't tend to use lyrics to convey messages directly, in part because narrative is not the only way to communicate with listeners. This was not the case with the approach that most represents the riot grrrl movement, which prioritized articulating its messages directly—as "in your face" as anything in punk history.

As much as Big Feelings departs from riot grrrl's manifesto-style politics, however, it also departs from the major feminist developments that took over from riot grrrl, the post- and popular feminist models offered by many contemporary pop stars.[14] Although Big Feelings takes place within the same pop-cultural context (and is thus affected by it), it nevertheless differs from the neoliberal, self-actualized, commercial feminism that is centered in the body and in narratives of resilience and self-improvement. Big Feelings is thus neither feminist in the riot grrrl sense nor postfeminist in the contemporary pop sense, but is what I consider a kind of post–riot grrrl feminism. As with other "post" categories, Big Feelings does not abandon riot grrrl postures totally, but updates them in a new cultural context, amplifying and building on select elements of the movement's legacy while leaving others behind. In particular, what is retained from riot grrrl is the powerful but unsettled possibility of reading lyrics with a queer orientation, a possibility that, as we will see later in the book, is often achieved through recourse to the signifiers of adolescence.[15]

3. The 1990s Are Critical for Big Feelings in a Variety of Ways, Often Manifesting as a Form of (Critical) Nostalgia.

As I've already suggested, the sound of Big Feelings is heavily influenced by '90s genres, including early grunge, '90s singer-songwriters, and earlier indie precursors such as shoegaze, among others.[16] Though genres from

14. For popular feminism (and its corollary, popular misogyny), see Banet-Weiser 2018. For postfeminism, see Gill and Orgad 2018; James 2020; Orgad and Gill 2022. For appropriations of riot grrrl discourse into popular/postfeminist paradigms, see Jacques 2001; Schilt 2003; Spiers 2015; Zeisler 2017.

15. For queer affects in the riot grrrl movement, see Siegfried 2019.

16. I use the term "singer-songwriter" here to refer to a particular *discourse* about genre—not genre itself—which usually locates a beginning in the music of James Taylor and Joni Mitchell. In my own writing, I try to avoid this label, along with the "confessional" description (about which more below), for their imprecision and gender implications, respectively. In terms of "singer-songwriters," the most relevant references for Big Feelings are Fiona Apple, Tori Amos, and the pivotal link to what was at the time described as "alternative rock," Alanis Morissette. All three of these artists align with Big Feelings' orientations toward performances

both the '80s and 2000s are also critical for the development of Big Feelings (see chapter 1), its sound is most often oriented around '90s aesthetics, making the sonic markers of this decade one of the critical factors in distinguishing the sound of Big Feelings from otherwise similar bands in the space of post-punk, post-rock, or indie in general. Often but not always, this lineage is explicitly recognized by contemporary musicians. Nineties nostalgia is furthermore not exclusively invoked through sound, but also appears visually and in many ways across music videos.

For example: in videos like beabadoobee's "Care," highly reminiscent of the Raincoats' 1996 "Don't Be Mean," washed-out colors mimic VHS home movies, while the singer herself sports various '90s-associated outfits (paradigmatically, flower-patterned sundresses). Meanwhile, at 0:23, two massive chords (B and A) hit like punches before the music lands on E, all three chords distorted with a particular '90s tone (compressed, full of stacked notes) that might well come from some of the same guitar pedals made famous by grunge music. I'm thinking for example of the Ibanez Tube Screamer (which Sophie Allison of Soccer Mommy also uses), and the Big Muff, each of which have been spotted on beabadoobee's pedalboard.

For Stephen L., a forty-eight-year-old music industry professional I interviewed for this book, the revival of sounds he associated with music from (for example) Juliana Hatfield produced a kind of comforting listening experience, one that he is familiar with both as a listener and as a guitar player. He talked to me about "Les Pauls and humbucker pickups," which he suggested make it easier to mask certain technical imperfections in guitar technique and make him feel spoken to as someone who grew up with those same materials. It is this combination of timbre and songwriting style that so clearly evokes a '90s sound, which is less about one particular guitar tone and more a cluster of associated ideas.[17] In "Care," timbre and songwriting collude with

that work through trauma and adversity in ways that feel personal, but which then resonate and perform community/political work among listeners drawn into an intimate public by those very disclosures. Another reason I move away from these terms throughout this book is the relative distance I see Big Feelings artists taking from even performing under their own names: most of the artists I mention in this book take band names (e.g., Soccer Mommy) even when they are the only or primary singer-songwriter in the project. I see this in part as a defense mechanism guarding against some of the (misogynist) connotations indexed by the image of a singer-songwriter (as well as the "confessional" mode they are expected to perform).

17. On the concept of the "sound" of a particular decade (in this case, the 1980s) being constituted by both the material particularities of specific instruments, as well as associations shared among large groups of people, see Lavengood 2019. I would also add that there are musical gestures that can invoke memories and associations with a particular decade. For

musical gestures like the interjecting melodic riff that concludes each chorus, demonstrating how thoroughly beabadoobee understands—and how adeptly she synthesizes—a variety of nostalgic sounds.

Despite the fact that I understand these sounds to perform a more active strategy of cultural critique than the word often implies, I stick with "nostalgia" in part because that is the word listeners used most often to describe their perceptions of the music. For example, Stephen went on to describe Soccer Mommy's music as "wistful . . . the word I would use is nostalgic, but that's not where everybody's coming to Soccer Mommy from" (Stephen L. 2022). Interestingly, however, younger listeners also described this music as nostalgic without any prompting. When I asked Deanna, a twenty-year-old musician and student, what she'd like people to know about bands like Soccer Mommy, Deanna responded by saying: "I'd say that they are creating a nostalgia for something that I never experienced . . . like, it feels nostalgic, it feels like the emotional impact of it has the same weight as feeling nostalgic about something. . . . It has the same kind of energy as that" (Deanna F. 2022).

The creation of a heavy emotional space through recourse to nostalgia—or something with that "same weight"—is a central element of Big Feelings that I discuss further in chapters 2 and 3. And as I elaborate there, I believe that '90s nostalgia functions in particular ways with regard to the two main groups of listeners to this music, which we can sort into "millennial" and "Gen Z" categories so long as we take them both with the large asterisks that all generational distinctions warrant. For the millennial listeners of Big Feelings, '90s nostalgia makes audible the distance between the past and present that not only foregrounds the loss of childhood (as all nostalgia does), but also the loss of the world in the particular way that we had been trained to imagine it. In the '90s, millennials were being raised during the last period where the myths of neoliberalism could be plausibly entertained: the fall of the Berlin Wall, the Clinton administration's "third way," and the (since derided) "end of history" made it possible to believe or feel (for a time, and especially if you were white), that neoliberalism's promises of widespread economic prosperity had or would soon come true. Millennials were by and large raised in this auspicious context, only to subsequently witness the dot-com bubble burst, 9/11 and its consequences, the 2008 financial collapse, and now the widespread trauma and inflationary pressures wrought by the pan-

example, the 1990s are clearly conjured by a particular type of note-bending on the guitar, heard on Soccer Mommy's "Flaw," among others. I suggest that this gesture, surely not exclusive to a particular period, becomes indicative of the '90s through overdeterminative examples such as the Smashing Pumpkins' "1979," a huge hit for the band in which such pitch bends feature prominently.

demic. In this context, to hear the sounds of the '90s is to recapture a time when dreaming of a bright future was possible, drawing attention to the long distance between those dreams and the reality we inherited.

For the younger musicians who are by and large making this music, there is also a sense of longing at play in '90s nostalgia; but it is not longing for a past they lived. Rather, given that this generation was not alive (or conscious) during the '90s, this is an example of what Andy Bennett has called "received nostalgia" (2010), in which a group projects desires and feelings onto a time period with which they have no direct experience. It is all too easy to imagine why this imaginary might offer a sense of possibility for young people: for Gen Z, knowledge of the world has never *not* been marked by the kinds of catastrophes wrought by neoliberal capitalism, the most salient of which is the collapse of the climate. For these musicians and listeners, '90s nostalgia is about inhabiting a temporality in which dreaming would be possible for the first time, a possibility that has been preemptively denied their generation, for whom the future has always implied catastrophe. Though obviously not all young people possess a progressive or radical understanding of the political conditions that have contributed to such crises, the young people disproportionately marginalized by those crises have more reason to understand than the privileged, who may be insulated from capitalism's worst effects. Increasingly, however, as more and more young people face skyrocketing costs for basic necessities, vast majorities are affected by crisis conditions. As a young woman named Nikayla recently put it in an ad for the youth-led climate advocacy group the Sunrise Movement, "I would like to be able to be 23 in the way that my parents were able to be 23. They fell in love, they got to travel, they planned for their future. They were able to live and be a little naive . . . We need a revolution—*so I can be young again*" (2021 [my emphasis]). From direct references to climate change (e.g., Why Bonnie's *90 in November*, Bachelor's *Doomin' Sun*) to music that prioritizes tenderness and care for one's community amidst overwhelming circumstances (e.g., boygenius's *The Record*), women and queer youth reflect the chronic anxiety of being young and unable to access any of the systems of power that would change things for the better, using the sounds of the past to stage complex critiques of the possibilities offered by the present.

4. Big Feelings Music Shares a Certain Harmonic Vocabulary That Makes Foundational Use of Chord Extensions, Setting Its Sound Askance from Rock Subgenres in a Masculinist Mold.

David Temperley writes in *The Musical Language of Rock* that "chords in rock are overwhelmingly triadic." Big Feelings, by contrast, makes use of those chord extensions "very common in jazz" but "mostly very rare in rock" (2018, 42). This is one of the key factors distinguishing Big Feelings from other feminist rock music that is more directly inspired by punk and queercore. For a quick contrast, it is instructive to consider a contemporary feminist rock band in the riot grrrl tradition. Take for instance, THICK's 2020 single, "Mansplain." There are several ways in which we can read this track as a direct evocation of a riot grrrl posture. Before the song begins, we hear a chorus of men's voices overlapping typical sexist commentaries about women in rock bands, saying for example, "Are those your boyfriend's drums?"; "I wouldn't really recommend a Fender to a woman but you're kinda tall, so . . ."; and "If they were guys, I'm not really sure people would be into this." The comments culminate when all but one voice drops out of the mix, foregrounding the remaining critique: "They sound great for women." Before the music has even begun, then, this introduction mimics the intro to Bikini Kill's "White Boy," which begins with recorded audio from an interview Kathleen Hanna conducted, including the sexist trope, "I don't think it's a problem cause most of the girls ask for it."

Once "Mansplain" begins in earnest, other Bikini Kill parallels emerge. The song has a relatively fast tempo, propelled by a quintessential punk drumbeat. The vocals have a clear melodic line, but are rather sung-spoken, including backing vocals that are both purposefully loose in terms of pitch and that sometimes escalate into screaming. Like the beat and the vocal delivery, the guitars in this track are also characteristic of punk-associated genres, consisting of relatively few chords (the verses basically sit on one chord alone, while the choruses have three) built simply (i.e., they are power chords or triads). Combine those musical elements with overtly political lyrics that center gender politics (filtered in this case through the contemporary discussion of microaggressions like "mansplaining"), and we have all the aesthetic hallmarks of a riot grrrl band, albeit in comparatively polished form.

It is not an accident that these sounds and lyrical contents are paired; rather, as has been well documented, riot grrrl bands specifically appropriated punk hallmarks in order to co-opt sounds overwhelmingly semiotically coded as masculine, read as aggressive or unapologetically angry, and connoting other traits which have traditionally been seen as unacceptable for or foreign to women (Gottlieb and Wald 1994; Marcus 2010). A large part of how masculine aggressivity is communicated in punk music derives from its harmonic construction: as I mentioned above, most masculine rock genres are built from simple, "strong" sounding chords, the most basic of which is helpfully termed a "power chord" (a chord composed of the first and fifth scale degrees). Combined with punk's unrelenting speed, volume, and its associated timbres (particularly with regard to vocal quality), the genre undeniably connotes combative aggression.

Big Feelings departs from this model in many ways. Its tempi are often much slower; its lyrics very often concern personal feelings (distanced from overtly political contexts); its harmonic vocabulary is more complex, and as I will discuss below, the vocal delivery is much more melody-driven. Picking up from '90s indie pop's feminized, lo-fi softness, Big Feelings' feminine excess is precisely reversed from the riot grrrl model: rather than appropriate punk aesthetics as a co-option of masculine tropes, Big Feelings doubles down on those sounds already associated with femininity and queerness. And while all of the musical elements are critical in sounding this different approach, I want to focus on perhaps the most critical element, which is the heavy use of chord extensions. As opposed to the bare-bones chords that in punk facilitate fast-paced sonic bombardment, Big Feelings creates lush and dense sound-worlds in part through the use of extended harmonies.

Consider "Bedroom Talks," a single from Fazerdaze's 2017 album *Morningside*. Beyond its clear similarities to certain tracks by Big Feelings precursors Broken Social Scene ("Looks Just Like The Sun," "Pacific Theme"), "Bedroom Talks" is notable for how it foregrounds three central Big Feelings dynamics: first, its reference to the quintessentially feminized space of a girl's bedroom places femininity at the center of its affective orientation, embracing rather than critiquing girlhood's stereotypical construction in patriarchal culture. Second, Fazerdaze here retains from '90s rock precedents a decidedly DIY aesthetic, not only in the music video (her friend Mark shot it on his iPhone), but also insofar as the title and musical production together recall the kind of drum machine–powered bedroom rock we can hear so clearly in Kathleen Hanna's *Julie Ruin* project. Third and most pertinently, the entirety of the song alternates between just two chords—I maj7 and IV maj7—chords that I suggest are critical for Big Feelings in a number of ways.[18]

18. Although my main point in this section involves the presence of chord extensions in general, it is also worth noting that this particular progression shows up *a lot* and in significant ways across Big Feelings tracks, including Soccer Mommy's "Cool" (chapter 2), De Souza's "Real Pain" (chapter 3) and Vagabon's "The Embers" (chapter 5). There are many reasons why this progression might show up all over the place, including the fact that I and IV are the two places in a regular Ionian/major mode where major-seventh chords occur naturally (and Big Feelings loves this major-seventh sound). Additionally, I want to suggest that another reason for their ubiquity might be the degree of relative stability they create: that is, these two chords can build a world between them, totally self-contained in the sense that they don't produce a feeling of tension that "needs" to be resolved by a cadence or further progression. While still maintaining a sense of movement, players can oscillate between two tone worlds that build on

In the 1990s, Susan McClary famously showed how opera and classical music utilized chromaticism and harmonic embellishments to signal feminine challenges to the male protagonist, or in absolute music, to the masculine, triadic cadence (1991). Inside the bounded space of the tonic key center, non-diatonic colors signified feminine conflict in the form of "madwomen" and "hysterics" that both male protagonists and coded-male tonic key centers must overcome by the end of the movement. As Anne Carson has written, the sonic dynamic associating masculinity with rational tonal harmony and femininity with non-diatonic excess (read as hysteria) is traceable to the Greek notion of *sophrosyne*, in which a certain model of male virtue could be seen as violated if women made too much noise (1995). In this sense, the riot grrrl movement reappropriates and intentionally defies sophrosyne by making loudness (and other qualities reserved for men) centerpieces of their aesthetic project. In their case, feminine excess was signaled by the mere fact that it was women making these sounds, screaming and playing fast, aggressive music in a world where only men had been known for doing so. Talking openly about their bodies, being unapologetic, stereotypically un-feminine, and otherwise taking no shit—these were the ways in which riot grrrl bands expressed feminine excess, consciously co-opting behaviors gendered masculine, musical and social practices that were not "for" them.

The feminine excess of Big Feelings is similarly self-conscious, but takes the opposite approach: rather than bombarding listeners with power chords, Big Feelings often utilizes chord extensions to complexify their harmonic movements, breaking outside the bounds of rational, masculine harmony by literally adding notes on top of it. This excess is not just literal (because there are more notes) but also affective and semiotic. The major seventh, in particular, is ambiguously coded. In Western cultures, the major triad most basically connotes feelings of happiness (the root-position triad in particular invites this simplistic reading), stability, confidence (and, extending McClary's framework) rationality, action, and therefore masculinity. The minor chord, on the other hand, connotes or is used to connote (e.g., in films) feelings of sadness, instability, disquiet—by extension, melancholy,

---

one another, rather than contrasting, helping to produce feelings of stasis, calm, or else intensification. These effects are also bolstered by the fact that the two chords share many possible common tones between them (especially when considering extensions like 9, sharp 11, and 13): taken together, there are various possibilities for hammering away on one voicing, while other instruments (principally the bass) switch from I to IV. This avoids any break in sonic continuity or affective momentum, allowing for an uninterrupted swelling or reverberant intensification of a major-7 sound-world, and thus bigger feelings. For examples of some songs that employ the I–IV extensively, see appendix B.

irrationality, emotionality, and therefore femininity. Adding a fourth note to the minor triad—the flat seventh—extends and nuances the minor chord's "melancholic" sound. But as I discuss further in chapter 2, adding a major seventh to the major triad achieves a different effect. Rather than expanding the major chord's straightforward brightness, the major seventh disrupts or complexifies it, adding an ambivalent quality that is both wistful and radiant. Partially because it is simply heard less often, there is no straightforward way to interpret the major-seventh sound outside of its contexts of use. So although all chord extensions add a dimension of complexity to traditionally "straight-forward" rock music, the consistent use of the major seventh (as in "Bedroom Talks") is of particular note here. It is a uniquely apt tonality for expressing feelings that are too strongly felt or ambivalently constituted to be reduced to words, to be represented and captured by sentiment.

It's true that such extensions appear in many earlier precedents, making it debatable how "rare" they actually are in rock music after 1970. But it's not just their presence that I mean to identify here; it's also how they are treated, how thoroughly they are used to build standard vocabulary, how they show up in such a large number of songs put out consistently by this group of bands working in similar aesthetic worlds, how they combine with other factors such as femme presentation or queer-coded thematics to signal a different semiotic resonance than past examples.[19] Combined with such factors

19. A note must be made here about the complicated case of emo, which I see retaining several points of overlap or intersection with contemporary indie, particularly insofar as a new generation of diverse artists are reappropriating its trademark sounds. Prior to emo's fifth wave, and following Jessica Hopper's essay "Emo: Where the Girls Aren't" (2021), it has been well-established that emo's ostensible progressivism vis-à-vis gender-bending physical performance and the expansion of possibilities for men to emote publicly was severely undermined by the kind of "beta-male misogyny" practiced by (once again) predominantly white-male bands (de Boise 2014; Bimm 2022). Interestingly, emo's focus on white-male pain was also accompanied by a musical exploration of "different chord progressions (there was a widespread use of minor seventh chords) and a greater variety of rhythms" (de Boise 2014, 227) relative to the straight ahead punk out of which emo emerged. But well unlike Big Feelings, emo's timbres and tempi differ substantially from the direction that indie had turned during the same time period; where (third-wave and later) emo glistens with high production value, bright textures, driving rhythmic intensity, and punk-adjacent vocals, indie doubled down on the indie pop lineage, where lo-fi aesthetics, soft vocal delivery, and slower, weightier song forms were becoming increasingly rerouted into the generative, creative space of young women's bedrooms (Bimm 2022). Thus I see fifth-wave emo and Big Feelings running in somewhat parallel directions: in the same way that even regressively masculine '90s alt rock has proven influential for feminist indie rockers, the musical vocabulary of emo has remained affectively compelling for young musicians and fans who may at the same time disidentify with some of its past cultural politics. In the same way that Big Feelings does with grunge, fifth-wave bands

and featured so foundationally, the use of extended harmonies by Jay Som or Soccer Mommy differs, I suggest, from a band like the Strokes, who nevertheless also utilize them to great effect.[20]

A racialized term as well as a gendered one, feminine excess gets mapped unevenly in our uneven culture, carrying different consequences, connotations, and modes of appearance for white women than for women of color. Yet, as I discuss further below, this indie rock movement has heard Asian diasporic musicians like Fazerdaze join Black artists like Vagabon—as well as white artists who do still constitute a majority in the indie rock space—in performing such self-consciously feminized affects as a constitutive element of their musical vocabularies. As I understand it, part of the political provocation of Big Feelings lies in the explicit foregrounding of feelings, regardless of whether or not mainstream culture—or even mainstream indie rock—has historically welcomed them. In this music, chord extensions intrude on or break through the relatively bounded sonic space of masculine rock, contributing to the feeling of excess emotionality that makes Big Feelings what it is. Instead of co-opting tropes of aggressive masculinity, Big Feelings dials up the stereotypically feminine concern with feelings, not in a parodic display but through a treatment that rises to meet the overwhelming experience of feeling in the first place. In this sense, Big Feelings is in line with feminist affect theory's attention to feeling and emotionality as a means of resuscitating critiques of rationality and patriarchal control (Ahmed 2014; Berlant 2000; Cvetkovich 2003).

By regularly and centrally invoking "extra" chord tones in its progressions, Big Feelings music produces a feminine excess in the space of rock. Thus, Big Feelings is not reducible to rock music about feminist politics; its politics takes place affectively, which is to say, in a way related to but distinct

---

like Glass Beach, Home Is Where, Pinkshift, Pool Kids, and Sweet Pill reprise and reappropriate harmonic vocabulary or guitar technique in order to recuperate what feels like the lost potential of the original genre, making it into the queer-feminist music the genre had initially (mis)promised, the music many of its listeners felt it was or could be, wished it to become. That both subgenres are replete with chord extensions is, in my view, no accident.

20. A helpful peer reviewer pointed out that the major seventh is also becoming more *generally* popular in contemporary pop music, as evidenced by Doja Cat's "Say So," Fifty Fifty's "Cupid," Sabrina Carpenter's "Feather," and Harry Styles's "As It Was." I see this development as both related to and distinct from the major seventh's appearance across Big Feelings: different because of how comparatively foundational, centralized, loud, and sustained the major-seventh sound is in indie rock (vs. its smooth and swift appearance in the aforementioned hits), and related because each of the tracks mentioned here is just as semiotically feminized as the ones I'm trying to point to in indie rock. In other words, insofar as the major-seventh sound is popular today, it's because queer and femininized music is popular.

from conscious understanding. We *feel* the feminist possibilities of this music; we resonate with and vibrate against it more so than we capture and comprehend it. This is why, at the outer limits of the concept, Big Feelings can appear even in rock that is also masculinist, as for example with the Smashing Pumpkins, whose black leather gowns, goth makeup, and yearning, Queen-inspired epics invite a queer reading at the same time that their egoistic front man embodies the worst of rockism's heterosexist male clichés.[21] Big Feelings is a concept that allows us to acknowledge the fact that the Smashing Pumpkins frequently used chord extensions to raise the emotional affect of their music to a red zone, over and above rationality, and that this can be a compelling, affectively non-normative force, even for those who rightly find details about the band's biography off-putting.[22]

5. Melodies Are Usually Tuneful, Clear, and Compelling, Saving Screams for Special Occasions.

This feature is very much in line with the previous one, merely adding that as the harmonic style shifts from punk toward a more grunge-oriented

21. "Rockism" refers to Kelefa Sanneh's now well-known (2004) formulation of a series of cultural norms that position white masculine rock as more artistically valid than other forms of popular culture (which in rockist discourse is generally feminized).

22. This is why I suggest that the Pumpkins' legacy is almost uniquely divergent in the space of rock music: whereas Sasha Geffen has written incisively about the ways that Kurt Cobain's social and musical life genuinely queered the image of a rock star (2020), the Pumpkins' queer affects occur through a divorce that allows their music to exist on different terms than biographical ones. In other words, while Billy Corgan's proto-incel oriented lyrics, virtuosic guitar playing, and political views can obviously appeal to aggrieved white-male masculinity, the harmonic vocabulary and extravagant aesthetic palette of the band as a whole also opens up the possibility for the music to resonate beyond (and in opposition to) that same audience. Aside from ample anecdotal evidence from friends and fans in the overlapping feminist/queer communities—as well as circulating internet memes conflating the Pumpkins with femme-coded imagery like Hello Kitty—the continuing influence of the Pumpkins on bands beyond the white-bro/guitar hero mold is evinced for example by a group like Wednesday, who have explicitly cited them as an influence, even going so far as to cover "Perfect" on their 2022 *Mowing the Leaves Instead of Piling 'em Up*. In the album notes, they write, "And if you listen to Wednesday's original music it goes without saying that the Pumpkins discography (at least 'til 1998) is a sound we reference often and tether ourselves to" (Hartzman 2022). See also for example Snail Mail—who both has a Smashing Pumpkins tattoo and who covers "Tonight Tonight"—as well as yeule, the project of non-binary Singaporean artist Nat Ćmiel, a sometime Sasami Ashworth collaborator who is outspoken about the Pumpkins influence on their music even as it often leans in a more pop/glitchcore direction. For a simple and effective illustration of the Smashing Pumpkins' use of extended harmonies, see for example "Here Is No Why," a soaring romance that begins on a repeated G-sharp maj7 chord.

sound, the vocals correspondingly shift as well. In the case of the vocal delivery and melodic composition, the approach feels more akin to singer-songwriters and pop-rock bands from the '90s and early 2000s, including (very interestingly) some of the postfeminist bands that I earlier contrasted with Big Feelings. Synthesizing these influences, Big Feelings works with the "the once-improbable combination of Sheryl Crow by way of Pavement" (Rytlewski 2022). As with the previous point, this is a lineage that is often acknowledged by the musicians themselves. However, also like the previous point, tracing this influence, for me, is not just about a list of artists that "inspired" the bands in question (although that is important); rather, it's about identifying certain musical tendencies as they appear and recede in various historical periods.

I read the reasons for this shift in two ways. Musically speaking, it in some ways "follows" that punk-influenced vocal delivery will not fit with the change in harmonic approach described above (if by "follow" we insist on songwriting as a co-constitutive kind of synergy between harmony and melody). Second, however, is the fact that Big Feelings is one of the first successful indie-rock projects to emerge well after the poptimist consensus (see James 2018).[23] In short, while many of these artists retain the traditional rock investment in a kind of canon, that canon has been given a kind of critical permission (and indeed, something of an imperative) to expand into other genres, most particularly pop and hip hop. Retroactively, poptimism as critical consensus re-legitimizes singer-songwriters from before the poptimist turn, such as Alanis Morissette, Tori Amos, Lisa Loeb, Natalie Imbruglia, and Sheryl Crow, as well as postfeminist figures such as Avril Lavigne and Taylor Swift, making artists who may have been previously dismissed by mainstream critics into essential listening for young musicians in the Big Feelings camp.

This, too, changes the political tenor of Big Feelings. As Joanne Gottlieb and Gayle Wald point out, the scream has been critical in feminist punk music as a means of expressing both rage and pleasure in rage: "Unruly and unexpected, these screams deploy punk values to violate the demand that

23. In brief, poptimism lifts up as artistically valid—worthy of both praise and critique—those popular music genres that were denigrated as superficial and feminized under a rockist paradigm, a permission structure perhaps best exemplified by the recuperation of Britney Spears' reputation, previously ridiculed by tastemakers. Insofar as poptimism has mounted a successful challenge to rockist hegemony, it appears today as a kind of common sense assuming that omnivorous listening habits are a mark of erudition, desirable and preferred, from a critic's standpoint, over outdated, narrow listening following equally outdated genre distinctions.

Figure 2. @theophelias, 2020, "Outfits I would wear to convince you to break up with your boyfriend and start a band," Instagram post, September 22. https://www.instagram.com/p/CFdFXr9hh_Q/?hl=en

women remain patient, uncomplaining, and quiet" (Gottlieb and Wald 1994, 262). By contrast, Big Feelings deploys the scream extremely selectively. As we will see with Indigo De Souza (chapter 3), the scream does appear in some Big Feelings music during moments of intense catharsis, breaking open a particular emotional space in a sound that is more often characterized by intimate, close-mic singing and compelling melodic contour. In fact, it is the contrast between overwhelming/loud/energetic instrumentals and detached, serene vocal delivery that characterizes much of Big Feelings' affective tension: the effect renders narrators and their circumstances somewhat distinct, where the instrumental music brings listeners into the affective experience of feeling a certain way, and the vocal delivery portrays the character as surrounded by and immersed in those very feelings as they are being narrated.

This emphasis on melody functions in several ways, first by referencing a woman-led indie pop genre that has been all but written out of rock history (see chapter 1). Simultaneously, it helps musicians tap a full spectrum of emotions while also guarding against the discursive association between women playing rock music and reductionist readings of their anger. Foregrounding the personal, Big Feelings follows the history of "vulnerability" and "confessionals" in women's singer-songwriter traditions,[24] and remains a feminist gesture inasmuch as "women remain the default managers of the intimate" (Berlant 2008, xi). To point this out is not to glorify the emotional labor that women are charged with in patriarchal society, but to identify self-reflexivity on the part of the performers; as we see in the discussion of harmony above, the focus on emotions, emotionality, and indeed women's relationships can be seen as a reappropriation of realms cast as feminine and therefore dismissed by hegemonic culture.

Book Structure and Clarifications

Throughout *Big Feelings*, I trace these five characteristics across particular examples, noting both points of overlap and divergence, as well as the singular ways that relevant tendencies are performed by musicians with unique vocabularies, artistic visions, and who are situated in their own constellations of contingencies. Throughout the following chapters, I am decidedly uninterested in telling a linear narrative that follows one or

24. For a critique of the term "confessional" see Pollard 2015. As I remarked above, I tend to avoid this word whenever possible. Certainly, Big Feelings artists like Soccer Mommy, Lady Lamb, and Indigo De Souza make music that is informed by their own lives; in keeping with Phillips-Hutton's study (2015), these artists also encourage reading their music as a personal expression through their social media activity, which sometimes contextualizes the topics they write about, and is in any case invested in crafting a public-facing persona that reads as authentic and intimate. The reason I try to avoid the word "confession" then is primarily because of the ways it threatens—as label—to foreclose or downplay the creative, generative aspects of their work, some of which cannot be read as disclosure at all. Instead, here I stick with the ideas of "personal" and "abstract" to suggest that while the personal lives of these musicians are clearly central elements of their craft, the latter is not reducible to the former. Moreover, I don't actually think that the idea of these songs being personally "real" or "authentic" is the central issue with Big Feelings. Rather, the form of the performance affectively signals that musicians and audiences share similar genres of life experience and similar genres of interpretation about those experiences, regardless of the specific content (which would account for the fact that songs can be either quite specific in their storytelling or hopelessly vague—while being equally a/effective for listeners). The point isn't "that happened to me too" but "we belong to the same world."

another artist and their career; instead, this book's aim is simply to take the music seriously, treating each track like a text, extending its tendrils back into the world. Where chapter 1 traces a prehistory of the Big Feelings orientation, chapter 2 sifts through Soccer Mommy's subtle formulation of a post–riot grrrl feminism: deferred in overt terms, Soccer Mommy's music produces feminist affects that both proceed and depart from previous third-wave articulations. Chapter 3 brings these discussions into conversation with the kinds of traumas—both quotidian and acute—experienced by young, queer, and otherwise marginalized groups, as well as the queer care practices that emerge in response, as exemplified in the music of Indigo De Souza.

Chapter 4 shifts toward Mitski, Jay Som, and SASAMI in order to engage the centrality of Asian diasporic musicians to the sound of Big Feelings. This chapter aims to not only acknowledge the long-overlooked history of Asian, Asian American, and biracial musicians in the indie rock space, but also to put generative pressure on the ostensible whiteness of both indie rock generally and Big Feelings particularly. Chapter 5 then focuses on community-building and space-making practices through the music of the Ophelias, whose latest record was produced by Julien Baker. Originally based in Cincinnati, Ohio, the Ophelias render a vision of the queer Midwest that is difficult to locate in mainstream narratives, demonstrating how sound can orient listeners and create spaces of belonging that otherwise remain elusive.

The final chapter considers Vagabon's queer Black interventions into indie through a focus on her powerful manipulation of genre and geography, arguing that her proliferating musical interests align with Black rock aesthetics in ways that frustrate mainstream discursive efforts to pigeonhole and categorize. Lastly, the outro considers the ambivalent politics of Big Feelings, interrogating the significance of this kind of popular music by placing its oblique, affectively oriented approach into conversation with our present sociopolitical conjuncture. Here and elsewhere, I suggest that while the whole book makes a case for reading Big Feelings politically, the music nevertheless performs a specific and limited kind of (juxta)political work that does not have the capacity to address structural inequalities in music or broader culture. As many popular music scholars have shown, uniting communities around shared sentiments is, if anything, a precondition for the kinds of political actions that are needed to (for example) level the systemically and materially uneven playing fields of both indie music and the music industry generally. Indeed, one of the primary challenges in uncritically celebrating the affective focus of Big Feelings is that it has traditionally been white women who are disproportionately allowed to express feelings in public, a problem separate from, but related to, the continued overdetermination of indie rock by/for white people.

This raises another way in which identity is critical to both understanding and participating in this musical scene, so long as identity is understood not as a rigid category but a series of experiences and orientations in varying degrees of coalescence: not only is it the case that public sentiment has always meant something different for white people in the United States, but it is also critical to acknowledge how indie rock specifically has been historically overdetermined by both whiteness and white people. To leave this unacknowledged is to reify the hegemonic status of whiteness by default, concretizing it through the common mechanism of making it invisible (and thus allowing its unmitigated proliferation—see Crenshaw et al. 2019).

For one thing, Big Feelings remains in the realm of whiteness insofar as it reaches back into those earlier '90s precedents for inspiration: invoking music from another decade is never only a stylistic choice, but one that brings along various cultural associations and semiotic resonances. To draw from grunge, riot grrrl, and other indie rock genres from prior decades is to reference musical spaces that were and in many ways remain associated with white performers and audiences, and thus to a certain degree to connote notions of whiteness within their musical expressions—this in spite of another reality that has been well established, which is that rock music was invented by Black women, and that punk, grunge, and indie all were created in part due to the important innovations by people of color who were subsequently erased from those histories (Mahon 2020; Brooks 2021).

For another, indie rock's institutional apparatus remains stubbornly segregated, with artists of color in the minority and experiencing the same kinds of implicit and explicit barriers that have made success more difficult across every industry in the United States (Sahim 2015; Tamanna 2019; James-Wilson 2020). So although there are both artists and fans of color in these indie rock scenes, it's clear that nonwhite practitioners have different experiences in them, and perhaps in part for these reasons, also tend to produce music that doesn't always fit neatly into the aesthetic categories I have been so concerned with identifying through the language of Big Feelings.

That being said, I don't ultimately conceive of Big Feelings as an inherently white affective orientation, but rather one that takes place within an indie rock space that has been long associated with whiteness. This distinction is important because that hegemonic association has always been built upon a fiction: biracial and nonwhite artists have been central to rock music generally, indie rock more specifically, and are particularly influential on the sound I hear as Big Feelings. So while the overall discursive climate and structural inequality of the music industry are essential contexts for considering Big Feelings, I also believe that the affective constellation itself is not reducible to whiteness. Rock isn't and never has been white music, but something *associated* with whiteness for contingent historical reasons. While it is therefore important to recognize public associations between rock and whiteness—as well as industry pressures that help maintain that conflation—the innovations that Big Feelings artists contribute to the genre are, as I have variously suggested, actively challenging those associations, changing what indie rock means, how it sounds, and who it is understood to be for. For artists like Indigo De Souza (Brazilian American), Vagabon (Cameroonian American), and Jay Som (Filipino American) to create in a similar space—to take rock's aesthetic and political terms and virtuosically manipulate them in the expression of one's subjectivity—is both a powerful act of reclamation and reformulation at once.

Throughout this book, readers will notice various prefixes attached to the word "feminist." The hyphenated treatment (for example, "Black-feminist" or "queer-feminist") is essential for pointing to the ways in which identity categories are not separate from one another, but rather co-constitutive. Of these prefixes, "queer" is the most ambiguous, and intentionally so. In this book, I follow, Sara Ahmed (2006), Cathy J. Cohen (1997; 2019), Kara Keeling (2019), and many others in understanding "queer" as a political, epistemological, and affective concept involving but irreducible to questions of desire, sexuality, and identity. Nearly all the affects discussed throughout *Big Feelings* take on a queer valence, whether directly or indirectly, via productive ambiguities around representations of desire, raising questions about sex and/as politics, about boundaries and belonging. I use the word "queer" in this book to variously reference an umbrella term for the LGBTQIA+ communities; nonbinary, nonconforming, and queer gender expressions; ways of being that don't neatly fit within any one or another of these categories; "a collective position relative to state and capitalist power" (Cohen 2019); or some combination of these factors depending on the musician, the music being discussed, and how such affects are performed. In other words, I use "queer" in its broadest possible sense not to conflate various categories of experience, but to include as many different types of experiences as I believe are hailed by this music's affective orientations. Similarly to the elision between affects and feelings, I hope that such an expansive understanding of queerness can help us to draw connections across categories and developments in the music in a way that mirrors its outward reach, its expansive invitations to community, care, and world-building.

Taken together, my hope is that *Big Feelings* provides a loose but evocative framework for theorizing musical and social tendencies that overlap to varying degrees in specific contexts and scenes, and which change with the participation of particular people in those contexts. It argues that across diverse examples, the musicians referenced here are exemplary of a distinctive approach to indie rock in which feelings are central, and through which listeners come to indirectly but no less powerfully experience queer-feminist affects, or expressions of emotional experience that resonate obliquely because of shared cultural contexts. Aware of the rapidly collapsing environment, the disproportionate power wielded by corporations, the weaponization of the state against racialized populations, the overt legislative assaults on women and queer folks, and more, Big Feelings makes space for self-exploration and joy that is hard-won, contingent, and still important. It does not make this space didactically, but through affects, orienting listeners toward community through a shared sense of what feels—and is—urgent.

1 • "All My Friends"

Historical Considerations and a Break in Indie Rock

I told you we'd make it
On for another
—Broken Social Scene[1]

This chapter addresses selective historical factors that matter for the emergence of Big Feelings, tracing important precedents and themes that are critical for contextualizing the music. It has to be selective, because Big Feelings draws on the sounds of multiple genres—including subgenres in rock (punk, post-punk, indie, shoegaze), pop (bedroom/lo-fi, dream, indie, mainstream), folk, and alternatives of all kinds—each of which have their own complex histories. Beyond genre, there are also extramusical developments that have contributed to the conditions that helped make Big Feelings possible. The internet, for example, has radically transformed music production and distribution since the 1990s, lowering barriers of entry for everyone—but perhaps especially girls, women, queer musicians, and others who have been traditionally marginalized by rock culture. From YouTube tutorials to low-cost digital audio workstations (DAWs), it has never been easier to learn how to write, perform, record, and distribute one's own music on a technical level. In the post–riot grrrl era—and largely indebted to that movement's ethos—the work of making rock music more accessible has also continued offline, with the Girls Rock Camp Alliance (and associated locals) hosting workshops all over the world for (cis and trans) girls, as well as nonbinary youth. These camps teach musical fundamentals but also prioritize the emotional health and well-being of their participants, building confidence, channeling anger

1. From "Almost Crimes," track 4 on *You Forgot It in People* (2002).

creatively, and solving disputes with equity in mind (Propst 2017). In this way, they foster the very kinds of queer-feminist care cultures and rock aesthetics that together pervade Big Feelings communities.

A critical precedent for the riot grrrl movement, as Mary Celeste Kearney has shown, was the women's music movement of the 1970s, which intentionally cultivated DIY logistics, safe cultural spaces, and queer-feminist folk music together (1997). Advocating a lesbian separatist ethos, the movement "felt it was both culturally and politically necessary that the structures and systems of recording, distributing, marketing and consuming womyn's music be equally free of the taint of masculinity, male-domination, and misogyny" (1997, 219), and thus pursued the kinds of alternative logistical ecosystems that would become famous when championed by men in the context of 1980s indie.

Further, significant cultural touchstones in live performance (e.g., Lilith Fair) and music discourse (e.g. *NPR*'s "Turning the Tables" series), have continued to produce powerful counternarratives to the implication that rock is masculine music. Of course, the dominance of post/popular feminist artists like Beyoncé and Taylor Swift has also contributed to an overall cultural atmosphere that is at least ostensibly more hospitable to women in popular music than the 1990s, when discourses about gender and genre largely adhered to rockism's stereotypes. Given these many and divergent factors, my aim in this chapter is not to tell a historical narrative that somehow culminates in the Big Feelings sound; instead, I want to raise select ideas and moments that may resonate against one another, as well as the themes of upcoming chapters. Of these, gender and genre are primary—but it is also essential to consider a third term before everything else: indie.

Indie in the 1980s and '90s: Rock vs. Pop

For more than two decades, the word "indie" has functioned more or less as a genre signifier in US popular culture. Though as of this writing, traditional genre categories are undergoing shifts inaugurated by streaming platforms and what Robin James discusses as a kind of vibes economy (2024b), one need only open the "indie" section of Spotify's playlist page to verify that the word remains relevant as a category for listeners. But however defined, its ubiquity as a musical descriptor belies both the concept's complexity and its history, which has seen indie move from a political-economic designation to a more ambiguous index of style.

Scholars agree that indie music as we recognize it originated in the context of UK-based rock bands, who, influenced by punk's DIY ethos, forswore involvement with major record labels out of an insistence that music's socio-political potential—as well as the integrity of the musicians who made it—would be irrevocably compromised by the profit-motives animating the corporate music industry. David Hesmondhalgh (1999) detailed this attitude, writing that indie's adoption of the moniker "independent" marked it as the first musical genre organized around a question of political economy rather than musical characteristics. Though indeed worth emphasizing, labeling indie in this way also had another effect: by consecrating a subset of British post-punk as "indie," an origin point was established onto which historians could focus their attention when seeking to understand the rise of independent musicking in popular culture. As a result, while there were many other popular musical movements that insisted on doing things without corporate involvement, such genres are seldom understood as "indie." As I wrote above, for example, the women's music movement of 1970s New York performed much of the same work, creating its own record labels, distribution mechanisms, and spaces in order to free the musical process from corporate and patriarchal influences (Morris 2015). Still, this movement was associated most of all with '70s folk music sounds, which from a historical perspective, seems to prevent writers from understanding it as a part of "indie" music given the overdeterminative associations between indie and white men playing rock music, particularly in the United Kingdom. We see this dynamic reflected in the overwhelming majority of scholarship and public accounts alike: though Hesmondhalgh's study focuses more on the independent post-punk record labels that formed in the '80s, subsequent work on indie has almost exclusively fixated on white men playing rock music, from the Smiths to Dinosaur Jr., Nirvana to Spoon (Azerrad 2001; Ballance et al. 2009; Bannister 2006; Fonarow 2006; Hibbett 2005; Phillips-Hutton 2018; Ruland 2022; Sellers 2008).[2]

These works have been critical for both rock music studies and popular music scholarship more generally. They contribute to our understanding of important scenes, as well as the operations of identity, politics, and power therein—particularly insofar as they foreground discussions of race and gender in the construction of rock music cultures, dislodging the presumed neutrality/invisibility of white-maleness. But at the same time, the apparent consensus linking indie music to white-masculine rock belies the complexity of

2. For notable exceptions, see Dolan 2010 and Roy 2014. Fonarow (2006) and Lifter (2019) do discuss indie pop, but are focused on scene-building and fashion (respectively), rather than music per se.

even those original indie music scenes, in which women, queer musicians, and artists of color operated both in the United Kingdom and abroad. Initially referenced interchangeably with "indie"—and emerging in many cases from the very same scenes as their more aggressively rock-oriented kin—what would become known variously as "cutie," "twee," or "indie pop" bands took a lighter, more melody-oriented approach to guitar-based independent music beginning as early as 1983. Combined with the fact that this orientation featured on the whole more women musicians, I suggest that the semiotics of this "softer" indie music contributed to its being written out of indie history.

For proponents and detractors alike, indie pop symbolically began with the release of the *New Musical Express* compilation *C86*, a cassette that brought together artists from various UK indie labels, including Rough Trade and Creation. While it initially set off a flurry of excitement and activity—and while it remained popular with listeners well after 1986—the subgenre of indie music with which *C86* became associated quickly faced a backlash. Almost immediately, many critics and musicians took pains to distance themselves from what had come to be seen as an unpolished, "jangly," and unappealingly amateur direction in the music. "We had no idea what a ruckus it would cause," said David Swift of *New Musical Express* (*NME*). "A lot of the bands were lame, it turned out" (quoted in Cavanagh 2024, 212). Frustrated at the stereotypes to which the "*C86*" sound was often reduced, many bands who participated in the compilation later disavowed the excitement it caused, as if misguided. Often, it seemed as if the bands most closely associated with *C86* were the most upset: David Cavanagh observes that those bands "at the top of C86's genealogical tree were among the louder to protest" (2024, 212).

Criticisms of the compilation and the resulting embarrassment on the part of those involved most often have to do with its poor production quality and the too-easy ways it was linked with ostensibly poor musicianship. At least some of that criticism has been held up as reasonable by those involved, either because a lot of these bands (in fairness) broke up after playing a few shows, or else because the ones who stuck around subsequently got much better at what they did. However, I suggest that we can't read reactions to *C86* in isolation; as it turns out, the indie movement it helped to birth included a persistent strain of bands who continued in the "jangly" tradition, writing intentionally pop-oriented songs that were more concerned with exploring emotional life than they were performing post-punk's political alienation and disinterested artistry. Well into the nineties, bands like Black Tambourine, Blake Babies, Belle and Sebastian, Blueboy, Boyracer, Korea

Girl, Lois, the Cat's Miaow, the Cardigans, the Darling Buds, the Primitives, the Softies, the Sea Urchins, Tiger Trap, Rocketship, Velocity Girl, and the artists on the *C86* mixtape (perhaps particularly Primal Scream, the Mighty Lemon Drops, and the Pastels), brought the halting, amateur performance of sincerity pioneered by the Raincoats into conversation with 1960s-inspired timbres and melodies, disavowing masculine-oriented postures of "cool" and embracing softness as an unapologetic critique of normativity. But like *C86* bands, what blossomed into an international indie pop scene was largely ridiculed in the British press in ways that can't be reduced to ostensible amateurism or poor sound quality (which was after all equally characteristic of much punk and post-punk).

Detailing the overall critical attitude of the indie press in the United Kingdom of the 1980s would be relatively impossible in this space, particularly given that back issues of *NME* and *Melody Maker* (the two most important indie publications) remain difficult to access from the States. Yet two points are clear enough: first, indie pop bands don't often make it into academic accounts of indie music with their louder and more stereotypically masculine counterparts. Second, those who have invested time digging into the indie pop phenomenon conclude that, overall, critical appraisals were largely negative (see Eastaugh 2019; Dawkins 2015; White 2016). For my purposes, it is the nature of those critiques that is crucial: performing the classic patriarchal conflation of femininity with pejorative qualities, the press castigates indie pop along the lines of both sex and gender by describing the music as "fey," "meek," "wimpy," "emasculated," and indeed "twee," universally understood as a slur before it was recuperated in the '90s. In an indie subgenre characterized by the relative prominence of women performers, the criticism is self-evidently misogynist; moreover, in a scene that was at least hospitable enough to allow bands like Boyracer and Blueboy to write explicitly about queerness, such reviews also take on relatedly homophobic dimensions.

For scholars of popular music, the foregoing discussion will prove unsurprising: as has been well-established, the "rockist" paradigm that dominated mainstream popular music epistemology for decades has consistently associated hard, aggressive music with both masculinity and artistic merit, while dismissing pop-oriented sounds that hegemonic norms associated with women, girls, and fan cultures, read as superficial and commercially rather than artistically oriented (Coates 1997, 1998, 2003; Cohen 1997; Wald 1998). That indie pop bands don't figure into academic studies of independent music accords with rather than contests the critical consensus that regarded this music as inconsequential. More essential for this chapter, I focus on critiques of indie pop in order to point out that insofar as it was consciously heard and recognized as effeminate during this period, it stands as an important precedent for the current moment, wherein associations with both femininity and queerness are central to perceptions of indie.

Post-2000s Indie: From Genre to Affect

Despite the importance of indie pop, shoegaze, and other post-punk subgenres shaped by the significant involvement of women, a series of retrenchments periodically reasserted the dominance of white men playing aggressive iterations of the music. The first and most disruptive of these crashed through Seattle in the 1990s, scooping up any band that looked and sounded like Nirvana (whose explosive success was unprecedented and shocking), scrambling entire indie scenes built on antiestablishment postures by creating a permission structure through which bands could become the very mainstream against which they had ostensibly railed. Even though there was a ton of overlap between what eventually became characterized as "riot grrrl" bands and "grunge" bands—particularly coming out of the Olympia, Washington, scene, a fluid, mixed gender, and by all accounts open community represented by the Beat Happening/K Records mentality (Baumgarten 2012)—mainstream press, media outlets like MTV, and large brands like the Gap picked up male indie rock bands for the construction of "alternative rock," leaving indie pop groups that ran in similar circles to occupy the "independent" space alone. Beneath mainstream popularity, this kind of indie pop continued to develop its own aesthetic characteristics, which were less hard-rock-oriented, and which would resurface in important ways after 2000.

Eventually, the alt-rock bubble burst, creating the conditions under which it would be easier to recognize "real" indie bands again. But a second shift came in the early 2000s, when the indie rock revival witnessed a consolidation of the term around bands like the Strokes, the Shins, and Bright Eyes. Robin James has argued that this streamlining was accompanied by a kind of musical gentrification wherein industry entities (perhaps most significantly, the recently monopolized Clear Channel radio behemoth) pursued and appropriated surface-level DIY aesthetics without sharing in any of the political or social commitments of earlier punk-informed iterations (2023). Informed in part by a post-nineties need for a different term than "alternative" (which had lost all meaning), one major consequence of this consolidation was that in media discourse and popular vernacular, indie became a question of style, exclusively: it was a certain sound, a certain look, a certain sensibility for moving through the world—thus the Strokes can be considered an indie band in spite of going platinum.[3] During this period, while indie was still associated with white men (think the Shins, Phoenix, and synth-based bands like MGMT), the gentrification James discusses saw indie turn most of all toward models of sensitive, "alternative" white guys who softened (and somewhat broadened) their sounds as part and parcel of indie's more sensitive, sophisticated, and (per James) middle-class semiotics.[4]

While I agree with James's reading (particularly as it pertains to indie's function in broader US culture), I also suggest below that 2000s indie is not reducible to bourgeois white masculinity, following feminist media

3. The idea that indie rock became gentrified also introduces the important and complicated issue of class into this discussion. Whereas it has been well-established that the initial wave of 1980s indie rock bands operated in working-class contexts (particularly in Thatcher's United Kingdom, where jobs were scarce and where many bands relied on social safety-net services in order to sustain their early efforts in the music industry), it is also accepted that 2000s-era indie was much more concentrated around college campuses, advocated via college radio, and synonymous with white middle-class cultures. In this way, characterizations of 2000s-era indie as bourgeois and hipster are something of a truism, perhaps most effectively represented by Vampire Weekend, whose hit debut appeared in 2008 and whose songs frequently reference locations on Columbia University's campus, where the group formed. Today, it is arguable that indie remains an extension of this middle-class/college-oriented lineage, though the question is complicated, in my view, by the inadequacies of traditional class categories for the lived experiences of vast majorities under what Wendy Brown calls the "ruins of neoliberalism" (2019). As I understand it, we don't get sorted into class categories so much as we live between them, particularly, as Stuart Hall would have it, during periods of interregnum. That being said, it is important to acknowledge that my own class position is decidedly upper-middle. Reflecting my position and perhaps relevant for thinking through contemporary indie writ large, most of the fans I was able to speak with for this book also went to college, and some of them were also pursuing advanced degrees.

4. As Matthew Bannister and others have demonstrated, while indie rock initially positioned itself outside and against normative rock culture, its construction of alternative forms of masculinity nevertheless relied upon and further consolidated classic white-male tropes from both public culture and "traditional" white-masculine rock (Bannister 2006; Houston 2012; Hopper 2021; Bimm 2022). For example, Bannister tracks a kind of "tortured genius" archetype in indie rock that casts men as simultaneously perpetrator and victim: "The trope of male suffering," Bannister writes, "allows men to have feelings without being responsible for them, because they are being 'made' to feel by somebody or something else" (2006, 136). In this way, though indie rock does provide a potential opening towards non-normative masculinities, the indie rock archetype itself fails to escape rockism's most persistent values, becoming reinscribed into dominant masculinity all while positioning itself explicitly against that same model. In this it joins both punk and metal, which likewise positioned themselves against a rock mainstream while maintaining white men as consistent protagonists (Waksman 2009).

scholarship that reads indie as transformed and manipulated by fangirl cultures during this period. Nevertheless, the main point I'm trying to make is that indie's reemergence in the post-2000s period solidified it definitively as a genre of music, however delimited. How a given band made their record, which label they signed with, and how the music was distributed became irrelevant for participation and appreciation in the scene, particularly to the extent that such factors ever mattered to fans as barometers of a given band's authenticity.

Accounting for Contemporary Indie

Though at the time of this writing it could be argued that indie remains a coherent genre category, I ultimately suggest that the most useful way of thinking about it is to follow Barry Shank's discussion of indie's overall aesthetic and political world-building. For Shank (utilizing the work of philosopher Jacques Rancière) we can recognize indie more through its "distribution of sense" than in its genre characteristics or political economy: in this understanding, indie communities form a sensory field that communicates core values affectively, organizing listenerships via the transmission and recognition of certain key ideas that are fundamental to the form—for indie, these include uncertainty, contradiction, and emotional honesty (2014).[5] Because such values can be communicated in a variety of ways, there is no particular sound or performance practice that *necessarily* signifies an indie sensibility, although there are certainly musical tendencies. Instead, the genre relies on a certain degree of consensus and shared recognition, which may shift over time and may indeed incorporate factors like business practices.[6] In this formulation, no one criteria is primary, since sense formations are thoroughly contingent on the people, historical circumstances, technological developments, industry pressures (and so on) that happen to be involved.

I follow Shank's perspective because it helps break out of the confusing effort to identify indie either using some kind of popularity threshold (which lots of bands crisscross), or else according to a certain set of instrument-based sounds (likewise). This view is particularly helpful in the current moment for

5. While Rancière himself does not use the language of affect, I follow Brigitte Bargetz in advocating the utility of viewing his "partage du sensible" in sensory/affective terms (Bargetz 2015; DiPiero 2022).

6. For example, Bandcamp is a platform that signifies indie credibility much more than Spotify, which artists engage simply because they have to.

how it also allows us to consider the ways in which indie's *sens* can communicate values like "ambiguity" with *any* sounds—so long as they are accepted and recognized by listeners—because the sonic indexes signifying such values are not fixed in perpetuity. This would account for the fact that from a post-2020 vantage, indie has been able to retain its core affective orientation while also expanding its sonic palette, including more and more textures and timbres under its umbrella, particularly in the last decade—all without becoming incoherent. Put simply, given that indie now includes iterations from folk, synthpop, rock, country, and many other sounds under its umbrella—and given the ways that mainstream pop artists like Taylor Swift have selectively incorporated indie sensibilities into certain projects (James 2024a)—I believe that it is more helpful to talk about indie as an *affect* than a genre.[7]

Shank focuses on Beat Happening to unpack indie's renegotiation of musical beauty, and Beat Happening in turn were deeply influenced by the Raincoats. Though often classified as post-punk, the Raincoats provide the earliest significant example of the kind of earnest, intentionally and insistently amateur performances of sincerity we now hear as fundamental for indie, and which can be heard all over indie pop, including American bands like Korea Girl and European groups from the Bartlebees to Marine Girls.[8] Both Allison Wolfe (Bratmobile) and Kathi Wilcox (Bikini Kill) have attested that "everybody in Olympia knew about the Raincoats" (quoted in Pelly 2017, 22), in large part through the efforts of Calvin Johnson (of both Beat Happening and K Records). "Johnson is a Raincoats evangelist if ever I have met one," Jenn Pelly writes. "He is often credited with pioneering the sensibility of a punk donning a cardigan sweater, but you can trace that back to the Raincoats as well" (2017, 20). Together with Heather Lewis and Bret Lunsford, Johnson's Beat Happening championed the Raincoats and followed their renegotiation of punk sensibilities from a militant amateurism

7. To the extent that this understanding of indie holds water, it also explains the difference between a DIY musician and a DIY *indie* musician. In other words, one reason that I don't talk about Billie Eilish as an indie artist is because Eilish is most commonly recognized and discussed as a pop musician. Despite the fact that her debut album was entirely produced with her brother Finneas in their parents' home, Eilish's music has somehow not been recognized or perceived as fitting within a sensory understanding of indie; it might have been independently made, but the result is something else. Again, while the means of production do matter as indie music criteria, they alone are not sufficient for determining belonging in the category.

8. For critical discussions of amateurism and/as performance in (post) punk and indie, see Haddon 2020 and Shank 2014.

into something more sensitive. As Shank writes, "the amateurism presented through out-of-tune guitars, dropped beats, and cracking voices" opened up a new sense of value, a new way to hear punk authenticity without its aggressive drive (2014, 189). What we can hear in both the Raincoats and Beat Happening is an adoption of punk's permission structure without its macho bullshit; its unvarnished expression without its posture of coolness; its social discontent without the racism, sexism, and homophobia; all its energy without, somehow, its militancy. It was like art school and punk music combined with the sensibilities of a children's librarian or a Sesame Street character—all of that creativity was mobilized towards a view of the world that was expansive and kind—not naive, but not self-righteous either.

If indie is a contingent, affective sense formation, we can track how bands perform its key aesthetic features over time, shifting in response to industry changes, historical factors, and more. And while the remainder of this book leaves aside the question of indie in favor of a more detailed discussion of particular artists, it is nevertheless striking—given the history sketched here—that at least by the time *The New York Times* first clumsily identified a flourishing of indie rock in 2017, indie had become overwhelmingly associated with women and queer musicians, a near complete inversion of the hallmark features discussed in scholarship equating indie music with men.

The Feminization of Indie

If there have always been women and queer musicians playing indie, what I am concerned with tracking here is a discursive shift in which mainstream understandings of indie have switched from an association with masculinity (throughout the '80s and '90s) to one with femininity (in some ways post-2000, but certainly today). On the one hand, Tony Grajeda has argued that the lo-fi aesthetics performed by indie bands like Beat Happening and Sebadoh—as well as more popular acts like Sheryl Crow and Liz Phair—helped feminize rock sounds insofar as lo-fi productions values have been gendered and variously denigrated by mainstream rockist discourse (2002). On the other, Alyx Vesey (2021) and Morgan Bimm (2022) have shown how indie became imbricated with visual media in the mid-to-late 2000s, where movies like *Garden State* and TV shows like *Awkward* (MTV) helped associate indie sounds with the emotional lives of young women and girls. As the streaming age dawned and record labels became less relevant to the lives of working bands, the increasing centrality of screen media to artists' career prospects affected how indie appeared in popular culture. It is in this time period particularly that indie's consolidation as a genre classification both shifted and solidified, becoming associated with the smoother, more introspective sounds of bands like Bright Eyes, Death Cab for Cutie, and the Shins, and standing in somewhat of a contrast with their indie brethren in the garage rock revival (the Strokes, the Hives, the White Stripes, the Vines), much heralded in the rock press as a return to the glory days of a rock music that had, by the end of the '90s, all but ceded mainstream popularity to pop and hip hop. Bimm and Vesey suggest that during this period, the softer sounds of Wilco, Feist, and Regina Spektor were being taken up by women and girls for how the music resonated with their affective orientations. Often enough, this resonance was facilitated directly through the choices of other women musicians like Bethany Cosentino and Tegan and Sara Quin, who were hired as music supervisors at MTV with the explicit purpose of attracting young female viewerships. Along with figures like Alexandra Patsavas—the music supervisor responsible for bringing music from Phantom Planet, Death Cab for Cutie, and Rilo Kiley to shows like *The O.C.*—this work consistently paired indie music with affective worlds of feminized feeling. Even still, this had to be a reflexive and reciprocal process. As Bimm reminds us, it wasn't just artists and supervisors remaking perceptions of indie; it was also listeners. "Arguing instead for the joy and possibility in reframing this era as a time of shifting benchmarks around what counts as 'good' art, musicianship, access, authenticity, and fandom," Bimm makes the case that fans have actively reshaped the social connotations and functions of indie in ways that are rarely noted in scholarship (2022, 3). Beyond the fact that rock cultures wouldn't exist without fans, fan communities have measurable and important impacts on the developments of genres over time, and often in ways that are entirely unanticipated by either artists or industry figures.

These developments, I suggest, easily link up with the feminized sounds of early-nineties indie pop, particularly the twee aesthetic that self-consciously resisted macho performances. Together, they contributed to a significant cultural recoding whereby indie as a label shifted its cultural connotations: what invariably signaled white hetero-masculinity now conjures not only femininity but also queerness, helping set the stage for the flourishing of music discussed throughout this book. Before this process of cultural recoding was complete, some less well-known indie bands were explicitly working from and appealing to the perspectives of a more expanded music audience. To finish with this chapter's historical considerations, I turn now to two early precedents for this affectively oriented approach to queer-feminist indie.

Emergent Example: Broken Social Scene

At the turn of the twenty-first century, the *Billboard* charts were dominated by groups like Savage Garden, Destiny's Child, Christina Aguilera, Santana, Eminem, and a host of others who had in common that they did not perform rock music. Radiohead's *Kid A* did chart; but the only other rock bands with any traction include Limp Bizkit and Creed, hardly indicative of important or interesting developments in the genre. Going by the charts alone, the unquestioned conflation between "rock" and "popular music" that had been dominant for decades—and which had arguably peaked in the alt-rock zeitgeist of just a few years earlier—seemed to be breaking up in favor of high production boy and girl groups, R&B, and the mainstream ascendancy of hip hop.

It is in this context that the mainstream rock press, anxiety-ridden over the potential loss of their own relevance, hailed the garage revival symbolized by the Strokes, the Hives, the Vines, and the White Stripes, casting them variously as the "saviours of rock and roll" (Smith 2009, 240). Roughly concurrently, bands like Neutral Milk Hotel, Death Cab for Cutie, and the Shins represented a meaningfully different interpretation of indie rock—one that was not as publicly dominant, but which would find its own cultural moment, later resurfacing in the softer, more eclectic sounds of bands like Beirut, Grizzly Bear, and the Dirty Projectors. It's not that rock critics ignored this latter, more introspective group altogether; in fact, both garage rock and indie represented two differing means of reasserting rock's relevance in the 2000s, utilizing two versions of rock's most persistent trope: authenticity. With the former, media narratives conjured historical authenticity, which the new group of garage bands were understood to embody by returning to the ostensible roots of rock and roll (whitewashing its Black origins) in an age overdetermined by high production value in pop and nu metal. With indie, the story remained largely as the indie story always had, where artists like Bright Eyes were praised for authenticity read as emotional honesty. The 2000s-era version of this latter story fits perfectly in accordance with Bannister's reading of '80s indie, in which intellectual, reflective, and uniquely sensitive white men had long signified authenticity in the genre, providing a readily available paradigm through which to read not only indie like the Shins but also emo like Dashboard Confessional.

What the press missed at the time was how gender and sexuality factored into the rock music of the new millennium. On the one hand, as discussed above, women and girls were taking up indie in ways that would expand its traditional association with men and heterosexuality. On the other hand, bands like Broken Social Scene made blueprints for an indie sound that would more explicitly take up the concerns of women and queer folks. Insofar as it is helpful to locate a "first" Big Feelings record, we could do worse than pointing to Broken Social Scene's 2002 breakout *You Forgot It in People* (*YFIIP*).

Released in 2002, *YFIIP* would eventually sell more than 200,000 copies, accruing indie cult status through a slow and steady buildup of live performances and indie press hype. But while *YFIIP*'s significance is better-established today, it wasn't necessarily understood as an important record for the mainstream rock press. The Strokes' *Is This It*, by comparison, would sell over two million copies while being championed by magazines like *Spin*. Appearing on the cover three times between 2003 and 2006, the Strokes are in good company with the White Stripes (October 2002, September 2003, Jack White in June 2009); the Vines (March 2004); the Hives (August 2004); Franz Ferdinand (October 2004; November 2005); the Killers (February 2005; January 2006; December 2006); My Chemical Romance (June 2005; March 2006; February 2007); Fall Out Boy (December 2005, March 2007); Dashboard Confessional (March 2003, October 2003); the Foo Fighters (November 2002, August 2005, November 2007); Radiohead (November 2000, July 2003, December 2009), and Eminem (August 2000, January 2001, August 2001, December 2002, April 2003), considering just the 2000–2010 decade. Garage rock, emo, and still-strong '90s alternative bands are well represented in these issues, but it is truly striking how many different ways the magazine finds to loop the Strokes into whatever conversation. There are multiple multipage profiles of the band across many years; fake press releases hyping "the coolest kids in New York City," who are "set to unleash the best album of the year . . . again"; stories about other artists framed by their encounters with the Strokes (e.g., Regina Spektor); stories about people simply *talking about* the Strokes (e.g., Courtney Love); and consistent appearances across any number of lists ("best band," "best album," "best song," "most important artists making music right now," etc.).

By contrast, the closest *Spin* gets to championing a band that differs from the hegemonic masculine norm is the Yeah Yeah Yeahs (on the cover June 2004, April 2006, March 2009), with occasional appearances from bands like Death Cab for Cutie (September 2005) and Rilo Kiley (September 2007). The editors do seem to like Bright Eyes a good amount (perhaps not as much as *Rolling Stone*, who literally labeled Conor Oberst "rock's boy genius")—but again, it's not that indie bands weren't praised during this period; it's just that the coverage was disproportionately stacked in favor of certain groups anointed with the rock press's investments. Beneath the surface of this mainstream, musicians and listeners alike were forging a different kind of indie rock commons.

Particularly given its near-universal relevance in my friend circle, it is striking to me that references to *You Forgot It in People* are scattered and brief across the mainstream rock press. It gets a glowing but tiny review from *Rolling Stone* in June 2003, for example, and later a two-sentence review (B+) in *Spin*'s September issue.[9] The point I'm trying to make here is that however much the record would go on to resonate with fans, there is still meaning in distinguishing between a rock mainstream and an indie underground in this moment.[10] Even as corporate pressures nearly break college radio, the search for genuinely alternative music is still being pursued by listeners and DJs who turn to the internet for hope—at least for a time (James 2023a; Jewell 2023). In 2002, just as the (indie) rock revival began to consolidate—narrowing its sound and successfully paving the way for the continued success of white men in rock bands (e.g. Arcade Fire, Arctic Monkeys, Vampire Weekend, the Killers, et al.)—relatively passed-over records presaged the current situation, in which indie is dominated by women and queer artists.

You Forgot It in People can be read as an important precedent for Big Feelings in several ways. Following a debut record of mostly instrumentals, the band's sophomore release is elevated by its layered vocal performances; but significantly, the lyrics are almost uniformly buried, dissolving into the overall texture as one more instrument rather than a focal point.[11] That the lyrics are secondary here is further enforced by their semantic content, which is altogether vague, imprecise, accidental. As with Big Feelings proper, the content of the lyrics is secondary to the role of the vocals as an additional voice in an overall project. That the lyrics are treated as coequal with every other sound is not to dismiss their importance, however; in fact, the few words listeners can make out work in concert with the band's sonic vocabulary to perform a distinct distance from rock hegemony. Song titles like "Anthems for a Seventeen-Year Old Girl" capture something of the nostalgic construc-

9. It also shows up in *Rolling Stone*'s "local favorites" chart twice (best-selling records for the week ending July 20, 2003, from Green Eggs and Jam in Asheville; September 28th, 2003 from Spaceboy Music in Philadelphia).

10. For another example, while the academic database *Rock's Backpages* includes 263 articles that mention the Strokes, only 17 mention Broken Social Scene.

11. Reflecting on the important track, member Emily Haines said, "I remember listening to the recording of 'Anthems for a Seventeen-Year-Old-Girl' and I couldn't really hear myself in it, which is the classic Broken Social Scene move—everything is obscured behind the wall of marijuana. I don't remember having any sense that it was going to have an impact" (quoted in Berman 2009, 87–88).

tion of *YFIIP*, while also dedicating music to a listenership not often explicitly addressed in rock history.[12] Likewise, "I'm Still Your Fag" laments a queer relationship lost to heteronormativity, marking the psychic toll of living without love. Like many post-punk and indie bands, Broken Social Scene has a mixture of men and women in the band. But uniquely, the collective nature of the group—which features a rotating cast of at times up to thirty musicians—makes room for multiple voices, literally and figuratively.[13] Relatedly, and like many Big Feelings records, *YFIIP* largely eschews standard pop song forms, stretching single sections, moods, and textures without giving way to what can be easily grasped as a "verse" or a "chorus." Combined with the same kind of unusual-for-the-genre instrumentation that was characteristic of bands like Neutral Milk Hotel, the heavy incorporation of soaring chord extensions, as well as a comparatively expansive deployment of texture—from serene strings to massive guitar distortion—*You Forgot It in People* presents an alternative path for rock music at the very same time that its seemingly eternal masculine blueprint was gasping its last breaths.[14]

---

12. One young musician impacted by this canonic song is Spencer Peppet of the Ophelias, discussed in chapter 5. In the interest of tracing points of resonance—or as Peppet describes, shared languages—I quote her at length connecting this song to another important touchstone in this book: the embrace of astrology and contemporary mysticism by young women and queer folks. "Astrology is one of my favorite shared languages," she writes. "I hear someone has an Aquarius moon and I think—oh, I understand. Someone has a lot of Virgo in their chart and we joke about planners or perfectionism, with the undercurrent of 'I see you, really.' I love astrology for this reason, the same as I love music and media and personality quizzes. It eases people into conversations about what lies underneath the teen magazine answers. It allows us to access those pieces without giving everything away. I think back to when I met my best friend the first week of college. She had a line from 'Anthems for a Seventeen-Year Old Girl' in her Instagram bio. It was my favorite song. We stood in the lobby of this new building, surrounded by new people who would swear to be friends forever and disappear after the first few months of school, and we saw each other. This song, so deeply important to me, was so deeply important to her too. It allowed us to be immediately vulnerable with each other in a way that we otherwise could not. She's still my best friend" (Peppet 2024).

13. Though not, as Carl Wilson points out, always seamlessly (2023a). Indeed, readers of Stuart Berman's *This Book Is Broken* will encounter anecdotes that portray typically sexist/male rock-band behavior, along with instances modeling something different, a kind of queer sociality. These modes coexist through the band's history in part because of how many different people were involved, as well as how those people changed over long periods of time.

14. In 2024, long after I had drafted this book, I was thrilled to discover yeule's cover of "Anthems" opening the lauded soundtrack for the emphatically queer/Gen-Z film *I Saw the TV Glow*, corroborating my arguments about the semiotic resonances of this music and its legacy for a new generation of women and queer artists. Moreover—and imagine my surprise—the vinyl version of the soundtrack is closed by Snail Mail's cover of the Smashing

Whether laudatory or more qualified, nearly all coverage of Broken Social Scene focuses around its communal structure, linking its collective composition to other large bands (the Polyphonic Spree, Arcade Fire) as well as the disparate genre influences that either made for incoherent listening or was evidence of a revolution in indie rock, depending.[15] Questions about how long the collective can last—particularly with its DIY integrity intact—abound. Almost universally ignored is that the collective structure of the band also allows for diverse perspectives to enter the songwriting, that the band might be cultivating an indie rock listenership beyond its stereotypical male fanbase. Save, so far as I can tell, a truly bizarre review that seems to conflate the band's queerness with its Canadian origins and presumed liberal politics (Phillips 2003), questions of identity are almost wholly absent from the album's mainstream reception.

Beyond the more overt ways in which feminized and queer perspectives enter song lyrics, there is also an affective orientation across *YFIIP* that is perceptible to listeners, well in line with my arguments about Big Feelings in general. For example, Ian Dahlman notes, "Love forms a significant part of the discourse surrounding Broken Social Scene, an affect mobilized to describe the connections between all members and to express what guides the collective spirit" (2009, 129). That is to say that the love in question is not per se romantic (although romance was involved among members of the BSS collective) and is decidedly not heteronormative. Insofar as collectivity, community, and chosen family themselves can be read as immanently queer, we can start to understand how the band's communal existence—what member Jason Collett called "an experiment in intimacy" (quoted in Berman 2009, 143)—might link up with their lyrics, song titles, and eclectic sounds to help attract feminist and queer listeners through resonance, both sonic and social.

A Break: Land of Talk

"Less a fetishized authenticity than a critique of the dominant mode of technology," Tony Grajeda writes, the "noise" of lo-fi recordings "upsets the

---

Pumpkins' canonic "Tonight, Tonight," helping to place these two differently queer vibrations in a shared lineage, just as I hope to do with this book, a lineage made so simply through the act of their being claimed by these young musicians.

15. This is also true of Ian Dahlman's master's thesis on the band (2009), as well as Stuart Berman's book (2009). That being said, both Dahlman and Berman take the question of collectivity much more seriously than the "isn't this weird" approach often found in the press, including compelling reflections on its social and musical implications for the band.

cliched depiction of slacker indifference underscoring lo-fi amateurism" by appropriating the 1960s and '70s avant-garde that was associated with masculinity in order to undermine or outmaneuver masculinized hardcore in the 1990s (Grajeda 2002, 247). Embracing what mainstream rock criticism marks as "inadequate or objectionable," lo-fi centers "fragmented incompleteness, indefinite structure, lack of resolution" (241) and other traits that Grajeda follows Susan McClary in understanding as feminized and devalued. As if self-reflexively aware of lo-fi's place in the Western aesthetic value system, Free Cake for Every Creature titles their intimate and out of tune debut *shitty beginnings*, the cover for which is a wobbly sketch of musician Katie Bennett's bedroom. From the hiss of tape to the halting guitar playing, this charming Bandcamp release testifies that the legacy of Beat Happening is alive and well. Released in 2013, *shitty beginnings* evinces both a continuing lo-fi tradition (even across the 2000s period, indie was dominated by big-name, male-fronted acts) and the extent to which lo-fi approaches had been thoroughly embraced by young women and girls by 2013. Positively reappropriating its feminized affects, this indie orientation can be also heard in earlier precedents like Wye Oak's *If Children* (2008) and P.S. Eliot's *Introverted Romance in Our Troubled Minds* (2009).

Bridging this kind of feminized lo-fi and the more quintessentially Big Feelings sound is Elizabeth Powell, the musical force behind Land of Talk (LoT). Best known for "muscular" records with "gut-level" post-hardcore riffs (Hogan 2007), Land of Talk has been described as a link between "today's Montreal and the Seattle Era that birthed Pretty Girls Make Graves" (Bevan 2008),[16] thus providing a critical early example of the Big Feelings combination of heavy, '90s/grunge guitars with ethereal, hookworm vocals. But before collaborating with Mark "Bucky" Wheaton and Chris McCarron to develop this sound, Powell was working things out in their bedroom.

Powell's 1999 cassette tape, *belle époque* almost entirely features acoustic guitar and voice, sometimes transcendently doubled, with the occasional glockenspiel accent. Already, LoT listeners will recognize here the unconventional harmonic construction (replete with chord extensions), the poignant use of repetition, the bittersweet affects that characterize later music, somehow both triumphant and introspectively nostalgic. Elliptical melodic lines embrace extensions like the acicular sharp eleventh, often landing on them squarely, at the end of a phrase. Throughout, Powell's irregular guitar tunings combine with the uneven production to produce a gauzy, romantic sheen

16. Note as well that Pretty Girls Make Graves is another mixed-gender band that cites rock history (via the Smiths) in their very name.

over everything, perhaps similar to other lo-fi indie, but to my ear infinitely more interesting in mood, arrangement, bone structure.

Posted to Land of Talk's bandcamp in 2021, *belle époque* captures an emergent Powell apparently fully formed as a musician. Some of its songs later appear, newly arranged, on *ELE_K**, a solo LP released with short-lived indie Sinistresound in 2003. *ELE_K** deploys a full band and a range of timbres and studio elaborations, from distorted guitars to intergalactic synth lines. This record also features early versions of future LoT tracks, such as the devastating and essential "It's Okay," here some thirty-five clicks faster than the version released with Saddle Creek on 2008's *Some Are Lakes*. Again contributing to the impression that Powell's musical voice was developed from the jump, this early work retains of all the energy to be found on LoT's 2006 EP, *Applause Cheer Boo Hiss*, the grunge-era heaviness communicated via timbre and combined with the glistening complexity of the harmonic construction.

With some lineup changes and several extended periods away from musical activity, Land of Talk has nevertheless continued since their formation, releasing their latest, *Performances*, in October of 2023. Though this record emphasizes synths over guitars, Powell's songwriting remains a compelling throughline, rendering melancholia in cinematic, existential terms. "Your Beautiful Self," for example, could almost be a ballad were it not for the driving drums, pushing the song forward while the slow harmonic rhythm of the chords pulls listeners back, a contrasting rate of speed that feels to me like a spinning movie camera, like a hand out a car window, one face standing still while the world spins behind it. This quality is always present in Powell's music, even when it's heavy: consider "The Hate I Won't Commit," for example, from 2010's *Cloak and Cipher*, which opens with a tremolo guitar tone that announces something huge, an anticipatory fuzz soon balanced by a choir of Powell's layered vocals, hymnal and cascading down an extended minor harmony. The contrast between the crunchy guitar, distorted main vocal, and serene, almost reverent background is one part of the contradiction that makes the track so compelling—but so is Powell's rhythmic sensibility, which is here both playful and deadly serious. Listen, in what might count as the "chorus" in this track (whose traditional function, in this song, is interestingly undermined), to the way the band sets up a rhythmic pattern twice before delaying it by a beat, keeping you guessing (1:14–1:36). The second time through the chorus, this play happens again, now displaced by *two* beats instead of just one (2:27–2:50).

The "serious" part comes at the end, a disgustingly funky breakdown that releases all the tension built up ever since that first opening chord. Built from a four-against-three polyrhythm between Powell's razor guitar and the rhythm section, the groove is anchored by a backbeat in the drums and the opulent mercury of Joseph Yarmush's bassline.[17] But while the groove—so thick with texture, so cathartic—remains the high point of the track, what prevents its rhythmic interplay from spilling into punk rock anarchy is the harmonic construction, the minor-seventh voicing with notes all crunched together, which produces a both-at-once feeling ambivalently stretched between remembering wistfully and rocking out in the present moment, between head-banging and crying. There is, in other words, an emotional complexity even in the breakdown, which performs all of grunge's timbral and rhythmic signatures while shading its corners, a dark harmonic nuance.

Like Broken Social Scene—with whom they toured and which Powell briefly joined—Land of Talk consistently presages the aesthetic and social hallmarks of the Big Feelings phenomenon. The prolific and varied use of chord extensions across LoT's output stands as particularly noteworthy both for how thoroughly the band adopts them and for how rarely we hear similar uses before the advent of Big Feelings proper. In part, I believe this has a lot to do with Powell's unconventional guitar tunings, which I view as a part of a long tradition that sees women, queer folks, and those otherwise marginalized by rock culture making their own ways forward in the absence of readily available mentorship from like-minded peers.[18] Powell's nonbinary gender identity is also one aspect of how this music resonates in the ways that it does, entering into the lyrics and the notes indirectly, the same way that every musician's subjectivity leaves traces in sound. Although the contemporary music industry remains largely toxic and hostile for women and queer performers, subsequent chapters of this book will discuss the ways in which marginalized indie musicians have found each other, forging communities and subscenes that protect and make space for one another. Powell, a pioneering "legacy musician" with demonstrable influences on a younger generation,[19] did not have this kind of protection, explaining in a recent interview,

---

17. What's even smarter, trickier than the groove on its own, is the way the band gets in and out of it: Powell teases the eighth-note pattern first (3:18), but in a slower version, where the hemiola takes place over two bars of 3/4 time, rather than resetting on each downbeat (as in the breakdown); the band plays this superimposition together, three times, before throwing listeners again by launching into the full-on groove, based in the original rhythm but now more rapid. The hits that take the band out of it are just as tricky, stopping abruptly after so many repetitions, easy to miss if you're not locked into the bass part.

18. On a more general level, these tunings also demonstrate a concrete link to grunge, in which such methods "replaced the technical precision of shred with an aesthetic variability . . . in which elements of dissonance often came to the foreground" (Waksman 2009, 271).

19. At least two verified examples include Julien Baker and Lucy Dacus, spotted by my friend at an LoT show in Los Angeles.

> Growing up in the Guelph music scene and being a young assigned female at birth person and performing femininity . . . I mean had I known about nonbinary or gender fluidity or that there was life beyond the binary for kids I would have been identifying as nonbinary since day one. . . . Being hyper sexualized by a lot of the older men in the Guelph music scene and beyond . . . I was not protected and I was not safe. We were all hardcore straight edge punk rock, apparently feminist, our politics all seemed to be tight. But there [were] still predatory men, predatory sex pests in the punk rock scene, in the Toronto music scene . . . and nobody was protecting me. Nobody. (quoted in Khanna 2023)

Such difficult experiences have informed Powell's identity and musical processes, not in ways that are directly discernible, but insofar as Powell channels their life experiences into poetry without premeditating what a given song is going to mean or discuss. In the same interview, for example, Powell discussed how references to babies in two recent tracks had less to do with literal children and more to do with the ways in which Powell is working through the trauma of not being held in safety while doing the work that they love.

As I described above, I consider Powell one of the pioneers of the now ubiquitous sound that pairs cacophonous '90s guitars with melodious, harmonized vocals—particularly in heavier Big Feelings bands like Bully, Indigo De Souza, Mannequin Pussy, and Wednesday. It's music heavy in both directions at once, with the timbral density of alt-rock guitar sounds and the harmonic density of the songwriting. This combination of force *and* beauty is stitched together by Powell's voice, commanding enough to stand up to the guitars and navigating melodies as unconventional as they are captivating. Something important is happening here, where the gravity of alt-rock supports a crystalline focus on song construction, on melodic and harmonic intricacy. Emerging but distinct from bedroom indie, Powell's approach models so much of the characteristic disjunction present in Big Feelings' embrace of the loud, the aggressive, the overwhelming in rock music—yet nearly always with the simultaneous insistence of the line, the melody, the *note*. It is this combination of beautiful and boisterous that makes Big Feelings sound like everything, simultaneously bitter and sweet, because it's made from every feeling and memory and relationship and place and thought articulated or not, every exuberance and heartbreak and banality and tenderness and violence and experience of the whole bundle's transience, already gone.

History, Affect, Politics: A Brief Note on Citation

In tracing an incomplete history of the current indie rock environment, this chapter has been concerned with raising important markers, moments, and figures so that they might resonate against one another, drawing out frequencies too often submerged in canonic tellings. From indie's earliest moments straight through to the present, mainstream histories of rock music have denigrated or ignored the women and queer musicians in the middle of everything, as well as the alternative sounds, stories, and semiotics they produced. And yet, today it is incontestable that indie music is the purview of these diverse artists, a striking reversal of conventional wisdom that belies the longer history of their involvement.

After attempting to outline some of this history, it's important to raise the fact that many contemporary indie artists are often aware of and actively invested in critiquing the stories told about rock music in popular discourse. And while artists like boygenius directly address such issues in interviews, Big Feelings artists have also embraced cover songs as a key site for advancing a worldview. Following Morgan Bimm's formulation of cover songs as a "reclamation and a reassertion of girls' and women's roles in indie rock history" (2022, 19) and in line with what Stephanie Doktor shows is a much longer history of "cross-gender cover songs" (2024) that comment on identity vis-à-vis popular music history, I understand cover songs to perform at least three related functions in the Big Feelings universe.

First, they help (de)construct rock histories, raising up important artists who may have been left out of more mainstream narratives of the genre while also critiquing/commenting on those more well-known references. Adopting Sara Ahmed's formulation of citation as a feminist praxis,[20] Bimm raises Soccer Mommy's cover of MGMT's "Indie Rokkers," noting how "Allison's refusal to change the lyrics or pronouns in a song largely focused on a sexual encounter also effectively turns the indie slowburn into a queer anthem" (2022, 27). We could say the same about the Raincoats' 1979 cover of "Lola" (originally released by the Kinks in 1970), which is particularly significant given the Raincoats' profound influence on indie.[21]

Though not a literal cover, we can also think here about Soccer Mommy's

20. Ahmed has written about this in several places, but I like her formulation in *Living a Feminist Life*: "Citation is feminist memory. Citation is how we acknowledge our debt to those who came before; those who helped us find our way when the way was obscured because we deviated from the paths we were told to follow" (2017, 15–16).

21. The Kinks are also cited by Sleater-Kinney, whose 1997 record *Dig Me Out* patterns its cover after the Kinks' *The Kink Kontroversy* (1965).

"Your Dog," which responds directly to the Stooges' "I Wanna Be Your Dog" in a way that also protests a stereotypical heterosexual relationship in which the woman functions as a token, accessory, or animal. "I don't wanna be your fucking dog" Allison sings, opening the track, "That you drag around / A collar on my neck tied to a pole / Leave me in the freezing cold." Beyond apparently contradicting the Stooges, the song further clarifies its subject of address as it develops, situating itself decidedly in the context of a romantic relationship: "I'm not a prop for you to use / When you're lonely or confused / I want a love that lets me breathe / I've been choking on your leash." Here the speaker's refusal to be treated poorly by their partner speaks in the language of classic white-guy rock, conflating the gendered implications of (bad) heterosexual romance with the rock canon in order to reject them both.

Second, cover songs help build community through the sharing of cultural referents, a function they have always performed, but which becomes newly political in the context of a genre traditionally overcrowded by men's references to other men. When Soccer Mommy and Jay Som cover each other's songs for the *Soccer Mommy & Friends* EP, they help to raise one another up while also cluing listeners into musical and social bonds among musicians, strengthening feelings of intimacy on both sides. I see this as an example of what Andi Schwartz identifies as "feminized social values, like friendliness, sharing, and secret-keeping—which become politicized as collaboration, citational practice, and sisterhood" (2024, 11). In this way, cover performances help Big Feelings musicians simply but importantly *share culture* with one another, and by extension with their fans, as if passing around a favorite mixtape or bargain bin discovery.

This can be especially significant when what Ahmed calls "citational chains" (2017) link together artists who have been similarly marginalized by rock culture. (For example, Jay Som and Japanese Breakfast were each tapped to record Yoko Ono covers for Ben Gibbard's tribute record *Ocean Child*.) But these kinds of connections are also being drawn in other ways, including what we might call a kind of "community logistics": Melina Duterte (Jay Som) plays bass for boygenius, for example, and has also maintained a strong friendship with Michelle Zauner (Japanese Breakfast). Laetitia Tamko (Vagabon) helped out on Duterte's 2019 album *Anak Ko*, and is friends with both SASAMI (Sasami Ashworth) and Mitski Miyawaki (Mitski). Duterte's latest project, Bachelor, was formed with Palehound's El Kempner in part as "an ode to queer friendship" (Velasquez 2021). Sophie Allison (Soccer Mommy) is also a part of this scene, having worked with both Duterte and Ashworth on the *Soccer Mommy & Friends Singles Series*. Allison also went to college with Spencer Peppet of the Ophelias, whose most recent record was also produced by Julien Baker. Like Karen O joining Japanese Breakfast onstage or touring with SASAMI, cover songs and collaborative projects create visible and audible connections that are especially important given that many minority indie musicians have lamented having only one, two, or no role models in the indie rock past.

Third, cover songs help indie music produce feminist affects, contributing to the recoding of rock music through what Alyx Vesey calls "citational feminism," a term for describing "the act of explicitly referencing feminine and female emblems of popular culture as an intergenerational expression of women's solidarity through creative inspiration" (2018, 74). When Soccer Mommy covers Pavement, Sheryl Crow, Slowdive, Taylor Swift, and R.E.M., for her EP *Karaoke Night*; when yeule covers "Anthems for a Seventeen-Year Old Girl"; when Snail Mail covers "Tonight, Tonight"; their construction of an alternative canon emphasizes the kinds of feminized rock music and overtly *pop*-oriented sounds that had been previously dismissed by rockist gatekeepers. I understand such interventions to be one way that Big Feelings artists are changing what rock music signifies, as well as its presumed audience.

Further, feminist affects can also adhere to the *mode* of covering songs: Phoebe Bridgers, for example, has covered the Goo Goo Dolls' pining '90s anthem "Iris" at certain live shows, also releasing a version made available for twenty-four hours in order to raise money for abortion funds. SASAMI has played covers (or snippets of covers) on Instagram and Facebook stories, sharing work in progress in ways that dovetail with Gen Z indie's culture of intimacy. I understand both examples as selective, a kind of specific, contextual sharing used to bring together certain groups in certain moments and further consolidating an intimate public around sensibilities-in-common: those who value intimacy and disclosure, who may feel something of their own (queer) experience in the unresolved romance of "Iris" ("And I don't want the world to see me / Cause I don't think that they'd understand"), who understand the stakes involved in the fight for reproductive justice.

Citing people is a way of writing history, consolidating narratives around the key figures understood to have enacted them. With enough repetition, those figures can even inadvertently help to preclude others, so that Elvis eclipses Big Mama Thornton, so that the Smiths snuff out Marine Girls. But if Ahmed draws our attention to "how certain bodies take up spaces by screening out the existence of others" (2013), Big Feelings artists show how alternative citational chains can help reclaim space for others even retroactively. In the context of indie rock history, this chapter's brief discussion of contemporary citational praxis is intended to show not only how cover songs help affectively reorient indie rock sounds in a feminist direction, but also how they perform an active refusal of the persistent and repeated erasures that have made this intervention necessary in the first place: the denial of women, queer folks, and people of color in historical narratives. As I show in the next chapter, such interventions are just one means by which contemporary indie bands are producing queer and feminist affects in sound.

2 • "I Wanna Be That Cool"

Soccer Mommy's Feminist Affects

> I don't know how to feel things small.
> —Soccer Mommy[1]

Performing as Soccer Mommy since 2015, Sophie Allison seemed to find success immediately, and by 2017 had dropped out of New York University to pursue music full-time. Since the release of her first album, *Clean*, she has been praised across pop music journalism for her dedication to the craft of songwriting, as well as the way that she can turn intimate musical disclosures into poetic sentiments that resonate widely. These musical qualities are indeed worth emphasizing, the kinds of observations so often denied to women rock musicians in the past, whose genders overdetermined how the press talked about their music, occluding any serious grappling with their contributions to the genre. At the same time, one of the reasons I am so compelled by Soccer Mommy's music on a personal level is that it *feels feminist*—that is, it holds out the possibility of affirming or reflecting back to me my political commitments and those of my communities. I'm not trying to say anything here about Soccer Mommy's politics, or even how I understand feminism as a project, as a lens through which to view the world; instead what I'm suggesting is that before those details come into focus, I hear something in this music that attracts my attention, that seems to invite me closer. While I offer my own listening experience only as a gateway into a larger discussion, it matters to me personally that this music feels like it works within the same kind of world that I inhabit and perceive, at least to a degree, especially and specifically because in the context of broader US culture, such indications still feel rare and precious.

1. From "Still," track 11 on *Sometimes Forever* (2022).

Although a certain kind of "popular feminism" is today visible everywhere, it is overwhelmingly individualistic, white, and profitable for the corporations who nominally embrace its message (Banet-Weiser 2018). It is not an intersectional feminism, and it does not question the role of systems of power such as capitalism and white supremacy in the construction of gender inequality. For those of us on the Left, for those who can't see themselves reflected in popular feminism's cold insistence on white beauty norms and profitability, this is a model that is affectively prohibitive, even if we might not be able to articulate why. Instead of attraction and gravitation, popular feminism produces profoundly alienating experiences for those on the outside of its vibrational pull, who need not have any particular ideological position in order to feel disconnected from what popular feminism sells.

As I've been claiming from the beginning, it is critical to stipulate that Big Feelings music most often doesn't address politics directly, and therefore doesn't provide a kind of comprehensive, intersectional-feminist political articulation around which to cohere. What it does is provide an alternative space for feeling feelings that popular feminism—caught up as it is with neoliberal resilience—prohibits from its framework. Instructed from all quarters to "girl boss" our individual ways out of what are actually structural problems, Big Feelings instead makes room for affective experiences beyond grit and resilience: sadness and depression, yes—but also desire and pleasure, queer community, feminist solidarity, and joy. Even without overtly politicized messaging around certain actions and their significance, Big Feelings creates sounds that express a more capacious range of human experiences, and the feelings that suffuse them.

Feminism is not reducible to a politics of feeling, and feminist affects do not equal feminist political actions. These related facts are why I resist celebrating Big Feelings music as a political project, or a new vanguard of feminism in popular culture. Contemporary indie rock of the type discussed in this book is not (nor does it purport to be) a solution for the structural oppressions that popular feminism refuses from its gaze, does not necessarily raise consciousness around issues of power, structural inequity, implicit biases, attacks on reproductive freedom, interpersonal violence, popular misogyny, and more. Thus it is possible to read Big Feelings as emblematic of political defeat, exemplified in the shift from the material political commitments of punk and riot grrrl to the *feeling* of politics across contemporary indie rock. Critics of the politics of representation might bemoan affectively oriented political activity as purely symptomatic of our post-truth, vibes, or hyper-abstracted finance-based economy, an immediacy paradigm (Kornbluh 2024) where being immersed in the sensation of something passes for the thing itself. While we're busy feeling feminist, fascist politics surges around the planet (which, incidentally, is still on the brink of disaster).

Though I do resist uncritical celebration of the political efficacy of feminist affects, I nevertheless also refuse to read Big Feelings strictly through the lens of exhaustion. Though perhaps not "properly" political, the feminist affects produced by Big Feelings artists remain meaningful, I suggest, for how they provide an alternative to the affective spaces that popular feminisms create, a different kind of cultural vibration along which to attune. If not for feminist politics itself, this space can be helpful for a variety of processes that may *feed into* feminist politics, including healing from traumatic experience, community-building, and introducing feminist themes and social praxes to those who might be inclined toward them if not for popular feminism's alienating affects. I view this as important pre-political (or as I discuss in chapter 3, juxtapolitical) work made possible via inducement, by the seductive force of certain combinations of sounds, lyrics, and presentations, the queer-feminist affects produced by artists who communicate from an orientation they might not name, but which is felt regardless. This work is necessarily vague and imprecise, the conditions for politics rather than politics itself. Nevertheless, I posit that this music attracts listeners with feminist inclinations, no matter how thoroughly developed or nascent their politics at a given moment. And I posit that this matters: contrary to interpretations of affective politics that leave off at its superficiality, it is exactly this surface quality that also makes it potentially powerful. Connecting people with fiber rather than steel, its structure risks snapping at the same time that it still lets light through, allowing the minimum vision necessary to see how our struggles overlap with others'. It is the kind of imprecise and intuitive resonance that allows Black activists in Ferguson and Irish citizens alike to see themselves in Palestine, that allows queers and feminists to find themselves in the same poetry readings, protestors to shout "water is life" and "Black lives matter" in the same march. Bypassing everything but solidarity, affective politics recognizes the urgency—in these conditions, all of us beset both differently and the same—of simply gathering in the same place under the same sentiments. The rest follows.

How Big Feelings communicates a feminist posture is difficult to say, because there is an important level on which it simply seems *obvious*—at least to those who are already attuned to the ways that feminists (tend to) present themselves, how they sound, the language they use, whether visual or aural. Culture works by establishing meaningful yet nonessential ties—ties between a certain way of doing and a group of people for whom that way is affirmative of something in their experience, especially critical for marginalized groups. When this happens, such ties become reinforced through repetition and replication, as markers of identity. This repetition codes meaning into gesture, producing affects that help us know where someone might be coming from. Perhaps affect, at the end of the day, simply describes whatever it is that helps something to seem the way that it is, as a kind of given, or what Gregory Seigworth and Melissa Gregg have called a phenomenon's "thisness" (2010). But at the same time, how something is perceived can't be taken for granted, as different communities interpret identical phenomena differently; that is exactly why feminist affects produce ambivalent politics, more invested in coalescing communities of like-feeling people than in trenchant political critique or an ideological struggle. Even the idea of "like-feeling people" faces obvious and immediate limitations; not only are indie listening communities diverse and multifaceted, but there are also always limit cases that create divisions within otherwise common viewpoints. (I think for example about the ways that fans have clashed with Big Thief for the band's past support of Israel as one such dividing line.) The affective resonance of Big Feelings artists does not necessarily or cleanly translate into a coherent ideological position; at most, where politics is concerned, its aesthetic appeal can turn heads, metaphorically and literally, reaching out to those who might be receptive to a certain frequency, to a sound that contains potential yet to be discovered, vetted, picked up, held.

Hailed by her sound, Soccer Mommy's feminist orientation reaches me as a sense built from a thousand small signals, none of which are on their own sufficient, and which collectively may be missed entirely by those who are not already clued in. Allison's nose ring is a part of it, I think, as are her tattoos, as well as her makeup, in this context, the semiotics of a cat eye. So too is the astrological reference in her song "Scorpio Rising,"[2] and the way that she

2. As I mention periodically throughout this book, one of the key thematic resonances across much Big Feelings music is the importance of tarot and astrology among the overlapping young/women-identified/queer communities, which I read as an extension of the longstanding feminist embrace of witchcraft. Beth Maiden writes in the foreword to *Queering the Tarot*, "Seizing the 78 cards we know as tarot and using them to reflect our experiences has become part of our community's lineage and literary canon" (Maiden 2019, xiii). Recent scholarship (Sheedy 2022; Lustig and Wu 2022; Yao 2021) has likewise examined the "explosion in popularity of so-called 'occult' practices like astrology and tarot, particularly among left-leaning people who tend to politicize their investments as forms of counterhegemony" (Sheedy 2022). Part of this book's methodology asks how such images line up with certain sounds to orient listeners into a shared aesthetic universe, where "aesthetics" always renders the material realities of our world through a particular perspective and experience. For many Big Feelings artists, astrological and tarot-derived imagery recur as a kind of resonance or echo not identical to the feminist citational politics I discussed in chapter 1, but similar insofar as

writes about relationships on "Your Dog," critiquing canonical masculine rock history along the way. Of course, the music is also a part of it. When I find a live performance of "Bones" on the WFUV YouTube channel, the accumulating energy near the three-minute mark moves me in equal parts for its nostalgic affect and its indie rock ambivalence, the way its force is tempered somehow, tinged by melancholy informed by the world, a kind of contained fire. So at the same time that I see in Allison's band a long and direct lineage linked to bands both overtly feminist (e.g., Sleater-Kinney)—as well as implicitly feminist (e.g., Hole)—I also see something new: Allison's detached posture, her calm affect, the way that her vocal lines float clean and high and in the most interesting shapes above the noise that she has created performs a kind of reserve that we don't see in those '90s bands that so obviously inform her practice. The timbre of her voice works together with the way she performs and the notes she has chosen to communicate something I can't fully grasp, compelling me to write.

Soccer Mommy is a part of a group of recent indie rock bands whose music produces feminist affects, without being super clear about any particular political issue—at least in her music. To understand a bit more about how this happens, this chapter considers Soccer Mommy's music in detail, which I then place into conversation with discourse analysis and reflections from some of the fans I interviewed.[3] Like many Big Feelings artists, Soccer Mommy's feminist affects are connected to her discussions of painful experiences which might be to a degree universal, but which I suggest are disproportionately resonant with marginalized groups under white patriarchal capitalism. I take up discussions of pain more specifically in chapter 3, connecting Soccer

---

they help signal in-group belonging to others searching for a place where they too might hope to fit. Bands introduce themselves at shows by instrument and "big three" signs; in banter in-between sets, they make appeals to common sense (e.g., yeule live on KEXP: "Everyone knows that Scorpio and Sagittarius are very hectic") that help hail listeners into a world. For those uninitiated, "Scorpio Rising" refers to a person's "rising" or ascendant sign, which has to do with one's public persona or outward performance of the self (as opposed to one's "moon" sign, which governs internal/emotional life). Together with the "sun" sign—the most commonly known sign, as it's derived from one's birthday—and these are the so-called "big three" in one's astrological chart. For more on contemporary occultism and queer communities, see for example Masters 2020 and Sheth 2023.

3. Despite this chapter's engagement with musicological and music-theoretical methods, my aim here is to put those methods to different ends than those to which they might more naturally incline, resisting the analytical impulse to categorize and classify and instead treating this music with more epistemic humility. At the end of the day, what this chapter and this book aspire to do is not to comprehend the music but rather to take it seriously, offering just one account of how this moment in popular music matters.

Mommy's use of '90s nostalgia with Indigo De Souza's performances of care. In this chapter, I want to think more specifically about the subtle ways that Soccer Mommy utilizes and alters the aesthetic vocabulary of feminist rock music. To do so, I read Soccer Mommy's track "Cool," detailing the ways in which her music both builds on and departs from key themes from the riot grrrl era, including lyrics that critique "girl/girl jealousism" while leaving open the possibility of a queer reading, as well as DIY aesthetics that overlap with and reinforce an adolescent, "girl"-oriented perspective. But while Soccer Mommy draws from and builds on riot grrrl aesthetic postures, her music also exemplifies Big Feelings' social and musical departures from past precedent insofar as its feminism remains affective, utilizing subtleties in harmonic construction to double down on the stereotypical association between femininity and emotion, positively reappropriating such tropes in the pursuit of creating community, catharsis, and safety in a world where such opportunities are increasingly difficult to find.

"Cool"

Soccer Mommy's 2018 single, "Cool" is a low-key, slightly dreamy rock paean with an unusually compelling melody (a quality for which Allison is well-known). The subject of "Cool" is Mary, a classmate whom Allison's character idolizes. According to the singer's perspective, Mary isn't cool because she is popular with boys, but because she rebuffs them: the second verse explains, "And she won't ever love no boy / She'll treat you like a fucking toy / She'll break your heart and steal your joy, like a criminal." Later, Allison elaborates, "Mary keeps you off her mind / She wants to spend her weekend right / Out with her friends just getting high, like a stoner girl." This latter verse in particular not only describes Mary's disinterest in heterosexual dating but also and importantly foregrounds friendships and broader community.

In these verses, Allison seems to be speaking to one of the anonymous boys in question; but the choruses are less clear. Allison sings, "Ooh ooh ooh ooh ooh ooh ooh ooh / I wanna know her like you-ou-ou-ou-ou-ou-ou / I wanna know her like you-ou-ou-ou-ou-ou-ou / I wanna be that cool / I wanna be that." Here, the subject of Allison's address ("you") could be a commiserative admission aimed at the same boy from the verses, who is perhaps hooking up with Mary even if doing so risks having his heart broken. Alternatively, Allison could have turned to one of Mary's aforementioned friends, one of the stoner girls Allison observes but among whom she perhaps doesn't fit. It's also possible that Mary is dating one of these girls; but, as I suggest is true in multiple ways across this track, the specific narrative is both less clear and less important than the feeling of yearning, swelling so large as to occlude unnecessary particulars. In Allison's chorus confession, more vulnerable than the verses, her protagonist continues to blur the lines between idolization and desire, singing that she wants to know Mary "like you," an envious sentiment implying that, while the speaker might be close with Mary, there is a sphere of intimacy that is beyond her reach, perhaps but not necessarily sexual, perhaps but not necessarily involving anonymous boys. Still, it isn't just that Allison's speaker yearns for a sexual or romantic relationship with Mary; the stanza also ends with her desire to be "that cool."

Allison's lyrical address provides one of the clearest examples of what it means to identify a post–riot grrrl posture, which does not completely distance itself from the themes and politics of the movement, but which also approaches those themes in new ways. Specifically, the purposeful ambiguity created in "Cool"—between idolization and desire—is characteristic of bands like Bikini Kill, whose famous anthem "Rebel Girl" proclaimed that the titular girl is "the queen of my world" and that the singer "wants to take [her] home" and "try on [her] clothes." In "Rebel Girl," Kathleen Hanna's character similarly describes ambiguous longing in relation to her "best friend," a deliberately blurred desire to both be *like* her and to be *with* her.

This parallel is significant for reading "Cool" insofar as I am concerned with tracking how feminist affects shift in indie rock from the 1990s—a critically influential period for Big Feelings—into the mid-to-late 2000s. While there are clearly connections here that attest to the lasting influence of bands like Bikini Kill, it is also important to note that "Cool" does not take up the most overtly anthemic, rebellious, or pointedly political declarations that "Rebel Girl" does. Whereas in "Rebel Girl," Hanna sings in defense of her character ("They say she's a dyke, but I know / She's my best friend, yeah"), and while Hanna repeatedly locates "revolution" in the rebel girl's movements (her hips, her walk, her kiss), there is neither a defensive posture toward others nor a pointed political orientation in Allison's lyrics. However, that does not mean that "Cool" is apolitical.

We have already seen that "Cool" becomes indirectly political via the lyrical foregrounding of women-women relationships, which can be read as feminist no matter how one interprets the platonic/romantic ambiguity. But there is at least one other important parallel to "Rebel Girl": the way that "Cool" implicitly takes place in the universe of adolescence, a construction that builds on the riot grrrl movement's important critiques of patriarchy by recourse to the language of girlhood, specifically. Like "Rebel Girl," which

Figure 3. @gomagazineny, 2024, "🙄" Instagram post, February 7. https://www.instagram.com/p/C3DcpDjreUA/

describes the heroine as having "the hottest trike in town," the first verse of "Cool" describes Mary breaking a boy's heart "after school," characterizing the scene as one that takes place, if not in childhood, then still in a phase of life where emotions such as desire, envy, and idolization take on heightened intensity. Not only does this song place listeners back inside the period of their lives during which, (stereo)typically, emotions are most strongly felt, but critically, this "envy" is also constructed in order to combat the kinds of "girl/girl jealousism" that the riot grrrl movement critiqued, instead foregrounding the power of what we might call the uncomplicated friendship of young girls (Bikini Kill 1991). As Joanne Gottlieb and Gayle Wald write of riot grrrl,

> there is . . . a crucial element of fantasy in their self-construction—a nostalgia for the apparently close relationships between girls prior to

> the intrusion of heterosexual romance and its spin-offs, sexual competition and sexual rivalry. (1994, 266)

In "Cool," we can see a similar critique of girl-girl envy (where the guy is the object in the middle), since here Mary is the focus of Allison's desire, bypassing boys altogether. Even if Mary is dating one of her girlfriends, Allison's envy isn't weaponized here as much as it simply pines for a more intimate sphere of Mary's life, no matter the particulars. A clear feminist political orientation is thus implied, if not stated outright, building on the dynamic that Kate Siegfried (2019) terms a "grrrl crush," a "way of being" (23) that is "decidedly political" (21) as a "specific expression of queer and feminist solidarity" (24). I have described this orientation, now taken up by a new generation, as a "post–riot grrrl" posture not to signal distance from the movement, but to suggest that artists like Soccer Mommy selectively incorporate riot grrrl politics while also evolving them into a new cultural context. As the rest of this analysis will suggest, this implication is bolstered by musical and visual elements that also allow this orientation to become *felt*.

Harmonic Excess and Ambivalent Semiotics

Part of how "Cool" communicates its intense and unnamable yearning is through harmony. On paper, Allison utilizes but a handful of common chords; yet a closer look reveals a world of subtlety underneath the surface. Consider the beginning, for example, which functions both as an intro and as the first half of the verse, blurring lines between the two and thus immediately conjuring the kind of ambiguity so central to this music: where the vocal line plainly outlines an A maj7 chord, the guitar is simultaneously hammering a D maj7, most likely achieved by layering an open-string, drop-D chord under its wistful C-sharp riff.[4] This division between melody and harmony, this quietly destabilizing pair, is significant in a number of ways, and is probably best understood using David Temperley's notion of a melodic-harmonic split (2007). For Temperley, such disjunctions are con-

4. Following the previous note, this transcription likely captures only a sense of what's actually being played. What's clear is that the guitar is playing a D maj7 chord with a topline melody; what's more mysterious is the exact voicing/fingering arrangement, particularly given the possibility that our ears are filling in notes (for example, an F-sharp) because of how (especially distorted) guitar overtones resonate against one another, as well as the possibilities opened up by overdubbing. I'm happy that this track resists completely disclosing its inner workings, keeping something for itself.

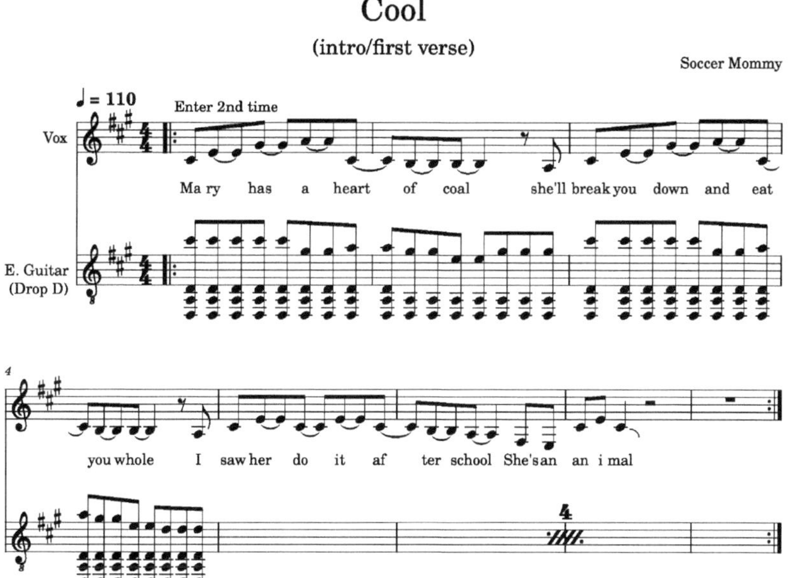

Figure 4. Soccer Mommy, "Cool," transcription of the intro/first half of the first verse

sistent features of rock music, where melodies often "manifes[t] an apparent independence" (323) from underlying harmonic structures. Rather than a simple flouting of "proper" music-theoretical principles, the split appears in specific ways, produces specific aural effects, and ultimately contributes to the overall consensus among contemporary theorists that rock music's harmonic language consciously departs from the "strong directional tendencies of classical harmony" (Temperley and de Clercq 2013, 192).[5] Here, Allison demonstrates this kind of departure by staging the all-important Big Feelings progression (I–IV) *simultaneously* instead of sequentially, thereby growing one emotionally huge sound.

The rest of the song finds other ways to maintain its affective world-building without breaking momentum. The choruses continue similarly to the verses, for example, but move more definitively between straightforward A and D chords (often with a slide back to the D) in a way that, rather than clarifying matters, actually reinforces the track's ambiguity: while it's true that the choruses present more discernible chord progressions, their cyclical

5. See also Clement 2020; de Clercq 2017, 2019, 2021; Doll 2017; Spicer 2017.

movement (from IV to I and back around again) displaces the feeling of tonic (a kind of harmonic "home base," a comfortable starting point to which we might expect to return) just slightly—an effect exacerbated by the extended periods outside the chorus when the tonic chord implied by the melody (A) occurs over what would be its subdominant (i.e., IV) chord (D), thus mitigating any sense of rootedness. In my hearing, this produces a quietly opaque effect, where the feeling of tonic is constantly deferred. Instead of moving linearly through clear beginning, middle, and end points, "Cool" continues to oscillate around variations of essentially one chord or sound, always already built through juxtaposition. In this way, the song mostly refuses to build tension, performing its own title by remaining within a consistently subdued atmosphere.

In keeping with the track's essential ambivalence, I suggest that the many deferrals in "Cool," its back-and-forth spirals, its in some ways indistinguishable, single universe, brings it in line with Mark Spicer's "fragile tonic" in rock songs, where "the tonic chord is present but its hierarchical status is weakened" (2017). Spicer goes on to suggest that this often occurs in rock songs where instability, ambiguity, or fragility are relevant for the narrative or total semiotic affect in the music—this is exactly what I suggest is happening in "Cool," where the kinds of lyrical ambiguities I referenced above are powerfully reinforced by the major-seventh sonority present here and across so much music in the Big Feelings camp, and which is literally doubled in this song, reinforced into an oversaturated haze, the biggest of big feelings delivered through slowly unfurling smoke.

Ultimately, no matter how we diagnose the complex construction of this ostensibly simple track, I suggest that the polysemy created by this major-seventh sound-world is one essential means of producing feminist affects, vibratory sensibilities with no guaranteed sound/politics relationship, but nevertheless strong tendencies. In other words, I am less interested in understanding the harmonic function here than I am in picking apart how the overall sonority of "Cool" resonates or signifies when combined with lyrical sentiments and visual presentations that reinforce a certain way of being. The major-seventh sound and its unitary world-building together saturate the listener in a kind of yearning or daydreaming, caught between celebration and disappointment. Because this affect might be considered particularly complex, it is capable of taking on a number of resonances or signifiers—but not without limit; at base, this is *not* the sound of mainstream cis/het guy-rock.

To unpack this point further, I first want to briefly address the role of chord extensions in rock music, before turning to the major 7 (and implicated sharp 11) more specifically. In the introduction, I suggested, following

David Temperley's corpus studies, that chord extensions are generally rare in rock, a genre whose most prototypical sound has been associated with two-note (power) chords or triads. I also raised the idea that Big Feelings' consistent and fundamental use of chord extensions helps produce feminist affects in the music due to the longstanding associations between harmonic embellishments and femininity, particularly in the figures of madwomen or hysterics. So the first point here is that both the presence of chord extensions and the extent of their use across bands like Soccer Mommy is important for understanding how feminist affect becomes successfully communicated to listeners—*especially when combined with other factors*, such as the lyrics addressed above. In this chapter, I also want to reinforce that point by focusing on a second, which is the way that the major-seventh chord specifically contributes to the "bigness" of Big Feelings, taking what has already been established as a musical device signaling feminine excess and intensifying it in new ways.

I make this claim in part based on the fact that the major-seventh chord is just that bit more unusual in the context of the rock genre space.[6] Where certain chord extensions like the dominant seventh (essential for blues-inflected styles) and others convey specific moods or tropes (e.g. the "Hendrix chord"), the major seventh is rare enough in the context of rock music that it frustrates simplistic semiotic interpretations, instead allowing the major-seventh chord to reinforce a degree of perceived *complexity*. Following Temperley's understanding of complexity in music as an attribute conveyed "by events or patterns that go outside the norms of the style" (2018, 143) the major seventh functions as a complication or a nuance that also produces *emotional* complexity, aligning it with feminized concerns.

But it isn't just the major seventh's relative rarity that contributes to its ambivalent semiotics; instead, both the quality of the chord itself and, importantly, how Big Feelings bands treat the chord also play key roles. In terms of the first point, it seems to me that there is something inherently contradictory about the sound of the major-seventh chord: it is both alluring as a major-mode sonority (major chords being one of the most common building blocks of Western music), while also containing within it perhaps the single most dissonant interval of all: the minor second. In whatever voicing, whether rubbed directly together or bouncing far away from one another, this jarring dissonance has none of the nefarious, cartoonish character of a diminished-seventh chord, but remains at turns haunting, melan-

6. Although I am comfortable making this claim, future corpus studies would be both warranted and welcome.

cholic, wistful, forceful, and (this I maintain) beautiful—by and through its very dissonance.[7] This is not to say that dissonance and beauty are opposed to each other, but rather that this chord is not as straightforward as others we might describe as pleasing to listen to. A sound so pulled between grace and discomfort can be considered quintessentially ambivalent, ideally suited for rock anthems of the kind we hear in Big Feelings: songs about pain and love, bittersweet transitions, or feelings that are simply too complex to articulate through clear referents. More to the point, insofar as the major seventh is capable of reinforcing *all* of those contradictory feelings, dialing up the major-seventh sound becomes one way that a song can hold onto many complex feelings all at once, both making space for emotional nuance and amplifying the affect of feeling so much. Unable to grasp the experience of being overwhelmed by feeling, the major seventh helps to reify that same too-much-ness in sound.

---

7. In order to at least partially address the semi-subjective nature of musical semiotics, I have periodically surveyed students about how they perceive major-seventh chords—doing so for a few minutes before class simply for the opportunity to hear lots of perspectives at once. On listening to a few different voicings at the piano, students consistently raised feelings of homesickness, of being back home after having been away, as well as ideas of staring at a night sky, and being in love with the world. As one student put it, "The word 'nostalgia' is really still sticking out to me. . . . It's like a super lonely, empty feeling, but it's still content. You're not upset, but there's so much loneliness. I'm content right now, but I'm still yearning for something that I can't probably ever experience again, cause that's just how life works." This view was corroborated by other students, who explained that the C maj7 made them feel anxious, or brought up feelings of "longing." One student pointed out that it was interesting to note consistent attributions of anxiety to "the people's key" also remarking that "C major is seen as the simplest . . . this triad that everyone learns . . . but when you add that seventh it totally complicates something that was so simple." When asked what kind of complication felt attached to happiness, one student said it felt like "a joy that you can't go back to"—a memory. An overwhelming majority of students consistently raised ideas of nostalgia, longing, bittersweet feelings, happiness with a complication attached, and cinematic scenes in which characters are swept up in moving events. Feelings of calm and groundedness were common, but almost always with a melancholic dimension. Sometimes, these observations were outright contradictory: "You're either kinda down in the dumps and it's raining out and it's like a sad movie scene—or you're insanely happy and you're reminiscing," said one. In this vein, there was lots of consensus about warm imagery ("summer," "strawberries in a salad," "a child's drawing of a sun") but also cold or dark imagery ("rain," "rain outside a cafe," "a starry sky above a meadow"). While these responses do not consider the major-seventh sound in the holistic context of a song, they nevertheless help to consolidate certain ideas around ambiguity, complexity, memory, and contradictory, ambivalent emotions. It is this capacity for the major seventh to potentially signify both grief and joy, dark and light, warm and cold, that I suggest make it compelling and effective for a kind of music invested in holding all the big feelings that its practitioners and listeners experience.

And it is this "dialing up" quality that I also consider unique to Big Feelings: unlike many other rock subgenres in which major 7 chords also appear, artists like Soccer Mommy embrace them more thoroughly and more forcefully, building entire songs around their affective force. Chordal sevenths are woven into central positions across melodic lines, or are hammered out in slow, huge, cathartic moments of repetition; sometimes, the major 7 sound extends and reinforces itself by reaching up to add that sharp 11, ostensibly even more unusual but here sounding a natural extension of the major 7's incandescent pain, a further and glaring refraction of its light. This can be heard in the intro, for example (where the guitar line hits the sharp 11 of a D chord); or else in the leadup to the second chorus, where a lead guitar wails a consistent G-sharp (1:46–1:55), layed out over both the D still implied by the rhythm guitar's riff and the A implied by the melody, therefore evoking both the 7 (of A) and the sharp 11 (of D) simultaneously.[8] In sum, because of the ways in which the major 7 and the sharp 11 are related, the latter is not an aberration as much as an intensification of the affect created by the 7, an over-and-above amplification of its sound-world. This overmuch sonority, this space of everything at once, is Big Feelings in a nutshell.

The point of all this is not to diagnose a particular harmonic operation per se, but to try to describe something of the affect, feeling, or orientation generated by the sounds. On this note, Christopher Doll veers into the language of affect when he writes that "we as listeners hear chords—we experience their presence—whether we know it or not" (2017, 5). Sounds exert force, even if that force is not fully graspable or consciously understood. By foregrounding harmonic architectures rarely heard in rock, we see one concrete example of the ways in which Big Feelings breaks open rock's tonal space, adding colors and intensities that increase music's emotional complexity beyond standard rock categories *and* reinforcing a feminist affect insofar as emotional complexity remains a domain of activism, concern, and proficiency beyond of the purview of traditional masculinity. After decades of mainstream and masculinist rock making use of simple chord structures—and given the long history of associating femininity with extended colors—the subtle and delicate ways that "Cool" makes use of such chord extensions places it along another register, generating feminist affect through complex,

8. Although not necessarily identical, the G-sharp in question also raises Brad Osborn's notion of a "subdominant tritone," (where a tonic major seventh in the melody produces a tritone over a IV in the bass), long used by film and television composers to provoke "a range of complex emotions, especially longing, relief, melancholy, or nostalgia" (2020, 66). For the rarity of the sharp 4/sharp 11 in rock music, see Temperley 2018 (particularly the discussion of a rock "supermode"), as well as Doll 2017 and Clement 2020.

deeply evocative harmonies and a catchy, decidedly indie-rock sensibility. In particular, the harmony being amplified here is the sound of the major 7 (sharp 11), that ambivalent and all-at-once feeling that overflows compartmentalization.

Feminism and Music Discourse

In this chapter I have so far been concerned with unpacking some of the ways that Soccer Mommy's music generates feminist affects, attracting listeners with a feminist orientation without didactic or otherwise overt messaging. As the conversations quoted in the next section will attest, these affects are perceptible even in the absence of any direct statements about politics by the artists in question. But first: thinking about Soccer Mommy specifically, Allison has even downplayed the idea that her music has something to do with feminist politics. Consider this nuanced exchange between Allison and journalist Vrinda Jagota:

VJ: Lately, a lot of people are celebrating women in indie-rock as if their presence is a new trend, even though women have always been making major contributions. How do you feel when people talk about that?

SA: I think that most women in music feel that way—that it has been a thing for a long time. I think everyone is kind of tired of being interviewed and asked "What's it like—women are doing so well right now." I think it's good to talk about it once or twice, especially in indie-rock, where women are doing really well right now and there is some truth to it, they are what everyone is talking about. . . . But women playing music is not a new concept. It just shows, it kind of tells how people think when it's so astounding to them, this phenomenon of girls playing music. It's like, "Why are you so shocked?" It's very surface level empowerment. And people are mostly talking about a very specific kind of woman—young, attractive women are what everyone wants to talk about. It can get a little exhausting. It's definitely fetishizing. Women of color aren't being celebrated as much. Trans women aren't being celebrated as much. And older women too.

VJ: It's hard because of course it's important to talk about feminism and to talk about different kinds of oppression, and you do want to talk about it if it in some way affects your work, but it's frustrating when your artistry is reduced by one aspect of your identity.

SA: I think people want it to inform your work more than it actually does. They want you to have this deep feminist meaning behind a song and you just want it to relate to anyone. I wasn't really thinking "I'm an empowered woman at this moment," I just was feeling emotions and writing. (Jagota 2018)

While it is certainly possible to read Allison's response as reflective of a postfeminist posture, I am disinclined to read it as a straightforward disavowal of the relevance of feminism in/to music, particularly given that when Allison is public about her politics, it bends in a progressive direction (see below). Rather, Allison's sharp observations about surface-level feminism and the kinds of women who typically get celebrated indicate to me a critical thoughtfulness around matters of representation that exceeds a kind of simple or outright rejection of feminism, focusing more squarely on the politics of what Banet-Weiser and others have described as *popular* feminism. In my reading, these comments reflect young women's broad agreement with feminist principles and frameworks, and simultaneously their awareness of and cynicism about the damaging ways in which capitalism today overdetermines what that word signifies, how it shows up in our culture, what work it has been called upon to do or not do.

Additionally, particularly given the history of the riot grrrl movement, contemporary artists' downplaying of feminist politics can also be read as an act of self-preservation, a renunciation that at least makes it more difficult for press outlets to group women in rock bands together under a label (which, as has been well-established, was part of how the press denigrated, dismissed, and ultimately appropriated riot grrrl politics into a lucrative, nominally postfeminist branding exercise), a move that was already underway as early as 1992, when Bikini Kill stopped giving interviews to the press (Schilt 2003; Dunn and Farnsworth 2012; Anderson 2013).[9] What's especially interesting here is

9. Relevant to my reading of Allison's above statement is the fact that she was included in *The New York Times* 2017 "women in rock" feature. On an episode of *The New York Times Popcast*, music writer Liz Pelly points out how this package mirrors past "women in rock" discourses, saying around 43:25, "(1) The idea of a women in rock article in 2017 is incredibly old fashioned. (2) The questions that were in the roundtable and also in some of the interviews do feel a little bit like square one. And I really hope that from 2017 onward we can get off square one and go to square two. Because something that would have been great is if this

that Allison's defense isn't really aimed at Jagota, who seems to be in agreement, starting this series of questions with the observation that "a lot of people are celebrating women in indie-rock as if their presence is a new trend."

Indeed, as a whole, press coverage of Soccer Mommy is not only positive, but also focuses on Allison's artistic contributions, with general tendencies to highlight songwriting chops, growth as an artist over time, and above all the intimacy she is able to channel. A significantly smaller minority offer qualified praise, in at least one case through language that does feel implicitly gendered insofar as it reserves its highest accolades for producer Daniel Lopatin rather than Allison herself (Richardson 2022). Still, that example stands as an exception through the coverage I have been able to collect, reflecting a shift in the predominant ways that the press covers such bands.

Among these, there are nevertheless several publications that take a "women in rock" approach, including one in the *Village Voice* that even draws attention to its own framing by quoting Jessica Hopper:

> "Stop talking about women's involvement and creation of rock music as if it is brand new phenomena, or their appearance on *Billboard* rock charts as a new incursion and not one happening regularly in the 40ish years of Rock Chart history," Jess Hopper, music critic and author of *The First Collection of Criticism by a Living Female Rock Critic*, tweeted just two weeks ago in response to a *Billboard* article implying that women are just entering the scene. As anyone with ears, a decent record collection, or a passing familiarity with Sister Rosetta Tharpe already knows, that's a pretty silly notion, as old-fashioned and blinkered as the equally predictable cycle of "Rock Is Dead" headlines that surface every few years. While male-fronted rock has indeed undergone a bit of an identity crisis in the last few decades, women have continued to turn out brilliant, emotional, entertaining-as-hell rock—and pop and hip-hop and rap and jazz and folk and country and on and on. This isn't a new phenomenon. It isn't a trend. But that doesn't mean it's not worth celebrating. (McKinney 2018)

piece got more into their music and what they're actually saying" (in Caramanica 2017). Later, Jenn Pelly adds, "So often women rock musicians get stuck in these situations where when they get interviewed like all anyone wants to talk about is gender and being a woman in a rock band or something." In my view, this criticism helps us to consider how resistance on the part of some musicians to a particular label and to the conversations that derive from gendered tropes is different than disagreement with any particular feminist positions or viewpoints.

Although it would appear that some of the more naked dismissals of women's contributions to rock music that characterized coverage in the 1990s are not repeating themselves here, the idea of framing gender in conversations about these artists persists—in part for what seem to me good reasons. Hence, a degree of guardedness and nuance from artists being asked about their genders or feminist politics is in this context understandable.

Ultimately, although it is an important factor to consider, I am less interested in how Allison herself intends these statements than in the effect of her music on the people who love it. If a certain caution around overt feminist politics is one aspect of Soccer Mommy's public persona, so too are the covert feminist dynamics analyzed in the earlier parts of this chapter. I suggested that these—as much or more so than literal statements by the artist—communicate a feminist orientation to fans, allowing them to coalesce around the music from a similar orientation. The question then would be, what evidence is there that this kind of affective orientation is actually perceived by listeners?

Feminist Affects and Listener Perceptions

For the rest of the chapter, I want to zoom out slightly, placing Soccer Mommy's music into conversation with other Big Feelings artists, particularly the subject of the following chapter, Indigo De Souza.

Throughout my conversations with listeners, one of my main curiosities was whether or not a feminist political orientation was part of the reason for their fandom—or if they perceived feminist implications in the music at all. Using Soccer Mommy as a starting point, I asked Deanna, a twenty-year-old musician, audio engineer, and student, if she associated feminism with the music.

> I think I would say no, initially, but there are songs . . . specifically I'm thinking of Beach Bunny in this instance, where she's singing about topics that are kinda political, or are starting to break into that territory. . . . So I think, unless it's . . . being directly talked about, I'd say not all the time. Although the kinds of people that are listening to that kind of genre are often associated with [feminism] and are often fighting for that or are involved in activism in their own way. I don't think [the music is] specifically conveying that or based around that. (Deanna F. 2022)

In this quote, Deanna doesn't identify politics as a core component of the music, but nevertheless recognizes the kinds of fans and communities likely to gravitate towards it. This way of characterizing musical community echoes Jacques Rancière's idea of the "distribution of the sensible," a "system of self-evident facts of sense perception that simultaneously discloses the existence of something in common and the delimitations that define the respective parts and positions within it" (2004, 7). I am interested here in the key phrases "self-evident" and "sense perception" in Rancière's theory: a distribution of the sensible marks out the political ground of community formation, where groups are organized by a shared apprehension of the world, as well as its implications for (un)belonging, so well understood as to be taken as commonsensical. Helping us to understand how sense perceptions become transmitted and shared, affect names what seems to invite social alignments in the absence of explicit invitations: Deanna's observations suggest that bands like Soccer Mommy participate in the constitution of a sensible world in common and in opposition to patriarchal hegemony; even when the music isn't "specifically conveying" feminist politics, "the kinds of people that are listening to that kind of genre . . . are often involved in activism in their own way."

Organizing people around these kinds of shared sentiments is a different kind of political action than the narrowly prescribed activity recognized and legitimated by the state, such as voting, canvassing, and advocating on a given policy platform. It is instead about setting up a contest between different ways of seeing the world, a clash whereby a group who Rancière suggests has "no part" in the official, dominant culture nevertheless makes enough noise to make itself of some account, to shatter the placid fiction on which the majority rests for its falsely earned assurance: the lie that the world they see is the "normal" one, the only one. It is this kind of politics, in the Rancièrean sense, with which Big Feelings most often engages. That being said, some bands (here Beach Bunny, but I also think of Bully, for example) are understood by Deanna as flirting with more overt approaches to politics, confirming that each band navigates this question differently, and reminding us that we should be wary of assuming one fixed approach to aesthetics or politics within any one band's oeuvre.[10] I am concerned with charting tendencies here, but each band displays a diversity of approaches both within their own output and relative to others.

---

10. A further complication is that, where feminist politics is more commonly deferred by Big Feelings bands (for what I understand to be a variety of complex reasons including but not limited to its own historical inadequacies and exclusions), questions of queer desire/identity/community are by comparison more frequently stated in direct terms. For a summary of what I understand as feminism's complexities and "failures," see Jolie 2024.

A second respondent, Katie, identified herself as a twenty-three-year-old white, queer musician, artist, and art teacher. Her response to my question also speaks powerfully to the ways in which I am trying to understand Big Feelings as an affect produced collectively, via music's multiply mediated formats:

DD: Does this music feel feminist to you, or is that not the right way to be thinking about your experience of the music?

KM: Yeah, it feels . . . the thing that this music *is* feels bigger than just gender. It's not wrong, but it feels outdated solely in that we're bigger than that now . . . or something.

DD: Even though they're not talking about those topics necessarily in their lyrics, it feels like there's something big about identity happening?

KM: Definitely. And I am conscious—[laughing] conscious/obsessive—about who the whole band is composed of. . . . I think about that a lot because where I went to college, there wasn't a single female instrumentalist in a campus band my whole time there, . . . but there were lots of token vocalists. And that really pissed me off—I was like, if it's gonna be a boys club just let it be a boys club. Don't put a woman in there so that nobody else in the crowd . . . even notices that they've never seen a woman play at this fucking college. (Katie M. 2022)

Notwithstanding its somewhat rockist distinction between vocalists and instrumentalists, this comment is critical insofar as it helps to underscore how personal/political/social orientations in music are not communicated exclusively by virtue of lyrics or even sound; it also has to do with who is playing the music and how—how they perform, present themselves, and so on. But elaborating further, for Katie this also isn't *just* an issue of personnel. Discussing Indigo De Souza, she continued:

KM: I think Indigo [De Souza] has a mostly man band . . . yeah . . . like looking at how they pose in pictures and who is writing their Instagram captions, and . . . I dunno, I think Indigo is an example of someone who's very like, "lowercase starts to sentences online," and like "multiple exclamation points" and shit like that, which somehow feels more "girl." So I definitely weigh how the other sounds are treating the song that's been written, as well as the song that's been written.

In this part of her response, Katie ties together the seemingly disconnected ideas of posture in an Instagram photo, caption writing, and the way that men musicians treat a song that's been written by a woman ("how the other sounds are treating the song that's been written"), testifying to the fact that this constellation of activities is perceptible as a holistic energy that affects how listeners approach and feel about the music in question—and that these factors matter to listeners.

Returning with this perspective to Soccer Mommy, we can also consider her extramusical activities as an important factor in orienting listeners. Allison regularly plays shows like the Abortion Access Benefit, and contributes to projects like the *Good Music to Ensure Safe Abortion Access to All* compilation, a mammoth forty-nine-track album of unreleased music that raised money for Brigid Alliance, Abortion Care Network, and Noise for Now over a twenty-four-hour period. I also think here of the fact that Soccer Mommy played political rallies for Bernie Sanders during his 2020 campaign, as well as appearing in various official campaign media on Twitter and other social platforms. However one might individually feel about a particular political candidate or their policies, such extramusical factors, as much as any lyrical content or interview statements, help listeners like Katie feel with the social orientations of the musicians and of the work they produce, online or onstage. I'm again stopping short of suggesting anything particular about Allison's political ideology, and especially not anything about her listeners; before all that, my claim is that a nonspecific series of postures and gestures helps incline fans in a direction that they might then choose to abandon or pursue, feel ambivalently toward or champion. It is a soft and unspecific alignment, the minimum prerequisite for tuning one's own listening toward a frequency that feels right, even provisionally.

Resonating with these themes, Alyssa, a twenty-five-year-old who identified as white and queer, responded to my question about feminism as follows:

AL: Yeah, I definitely would describe it as feminism—or woman or queer or any of those words—cause even if the artist themself isn't outwardly queer, they do kinda reach out to those audiences. . . . And I think it probably is kind of like a new wave of riot grrrl but in like a different font, I guess?

I think women, or queer identities, anybody who's a minority or whatever, can relate to that, so it is a relatability, I think, because it's nice to see parts of yourself reflected—because you're like, '*Fuck*, I'm not alone'—it's so silly, but it's like, I'm not alone in this; this is like a universal theme that other people have . . . just heartbreak or whatever it is. And I feel like with [Indigo De Souza] it's not just heartbreak; it's all these emotions that other people [are not] really talking about.

DD: What I'm trying to get a handle on too is like: OK there's a bunch of bands that feel to me like they're really concerned with feelings and emotions and staging those for people to experience. And the other part of it is—trying to pick up on something you said earlier—I feel like that matters more to some people than others . . .

AL: Sure, no it *really* does.

DD: Can you talk to me about that?

AL: It's for very specific people, I think. . . . I think people could watch her and be like, "Oh wow that's cool." . . . But then I think some people are maybe blocking it, where they don't want to think about those types of narratives and emotions . . .

[White men are] not gonna get it because it doesn't involve them, unless they make themselves involved. I know a few men who love Indigo, and they are the type of men that get things, and they are the type of men that talk about things that nobody else wants to talk about . . . that [are] important to talk about, and [they] make sure that they're doing their part . . . with, you know *Roe versus Wade* or whatever it is right now. So I think those types of men get it. (Alyssa L. 2022)

I am grateful for the way that Alyssa synthesizes here many of the ideas this book tries to think through, including their conflation of (or easy transition between) feminism and queer politics, as well as her stipulation that the personal identification of any one artist is relevant, but not the end of the story in terms of how the music speaks to fans. Finally, the contention in the final paragraph—that white men who take it upon themselves to be involved with issues like reproductive rights are those white men who are most likely to find value in Indigo De Souza's music—is exactly the kind of sociomusical connection that *Big Feelings* tries to articulate: in some ways, the entire purpose of this book is to show how a certain '90s-leaning indie-rock sound is being recoded in our present moment as one that is implicitly but no less forcefully feminist and queer, such that enjoyment of the music is at least in part predicated on a level of intimacy with those communities, orientations, and ways of being in the world. While the dominance of material and epistemological structures of past white-male indie rock are being critiqued and reworked, Big Feelings doesn't operate form an identity politics so narrow as to exclude or prohibit individual white men from helping in this project should they want to.

Feminist Praxis/Queer Care

In this chapter, I've been concerned with placing one Soccer Mommy track into conversation with a variety of extramusical dynamics that help inform it. In the following chapter, I use another Soccer Mommy single to introduce an explicit discussion of '90s nostalgia and its function across many Big Feelings artists. Overlapping with but also expanding Soccer Mommy's affective feminism, her use of '90s nostalgia raises particular sets of difficulties, traumas, and anxieties experienced by young people in the US context, thus facilitating and in some ways necessitating a turn toward practices of care as a means of managing life. While feminism and queerness as political orientations are not necessarily synonymous, this book's cases are most fruitfully discussed when considering the overlaps, conflations, and productive solidarities that can occur between and among queer-feminist communities and concerns. As I elaborate in chapter 3, the practices of care we can feel performed by artists like Soccer Mommy and Indigo De Souza are informed by queer cultures that have long struggled to find, and therefore highly value, the kinds of soft and accepting safety that allows people to flourish.

3 • "Real Pain"

'90s Nostalgia, Queer Care, and the Layered Semiotics of Trauma

I will hold you
It's gonna be alright
—Indigo De Souza[1]

By the spring of 2020, I had been listening to Soccer Mommy for about a year. But it was perhaps more than coincidental that I really dove into her catalog during one of the darkest periods of my recent life. Caught up in a wave of COVID layoffs at my university, I knew that the odds of finding my way back into full-time academic work were statistically meager and imagined that my career was over after just seven months on the job. During this time, I was living alone in a new city, newly shuttered. My world shrank into my apartment, which was nearly constantly filled with the sounds of the musicians I am writing about in this book. During this time, "Circle the Drain" (discussed below) captured like no other song how I felt—because of this track in particular, I, like many listeners, began to experience Sophie Allison's explorations of personal struggle less as "confessions" about her own life and more as portraits of a certain kind of generalized pain—pain that, during the pandemic, (even more) people began to experience in ways that were so widely acknowledged as to take on the feeling of a cultural zeitgeist. Suddenly, lyrics describing a certain moment of heartbreak could feel resonant with other depressing experiences, because in the context of widely shared pain, the content matters less than the form.

In the previous chapter, I described how Soccer Mommy's music creates feminist affects through multiple, co-constitutive dimensions of music per-

1. From "Hold U," track 8 on *Any Shape You Take* (2021).

formance: visual, lyrical, sonic, and extramusical. Chapter 3 builds on this argument by taking up '90s nostalgia more specifically, probing the ways that it bears on genres of pain that are commonly experienced by young listeners, particularly those who both experience pain as an outgrowth of their marginalized status in US society and who understand—even subconsciously—that marginalization as an overdeterminative factor in their difficulties. Placing Soccer Mommy and Indigo De Souza into conversation with one another, this chapter traces how generational nostalgia and discussions of pain work together in their music to produce queer-feminist affects by channeling the taken-for-granted, always-already nature of crisis in the United States and then performing the extreme emotions that daily living won't permit us to divulge. Ultimately, I suggest that Soccer Mommy, Indigo De Souza, and other Big Feelings artists who stage such difficult, affectively charged emotional experiences provide a kind of vibrational-therapeutic care for listeners, a somatic function that is further reinforced by fostering concert cultures that prioritize health, safety, and tenderness. In contrast to the polemical "girls to the front" culture advocated at '90s feminist rock shows, Big Feelings both softens and expands its culture of performance. Moving outward from the previous chapter's discussion of feminist politics, here I focus primarily on the nexus of trauma, care, and queer identity that this music and its concert cultures raise, overlapping with and reinforcing the feminist affects in Big Feelings writ large.

The first part of this chapter focuses on Soccer Mommy's portrayal of bad feelings in the music video for "Circle the Drain," before bringing her music into conversation with Indigo De Souza, both of whom I have seen in concert. It is important to this chapter that I bring in my experiences of live music, in part because that context helps to elaborate more fully how Big Feelings both fits into and also exceeds the category of sad-girl cultural production that has gained attention in recent feminist media scholarship (Alderton 2018; Goldfine 2017; Hayes 2023; Thelandersson 2023). Particularly focused on internet subcultures, this work has emphasized the gendered dimensions of chronic anxiety, drawing attention to popular culture that centers feeling bad in contradistinction to what Shani Orgad and Rosalind Gill call "confidence imperatives" imposed by internalized neoliberal ideals (2022). When the hegemonic construction of femininity demands that women be resilient—that is, both suffering and subsequently performing victory over that suffering—it can be potentially subversive to refuse this kind of confidence. While recent studies suggest that much sad-girl culture participates in the kind of vulnerability discourse that ultimately serves/reinforces corporate interests (what Thelandersson terms "profitable vulnerability"), *some* sad-girl cultures also present "more spacious ways of feeling bad" that connect mental distress to "power structures and inequality," ultimately constructing "girls and young women as political subjects with agency" (Thelandersson 2023, 12–13).

In agreement with recent theorizations of sad girl's politics, I do hear in Big Feelings a refusal of postfeminist resilience imperatives, an insistence on sitting with and potentially processing the bad feelings that are caused by patriarchal capitalism, and which recognize the imperative to overcome one's trauma on behalf of that same system as a certain capitulation, rather than a genuine healing. But at the same time that sad-girl cultures help to contextualize the focus on traumatic experience throughout this chapter's case studies, there are several reasons why I ultimately decline to identify Big Feelings with the sad-girl archetype as it has been established. First, some of the most prominent figures in the contemporary indie scene have explicitly pushed back against this label, rejecting it as perhaps this era's version of the "angry woman" trope: a flattening stereotype that does more to reduce women's contributions than to theorize/appreciate them.[2] Second, while sad-girl cultures rightly insist on the validity of feeling bad, Big Feelings artists as I hear them take the process one step further, from an acknowledgment of how fucked up the world is into a space of healing and reconciliation. This is why Big Feelings artists demand permission to feel and express a full spectrum of emotions, which, while always conscious of the social world in which they occur, may reflect a range of possible reactions to that world, from boygenius's tender meditation on intimacy ("True Blue") to Indigo de Souza's effusive celebration of community ("Hold U"). The emphasis on healing and provisional acceptance is why I ultimately understand Big Feelings as more in line with "soft" aesthetics also developed through internet subcultures, which I return to below in discussing Indigo De Souza's performances of vulnerability and care. As Andi Schwartz writes, "discourses of healing" are "central to soft femme digital culture" (2020, 4), which acknowledges the ubiquity of bad feelings while simultaneously critiquing the structural causes of those affects, making room for recuperation and even joy.

More than any particular affective response (sadness, depression, cathar-

---

2. "**Dacus**: I bristle at the idea of being like a neo-lib wet dream of a girl. [*laughter*] You know, like, feminism on a shirt at Target. I want to steer so clear of that and the sad girl. They're in the same soup. **Baker**: Also, it feels like the argument is trite at this point, like why there's a double standard for women disclosing emotion, and it always being interpreted as sadness instead of just emotionality. But then I'm also like, 'Who's *not* [sad]?' Life is suffering, that's the first noble truth. Music is about three things: love, politics, and suffering" (in *Pitchfork* 2023).

sis, overcoming)—this chapter tracks how traumatic experiences intersect with '90s nostalgia in contemporary indie. Following Ann Cvetkovich (2003) and in conversation with Jessica Holmes (2023), I treat trauma as something beyond a medical question, as a spectrum of experience that may include such medically mediated experiences while also making space for more quotidian genres of pain. Trauma is critical for understanding the political valence of Big Feelings insofar as it names "experiences of socially situated political violence" and "forges overt connections between politics and emotion" (Cvetkovich 2003, 3). In tracking queer-feminist affects across Big Feelings music, I hope to add to this conversation by studying the uniquely nuanced dynamics that music raises, particularly music that is more affectively than ideologically oriented. I want to nuance the "profitable/subversive" distinction around emotional vulnerability by showing how Big Feelings doesn't necessarily or always stop at insisting on the validity of sadness; rather, Big Feelings artists are also helping to construct alternative notions of care that do not so much "overcome" trauma as they provide paths for processing it, modeling an ambivalent and both-at-once orientation toward pain. In this sense, Big Feelings participates in long traditions of queer care, in which trauma is not disavowed or repressed, but is instead enfolded into practices that help marginalized communities to understand their own pain, to both fight and find joy in the middle of it. Additionally, this reading of Big Feelings, in which generational trauma plays out via personal, affective performances, also resonates with the project of nostalgia insofar as rock music from the 1990s famously took depression—or what Sarah Ferguson calls a "politics of damage"—seriously (2012).[3] Big Feelings writ large returns to a sound already culturally coded with such a politics and claims a place within it for the non-men musicians who were by and large excluded in its previous iterations, applying its trademarks sounds to their concerns.[4]

3. And while any number of canonic '90s alt albums might come to mind here (including/not to mention Nirvana's), for me the one that still stands out is Everclear's *So Much for the Afterglow*, the absolute entirety of which is shattering, but these days it usually just takes the opening bars to get me weepy. In the earliest days, it was this and the Cranberries' *To the Faithfully Departed* that taught me how to drum, so much repetition involved in my practice that the dark themes only sunk in gradually, at an age when you can't attend to how things are shaping you.

4. In a profile of boygenius, Lexi McMenamin puts it this way: "There is something radical in making music that we came to love in part through bands I won't name because they've been accused of abusing women and their fans. Raised on '90s alternative and 2000s emo and pop punk in the shadow of the Iraq War, Boygenius is making the music they never got to have" (2023).

It is also critical to grapple with '90s nostalgia across Big Feelings in part because it is one of the most consistently referenced characteristics in discourse about the music. As with beabadoobee, Snail Mail, and others, most critical reviews or interviews of Soccer Mommy (particularly regarding their first major release) note the audible influence of the '90s and early 2000s, as does Allison in turn: "I feel like that's because that was the culture when I was, like, a 5-year-old," she says in one interview (Zoladz 2020). "I was imagining being a teen and being a young adult and how cool it was going to be. So I feel like that's why I, and a lot of people my age, have this attachment and nostalgia for that kind of stuff. It's what we looked up to when we were kids." This reflection captures something important about Big Feelings' orientation toward sounds characteristic of '90s alternative: here, nostalgic sounds are those that allow us to recapture the feeling of looking forward ("I was imagining being a teen") precisely by looking backward. Rather than simply returning to a time gone by, Allison's comments about nostalgia index something meaningful about her generation's aspirations to recapture lost possibilities for *the future*.

It can be tempting to read the '90s resurgence among young indie rockers as reflective of a more general trend in popular culture, evinced (for example) by reboots of popular '90s shows and think-pieces trying to make sense of why low-rise jeans are making a comeback. And there are indeed such obvious ways in which capitalist postmodernism regurgitates cultural markers cyclically, once they can feel fresh again. But at the same time, I maintain that nostalgia, despite its ubiquity as a mode of consumption and production, also raises particular issues for both the producers and consumers in ways that remain singular across media formats and discourses. "Nostalgia is only for the broken hearted. For the displeased or disaffected, the ones who need to look to the past to give meaning to the present" (Abdurraqib 2024, 259). More a mode of expression than a simple marketing trend, I want to think about how nostalgia and trauma work together through a single from Soccer Mommy's 2020 album, *Color Theory*.

"Circle the Drain"

As its title suggests, "Circle the Drain" is a song about depression. Reading the lyrics in isolation, we are presented with a relatively straightforward portrayal of a character experiencing a mental health crisis through a series of metaphors. For example, Allison sings in the second stanza, "It's a feeling that boils in my brain / I would dial back the flame / But I'm not sure I'm able / I'm wobbling out on the wire / And the lights could go out / With the break of a cable." Here depression is experienced as a feeling bubbling up in the back of the mind, threatening to collapse the flimsy foundation on which the narrator's life is precariously balanced. Later in the song, we catch glimpses of what happens in the moments when that cable does snap, or the balance can't be maintained: "I'm trying to seem strong for my love / For my family and friends / But I'm so tired of faking / 'Cause I'm chained to my bed when they're gone / Watching TV alone / 'Til my body starts aching."

The image of Allison's character endlessly zoned out in front of the TV, "cling[ing] to the dark of [her] room," while "the days thin [her] out" seems to completely invert the experience of "too much feeling" that I have used to describe Big Feelings in general, instead portraying a debilitating inability to feel adequately. More to the point, the implication here is one of overload—of feeling so much that something has broken. Such a reading tracks with comments from my interview respondents (see below), which themselves reflect Ann Cvetkovich's well-known formulation of trauma in *An Archive of Feelings*, where she writes that "traumatic experience and its aftermath can be characterized not just by too much feeling, or hyperarousal, but also by an absence of feeling, or numbness" (2003, 43). Critically, this trauma is, in the narrative space of the song, not informed by any one particular event. To the contrary, (and back to Allison) "Things feel that low sometimes / Even when everything is fine."

Whether or not this song describes a real experience in Allison's life, I am more interested in thinking through how this performance might be taken up by fans and listeners, in line with this book's overall focus on the nonconscious, extramusical, and otherwise affective resonances that necessarily take place relationally, in negotiated contact between artist and listener. Building on my description of Big Feelings lyrics as both "personal" and "abstract," a critical feature of both "Circle the Drain" and Indigo De Souza's "Real Pain" (discussed below) is the way that they defer discussing the source, cause, or issue behind that pain. This is significant for how it holds open the possibility that fans will feel along with the emotional affects being described/generated by the music. Keeping the particulars open, listeners become more able to resonate with feelings of depression that are not limited to those caused by one or another specific issue, but are either more widely shared or else open enough to allow listeners to map their own experiences onto the sentiments being expressed.

That Soccer Mommy fans might relate to the feelings of depression expressed here can be considered something of a foregone conclusion in light of the widespread anxiety experienced by young demographics in the United States, particularly since the pandemic. Indeed, as mainstream news and scholars alike have observed, Gen Z as a whole experiences stress, anxiety disorders, depression, and other mental health struggles at higher rates than other cohorts, with 70 percent reporting these as major struggles among their peers (Horowitz and Graf 2019; Bethune 2019; C. Schwartz 2022). And in the same way that even mainstream news outlets seem to be aware that Gen Z is struggling, the sociopolitical factors informing this widespread depression are not mysterious. Gen Z grew up training for active-shooter scenarios in school; grew up watching Black people get murdered by police; grew up watching the world break its promises to their millennial elders, saddled with student debt or medical debt or both, matriculating into a gig economy, unable to afford homes or even apartments without roommates; grew up acutely aware of the climate crisis and the certainty that they'd live its consequences in the face of political intransigence; grew up experiencing key moments of high school or college through the mediated dissociation of a Zoom window. Young women are still entering an economy stratified by the gender pay gap, where women of color always fare worse. Queer-presenting workers are still not protected from workplace discrimination and are in many places increasingly subject to state-sanctioned harassment. Most young people grow up in towns that are as or more segregated than they were fifty years ago, experiencing the attendant economic, health, educational, and other disparities that result from marginalized communities being pushed to the metaphorical and literal margins, where neighborhoods are more likely to have lead pipes, are more likely to be situated near industrial manufacturing, are more vulnerable to damage during extreme weather events. Distinct from their millennial elders, Gen Z also grew up with the smartphone's toxic influence on mental well-being, self-esteem, and cognitive focus. Across the board, today's young people are no more likely to be able to afford hospital expenses or retirement planning or higher education than the previous generation, which was the first in contemporary US history to be statistically worse-off than their parents (O'Connor 2018; Picchi 2018; Rockeman and Saraiva 2021). Now, they are preparing to enter the workforce during an inflationary period with historic levels of student debt. Such crises have been building for a long time—but they had not yet saturated public consciousness in the 1990s, which, as I suggested previously, can be retroactively idealized as a moment of triumph for the neoliberal consensus. Today, by contrast, it is better established that neoliberalism is not only a failed project for the 99 percent, but also a chief contributor to anxiety and depression (Becker et al. 2021; Petersen 2020). Utilizing such contrasting

Figure 5. Soccer Mommy, "Circle the Drain," screenshot from the music video

views of the '90s and now, I suggest that the sonic and visual representations in "Circle the Drain" speak to our currently shared social conditions specifically through a disjuncture between Allison's character and the nostalgic 1990s atmosphere she inhabits.

As we have already seen, Soccer Mommy deploys '90s affects selectively and strategically, which is to say, as a particular tool in their musical project, a tool that they do not always employ and to which their music is not reducible. That said, when it is deployed, it is deployed comprehensively: both the timbre of Allison's guitar tone, as well as the songwriting structure (the two-beat harmonic rhythm of the song, for instance, and the voicing of common chords) evoke '90s alternative immediately and purposefully, to the extent that keyboard samples from '90s-era floppy disks were used during the recording of *Color Theory* (Cornish et al. 2020). At the same time, these associations are reinforced by the music video, the entirety of which is filtered to appear as if on VHS, complete with the kind of characteristic, RGB-colored glitching that might make any millennial reach to adjust the tracking.

Directed by Atiba Jefferson, the subject of the video—a group of friends skateboarding in an abandoned water park—is also immediately evocative of the kind of Gen X malaise so often represented in '90s media (e.g., "1979") but which was, for Allison, inspired by Avril Lavigne's work in the early 2000s. Both decades blend in the fantasy space of this video, which sonically

Figure 6. Soccer Mommy, "Circle the Drain," screenshot from the music video

and visually produces nostalgic affects that I suggest are not reflective of fashion trends as much as they constitute a key mechanism for of critique and commentary, helping listeners to feel struggles common to a young generation gazing backwards longingly.

If we continue thinking the music and the video together, both seem to eventually establish a strange kind of contrast with the lyrics. The longer the song progresses, the more it becomes clear that Allison's character—as portrayed in the video—is having a *good* time. While it does take her a while to get to the park and join her friends, possible readings wherein she might have been left behind don't seem plausible once she does arrive; rather, she skateboards, performs, goofs around, and laughs, ending the day high-fiving and playing air guitar.

This would appear a strange video, then, for a song about depression. Allison has acknowledged this tension in an interview, saying of the track, "I wanted it to feel like this really sunny, beachy, summer jam from the early 2000s while also hiding feeling bogged down. Because that's kind of what happens with people a lot of the time: The outside can be going through life [like normal] and then the inside is struggling" (quoted in Cornish et al. 2020). This quote surely helps to contextualize the perhaps counterintuitive images presented in the music video. But in addition to this reading, I suggest that it is also important to think through the affects generated by the musical, lyrical, and visual elements of "Circle the Drain" together—this might lead to interpretations of how the song functions, over and above the artistic intentions infused into it by the artist herself. In other words, each element of the multiply mediated "object" we're identifying as "Circle the Drain" can be thought collectively, as each ostensibly separate element actually co-constitutively informs how we understand the others. On this view, the video's disjuncture with the lyrics would also have to be read through the overall context of '90s nostalgia in which everything is housed; from *that* vantage, the carefree visual scene at odds with the lyrics is one that we are invited to read as taking place in the past—if not the literal past, then in the fantasy space of a nostalgic past. Following this implication, the disconnect between the visuals and the lyrics occurs because the depressive state being sung about and the fun afternoon being shown to us *do not occupy the same time-space*. It is in the imaginary past—a past that Allison has already attested allows her to look forward into the future—that we find her character's happiness. In other words, while the song alone easily supports an interior-vs-exterior reading, the video more strongly suggests that Allison is not hiding something from her friends but is rather genuinely enjoying herself; the catch is that this enjoyment is a memory, where the narration of the lyrics takes place in the current moment.

In my reading, the element of fantasy is critical: I am not suggesting (nor does the video suggest) that the 1990s were in fact ideal, that they weren't characterized by neoliberal austerity, wars, white supremacy, patriarchy, or any of the other traumas to which Gen X culture so often responded. This is not a direct or literal longing for the past, which witnessed many of the same structural violences that persist under neoliberalism today, and which was for Allison, born in 1997, a time before she would have had any real consciousness of the world. Rather, it is the kind of yearning proper to nostalgia, which locates lost possibilities in a past that never was. In some ways, longing for an imaginary past is simply how all nostalgia works. But critically, this is not a longing oriented toward nostalgia's conservative imaginary, which makes appeals to a "simpler time" gone by. By contrast, Big Feelings deploys nostalgia both self-consciously and in order to lament the current moment out of an impossible desire to reclaim the potential for a different future after that possibility has already been preemptively stripped from us. It only idealizes the past insofar as it happens to be the time-space in which future outcomes could still be altered; nostalgia here is not characterized by the desire to go backward but to reclaim the possibility of imagining a different future than the one we have actually inherited, becoming an indictment of the present through recourse to the past.

Given all this, and again thinking with Cvetkovich, we can read Allison's (character's) depression not as an individual clinical pathology but as a shared social condition, reflective of what Ann Powers identifies in Billie Eilish's music as an expression of "the pressing mood that has, in recent years, turned 'overwhelm' into a noun—not a condition that can be alleviated but a total environment" (Powers 2019). Considering the context of Gen Z's mental health struggles together with the always-glitching time-space referenced in the music video, the trauma portrayed in "Circle the Drain" invites a kind of universalist question—"Haven't you felt this way, too?"—and can thus be read as simply representing the condition of being young in 2020, the place from which we are imagining the affective world of the 1990s.

It should be clear how a musical portrayal of depression could resonate with young listeners generally, who grapple with the structural and historical conditions outlined above on a daily basis. But furthermore, music like this might resonate particularly with "girls like [Cvetkovich]" (2003, 3), the young, feminist, queer, and/or trans youth facing the realities of cis-hetero-patriarchy, disproportionately at risk for suicidal ideation and violence, both structural and personal. Recent data confirms that overlapping groups—women, LGBTQ+, and Black people—have higher rates of depression, anxiety, and suicide risk, even relative to the already alarming reports about Gen Z as a whole (Centers for Disease Control and Prevention 2023a, 2023b; Chatterjee 2023; Tanner 2023). Feminist, queer studies, and Black studies scholarship has long tracked the ways that the conditions of everyday trauma for some are heightened so as to become enfolded into one's experience of existing. For example, Angela McRobbie's "gender melancholia" (2009) and Kelly Oliver's "social melancholy" (2020) both name depressive consequences of being a woman in the world. Decoupled from clinical pathology, gender melancholia tracks how negative affective states for women are produced from gendered expectations to both identify with and to have always already overcome the struggles particular to women in patriarchal society. Relatedly, social melancholy identifies a loss of positive self-image under conditions of structural, gender-based oppression. "Confronted with abject images of themselves from mainstream culture, even as they are part of that culture, girls, women, and mothers suffer from the loss of a lovable image of *themselves*" (Oliver 2020, 32).

Over and above whatever intentions Allison infuses into her music, the question of how it hits listeners in their lived experience remains a distinct and critical consideration. Returning to the beginning of this discussion, we find the narrator of "Circle the Drain" in a state of depressive catatonia, a state performed by Allison's flat affect and close-mic production choices, portraying feelings that have become too big to bear. Read through the idea of social melancholy, "this catatonia is not just the result of individual pathology but also the result of social melancholy caused by the devaluation of women as well as their emotional and physical labor. In a sense, the depressive has given up on words and on society because they have given up on her" (Oliver 2020, 37).

On Social Conditions and Musical Enjoyment

As of this writing, every young listener with whom I have spoken has expressed feelings of depression, anxiety, and fear around current events and their prospects for the future. They consistently raised a common set of concerns, referencing the Black Lives Matter uprisings in 2020, the COVID-19 pandemic, and the recent assaults on minority rights—most specifically the rights of women, trans, and queer people—as issues producing anxiety and depression. For example, when I asked a student of mine, Sarah, about her perspective on the broader world, she responded by saying,

SF: For me specifically I think about abortion, I think of . . . I see a lot of headlines—I know I shouldn't just run on headlines—but I see a lot of headlines about like, "this bill about trans rights or gay rights or Black lives matter," and it's just like . . . all these [rights] are being taken away, and it's just so *bad* and I don't know . . . it's hard to see the light at the end of the tunnel because it seems like the government is completely redoing all the progress that we had.

DD: Do you think about the climate often?

SF: [Overlapping] Oh my God yes! I don't know why I didn't think about that. . . . The climate is one of the biggest fears of mine. . . . It's a reason I don't want to have kids: it's like, why would I want to bring a child into this world that's . . . I feel like we're just gonna go up in flames. And then I'm like, "Why am I in college?" Cause like, I'm wasting all this money, and I might not even be able to use this degree cause we're all gonna die. (Sarah F. 2022)

My later interview with Alyssa produced a similar sequence of reflections:

AL: I feel like ever since the pandemic and everything with Black Lives Matter, I feel like everything has been very high and intense for anybody who experiences any type of [marginalization]—for anybody who experiences hardships because of their identity . . . with *Roe versus Wade*, women or anyone with a uterus having to face the possibility that their state won't provide them with the healthcare they need—that's absolutely insane, and it's dehumanizing. . . . And then they're talking about taking away gay marriage again, and it's like: I just started embracing my queer identity in the past four years, so . . . I mean, I don't know about marriage, but that's something that should be an option for me or anybody else, regardless of who they are. So that's hard! Because when you're being faced with all this neglect and hate toward people that you love and see and are in community with, it is like a soul-crushing thing to see that every day. I think it's a battle that you have to wake up and do every day until things start to change. . . .

So that's kind of my take on it from the past two years. . . . I mean, it's been longer than that, but the two years with COVID, I feel like everybody is worn the fuck out. Losing jobs, having to pay for everything, [inflation] going up—is absolutely insane. I think everyone's on edge right now. But I think that also plays into how people are so tied to their music, because they're looking for stuff to . . . in a way music is a healing tool, I think, for me. It's definitely helped me with anything that I've faced, so I feel like that's even more so why music is getting to be that way now: because there's so much happening, and people need those paths or roadways to find some type of thing to hold onto, I guess.

DD: A lot of the people I'm talking to are in your age bracket. Are you worried about the climate?

AL: I didn't include that in my speech, but heck yes I am, oh my God. Like I said, I'm from the low country in South Carolina, and with everything happening . . . I wouldn't be surprised if in a few years . . . it is under water . . . Our flooding issues are so bad, and you look at Florida . . . how are they going to keep recovering from those things? When hurricanes come—and they are gonna keep coming, and they are gonna keep getting worse—those are going to take away the whole coastal ways, and then everything with the ocean, it's . . . yeah. I am super incredibly nervous about the state of what's going to happen and . . . I dunno, I feel like that's another reason why people should be allowed to decide if they want kids or not. Like, who the fuck wants to bring a kid into this situation right now? Not me. (Alyssa L. 2022)

Both of these responses stand out to me first because of the way in which the respondents seem to struggle knowing which crisis to address first (because there are too many), and second because of the ways that they tie together the climate crisis with other structural disasters, such as the unhinged cost of higher education in the United States and the stripping away of young people's reproductive autonomy via the *Dobbs* ruling—all of these problems that affect Gen Z most acutely, and which are caused by the same structural conditions. Finally, Alyssa's response specifically links the experience of these crises with music-listening, suggesting that artists like Indigo De Souza and Soccer Mommy provide "healing" and "something to hold onto" in the context of widespread, chronic instability. That instability is becoming a more universalized condition among young people should, I suggest, be taken seriously. As my student Dan put it, "I don't think . . . it doesn't make sense to me to plan into the future more than three months. . . . You just can't look ahead. You just have to make peace with that or joke about it or something" (Dan G. 2022). This reflects what I referred to above as the "always-already nature of crisis in the United States," or what Berlant calls the "long meanwhile of life in the crisis ordinary" (2022, 19).

I want to consider here further examples of the ways in which interview respondents connect issues of generalized anxiety and musical experience. For example, in a conversation about the band Big Thief (one his favorites), Dan explained:

DG: I think there's a certain type of person—if we were to generalize types of people for a moment—that is attracted to this music because of the way that it reflects and brings out and validates feeling depressed, feeling extremely anxious. I know that myself, I mostly associate with people who have mental health issues just because that's like . . . those are the people that my brain connects with, you know what I mean? I meet new friends and they're either depressed, on the spectrum, or have a ton of ADHD—always. Or like, a fun mix of all of 'em. And from the time that I've spent in these scenes meeting people, it's completely synonymous. And there's a reason for that! Ideally, what we can do as musicians—because we've had it done for us—is create something that people can gain feeling from. . . . And I think this is a fanbase of people, again to generalize, that feels the way that this music reflects, and then gains something from that. I mean like, they can feel like this is for them. The fans that I know that go see this band are like, this is it: this is their band. And they walk away crying, you know what I mean? As do I. As do I. (Dan G. 2022)

Likewise, while Deanna shared that her own personal life is "getting better every day," she also situated her experience within a broader context:

DF: In terms of things that are happening externally outside my own little bubble . . . [I'm] feeling pretty desensitized. It's like kinda fucked up, everything that's going on, it's been fucked up. I get articles in my email and I read through them and I'm just like not even shocked by the things that are happening anymore and I feel . . . not to be so pessimistic, but I feel a little . . . what's the word . . . powerless, I guess . . . so I'm kind of focusing on rebuilding myself up and kind of watching from the sidelines as everything's [breaking?]

DD: Does the music help you do that?

DF: I wouldn't say it directly does that, but I would say it helps me feel what I'm feeling—which is a piece of the puzzle. (Deanna F. 2022)

Every single respondent I spoke with shared similar sentiments, often connecting the general relationship between music-listening and the state of the world. Beth told me,

BC: The problems that I'm dealing with right now don't really have answers, so for me to try to find the answers . . . it's sort of impossible? So the thing that I can do to kind of help myself with that is just to feel like, accepted and comfortable, and to feel like problems are OK to have. . . . That's kind of the sense that I get with all of this music that completely blatantly acknowledges all these struggles that I find so familiar . . . with relationship struggles or just existential depresso, or just . . . trying to figure out your identity. . . . It just feels like a place [where] questions and problems are OK and understood and accepted.

I'm not feeling a specific "the world is burning down and that's why I'm listening to Billie Eilish today." . . . I think it's more that I tend to just carry a lot of emotion around. . . . No matter where I go or what I'm doing, there's always a little bit of sadness or frustration or anxiety, and I think that's partly mental health but I think that's also just being aware of a lot of shitty stuff happening. (Beth C. 2023)

Based on responses like these, I insist that the Big Feelings raised in the music I am discussing here are rendered meaningful in part because of the ways in which contemporary living conditions are experienced by listeners in this age group. Any personal experiences raised in the music are always already refracted through the collective situation within which those experiences take place. While it can be tempting to read in Big Feelings the same myopic emo-band cynicism that Karen Tongson writes is "alienation that comes with privilege rather than a striving toward affiliation with others who share the same plight" (2006, 63), taking "Circle the Drain" into this broader context renders its representation of depression more as a recognition of shared grief and the intractability of huge structural problems like climate change and systemic racism, which have gone unaddressed and compounded for decades. Following Kate Hamori's discussion of Olivia Rodrigo (2023), we might also think about how, for example, Allison's bedroom-bound character might also resonate with young people trapped inside during the darkest days of the COVID lockdowns—often after moving back home—experiencing another crisis that was traumatic in part because of how the government abandoned people's needs. Indeed, while many respondents described the kinds of generalized bad feelings with which this chapter is most concerned, the general and the dramatic can also overlap with one another, as for example during the height of the pandemic, during which time two of my interview respondents experienced significant and direct losses. "I think the [sad-girl thing] is special because it can reach people at their lowest," Destiny told me. "It allows me to stay quiet and also be heard" (Destiny M. 2023). Likewise, Sam talked about listening to Mitski's "Drunk Walk Home," during acutely difficult periods, saying, "I would just let her scream cause I had a baby sister to take care of and I had to be the strong one. So I was like, 'Mitski you can just do the screaming for both of us'" (Sam H. 2023).

Katie also described her experience of the broader social world as "crazy fucked, and there's a lot of things I'm ready to burn" (Katie M. 2022). But rather than describing music as a means of relating to her own feelings, she instead talked about making art with her friends and being in community as renewed priorities, particularly post-lockdown.

> KM: I no longer sit down and think hard and cry at Instagram, and that shift to me is also reflected in my relationship to music. . . . I don't sit around and record things by myself anymore because I can't bear to make music alone. . . . I'm not thinking about [current events] in the ways I recently was, and I'm not consuming [news] absentmindedly in the way I once was. . . . It's a more . . . I think about it sometimes, maybe if I've got friends over making art it'll come out in really cool art. (Katie M. 2022)

What I hear articulated in this description is not a refusal to pay attention to the world so much as a refusal to engage with what is so obviously traumatic beyond a limit—deeply informed by the isolation of the pandemic, fans like Katie participate in political activity tempered by a kind of self-preservation, where community and mutual care are integral to processing what's happening. When I followed up with Katie about what she meant by "crazy fucked," she clarified in exactly those terms: "Like, really what's fucked is capitalism. And the way that feels like it relates specifically is how art has to be a commodity, how people are all struggling alone and may be encouraged to 'take mental health days' or what have you, but only on an individual level. What's fucked is the resistance to real community care" (Katie M. 2022). As we can hear in her words, Katie and listeners like her are attuned to capitalism's inherent hostility toward any notion of collective caretaking, even as its systems cause the injuries that will require care in the first place. The remainder of this chapter will be dedicated to showing how Big Feelings artists—their music, their performances, and the cultures they foster—provide a kind of care for listeners that draws on the centrality of community in queer culture, queer theory, and queer life.

Indigo De Souza in Concert

On an early evening in September 2021, I stumbled into one of the best shows I've ever seen. Unable to make it, a friend gifted me his ticket at the last minute, so that I unexpectedly found myself walking from my German Village apartment to Columbus, Ohio's Big Room Bar, a venue whose name belies its intimate layout: in this single room with a bar at the back, musician and audience are almost literally coequal. I had only recently begun listening to De Souza's music, and I was hardly prepared to deal with it coming to life in that place. Arriving without any preconceptions, the show simply overwhelmed me. Every aspect of the performance conspired to make this happen. The band was tight and heavy, funky and devastatingly sincere. De Souza's voice had none of the charming, indie rock imprecision I can hear retrospectively in some early YouTube clips; it radiated command, bringing everyone in the room into each song, each space with her, no matter its affects or the feelings it sought to conjure. But in addition to the music itself, my experience that night was also caught up in the crowd's reaction: as I felt them collectively chant back the "FUCKED UP" stanza in "Kill Me"; watched young girls with pixie cuts and tears in their eyes scream "I love you!" and "You're so beautiful!" to a rock star mere feet away; watched a mass of people diverse across categories swell toward the stage while leaving space for the others around them, checking; I was swept up in the energy of that room in a way I hadn't been for a long time, or maybe ever.

As soon as I left the show, I regretted not trying to interview some of the audience that night—but I also don't know that I would have been able had I tried. I wanted to ask them about their experience, why they loved De Souza's music, and how it was that she seemed able to hail a crowd simultaneously diverse and yet unified in their comportment. What I mean by this has to do in part with the feeling of the room, a culture that felt warm and gentle, even as certain musical moments elicited guttural screaming from both audience and band alike. Part of it had to do with how both De Souza and the Ophelias (who opened) insisted on and thanked us for wearing our masks, with the fact that everyone seemed to be there to experience something together, concerned with creating the conditions for others to do the same.

Since attending that show, my generalized impressions about audience culture have started to sharpen into a theory about what made it so affecting for me, and (seemingly) the other fans in attendance. Because I had missed the chance to talk with my fellow concert attendees, this was one of the first questions I had for Katie, who was particularly excited to talk with me about Indigo De Souza; her responses capture many aspects of those performance dynamics that I experienced, and in ways that I heard echoed across many of my interview conversations. Describing a concert by Lucy Dacus and Indigo De Souza, Katie told me:

KM: It was in a bit of a COVID wave in Virginia, and so masks and things weren't required . . . so one of the most notable dynamics of the night was, there were signs around the venue that were like "Lucy says please wear a mask." And both artists were pretty straight up into the mic, like, "Hey here's how we want you to be as audience members: first off, please wear your masks, second, like be kind to each other, don't be bumping into each other, like share this together." And that was *sick*, that was so good. I was bringing a beloved straight dude friend who I've always been bugging to consume more shit from queer ladies cause he always ends up loving it . . . and so I brought him and I got to see him kinda like totally buy into the crowd as well as the music. . . . So when he saw everyone else singing along he was like, "Fuck I need to know this song or else!"

DD: What is it about both the artists and the crowd, do you think, that made that kind of dynamic work?

KM: I think [Indigo De Souza and Lucy Dacus] are already transparently soft and squishy in their art and in their online presence, which I guess is optional. . . . You don't really have to have an online presence; you can just convey your vibe through your music entirely. But it definitely helps that like Indigo's Instagram captions are sometimes like, "Hey I'm really not doing OK and I'm canceling this show cause I need to be doing better"—and that's such an easy pipeline into a good show. Compared to like . . . the worst time I've had at a show recently was Alex G, cause he was awesome and the audience was full of like . . . just the *worst men*. I didn't like them at all!

DD: You were talking earlier about her posting like, "Hey I really need to take a break for my mental health," and I'm imagining that there are some people who really resonate with that kind of a statement, and some people who maybe don't quite understand that as much. So my question is—and obviously you don't have to share more than you're comfortable with—but is there stuff from your personal life that makes you feel like you can relate to this artist? Is that part of why you like their music?

KM: Absolutely. But I feel like, at least with this specific artist . . . I relate to her as someone that I would want to be friends with—not necessarily someone who I see myself in . . . but this kind of . . . "Oh you're feeling this way? Here's what I want to do to support you."

DD: Yeah. And do you feel like . . . OK so maybe you don't directly relate to the experiences she's having, but do you feel like there are certain sentiments or . . . like this idea of being able to take a break for your mental health: to me, that seems like something that is being talked about more among people of, if I may, your age, than perhaps it had been in the past. Do you feel like there's a common understanding there among her fanbase?

KM: *Totally*. I do! I feel like that's a massive assumption that she makes. . . . She kind of banks on the fact that the people she wants supporting her will understand. And I sense that sometimes in . . . I think she was playing Cornell recently or something like that, and she seemed worried to me that the crowd wouldn't buy in, that the crowd wouldn't have the attitude that lets her be vulnerable—but here she is being vulnerable and she can't really stop. So yeah, I feel like that's totally an age thing, and . . . something in this life I'm livin, whatever that's attributed to . . . is starting to value a specifically feminine queer care sort of situation. I feel like there's a growing culture . . . of supporting each other and being honest with each other about doing poorly and making art with that. (Katie M. 2022)

In these comments resonate several points that I consider fundamental for this book. First, and building on the ideas presented in chapter 2, Katie describes the ways in which a social orientation is communicated and cultivated beyond any particular issue that might be the subject of a given song's lyrical subject. Rather, a personality, "vibe," or approach is cultivated both sonically and extramusically, for example via social media, where De Souza frequently shares sentiments that help fans orient toward her perspective: "Imagine," she writes in one Instagram post, "if every person just poured love and intention into their direct community. If every person chose to heal and learn and expand. If we actually took care of one another" (@indigofaraway 2022).

In retrospect, Katie's descriptions from the previous chapter of Indigo De Souza's stylized performances of girlishness ("'lowercase starts to sentences online,' and like 'multiple exclamation points' and shit like that") combine here with an insistence on care and healing to unequivocally communicate soft femme aesthetics to an internet fanbase already sensitized and familiar with the semiotics of such choices. So although Indigo De Souza strategically performs the heaviness of grief, softness and healing—specifically in a queer/femme register—are central to how and why that trauma appears. Therefore, (second) Katie's identification of a "growing culture of supporting each other and being honest about doing poorly" renders a kind of political act: in a world that disproportionately harms women, queer people, and other marginalized groups, to carve out spaces where those same people can foster mutual support—especially when this happens out of an explicit understanding of the exact nature of the political harm necessitating such support—can be understood as (juxta)political in ways that I explore further below, a response to political conditions that in turn produces its own political implications. Again, this is not a matter of individualized bad feelings or personal journeys toward healing; it is rather a politicized discourse, here performed via soft femme aesthetics, in a way that moves beyond any narrow demographic boundaries to be explicitly inclusive of overlapping experiences: "Healing one's relationship to the self or the perception of the self after having gone through something traumatic, like sexual assault, or experiencing the ongoing trauma of enduring sexism, homophobia, ableism, or racism, or living with chronic illness or disability is a common theme among posts that address healing in femme Internet culture" (A. Schwartz 2020, 4). Reading through this list of traumas helps to understand how, though Katie's quote and Schwartz's notion of soft femme cultures both help to contextualize Indigo De Souza's performances of care as femme-oriented, such performances also extend outward from femmeness, making space for the concerns of non-femmes, creating spaces of assumed commonality and shared permission for feeling into the ways this world damages all of us differently. Listen-

Figures 7 and 8. @indigofaraway, 2022, "Stop sleepwalking through it all," Instagram Post, November 3. https://www.instagram.com/p/Ckg5dyOvxjv/?img_index=3

ers who are attuned to these frequencies gravitate toward Big Feelings music because they feel this awareness as resonance, not because the music speaks directly to the issues most relevant for any one person's circumstances. "We don't have to find ourselves represented in the stories of others to understand or engage with them" (Grover 2023, 6).

As I discussed in my last book, care praxis has a long history emerging from queer/feminist scholarship in which it is often linked with but not reducible to friendship, where friendship is understood as "as a way of life" (Foucault 1997). For writers like Audre Lorde, bell hooks, Lisa Duggan, and others, (self) care emerges as a concept of particular importance in queer theory because of the ways that heteropatriarchal social structures make necessary other ways of being and doing for those who fall outside of its frameworks. Care and kinship outside the bounds of normative family structures have been not only historically necessary but also desirable insofar as queer relationality cannot be contained by what heteropatriarchy, particularly under conditions of neoliberal capitalism, offers as a model for living. Here we are back to Berlant's formulation of queer work as "skeptical about ordinary modes of attachment" (2022), branching out into other ways of relating to one another out of both necessity and desire.

This is one way in which artists like Indigo De Souza generate queer-feminist affects in their music, not regardless but in excess of however they might identify their own orientations toward objects of desire: De Souza creates cultures of care in her concerts by modeling certain kinds of behavior, what Katie described as "soft and squishy," both in performance and prior to it. As I suggested above, this posture is expansive and inclusive, rather than the kind of polemical inversion that (rightfully) insisted it was time for girls to move to the front. That is, the culture at De Souza's ideal concerts are not demarcated around gendered lines, but rather around behaviors demonstrating kindness and mutual support.

At the same time, the issue of care is not limited to matters of health—whether physical (as in the crowd helping to protect one another from COVID-19) or mental (as when De Souza cancels a show in order to guard against burnout); it is also emotional. Here, finally, I suggest that the kind of affective intensity staged by songs like "Real Pain" helps to perform a managed catharsis in which audience members willingly surrender the fantasy of their own sovereignty over their bodies, instead placing their trust in a band that will guide them through vibrational forces which may unearth past traumas, but in doing so, also help fans to process them on terms that have already been established as safe.

"Real Pain"

The most illustrative example of this dynamic might well be Indigo De Souza's 2021 single "Real Pain": while the track begins as a seeming lament about lost love, it very quickly transforms into something more, what seems to me a kind of sonic placeholder where listeners can identify with the feeling of pain itself, regardless of the particular situation that caused the pain to begin with. The rest of this section brings a close listening of Indigo De Souza's 2021 track "Real Pain" into conversation with fan interviews in order to unpack the ways in which De Souza's music creates spaces of queer care in performance by recourse to what Lauren Berlant calls a "good non-sovereignty."

For Berlant, good non-sovereignty is the very promise of the political: good non-sovereignty happens when we can afford to be swept up in something, because we trust the communities in which we are enmeshed. Indigo De Souza creates good non-sovereignty in performance by asking her listeners to take care of one another, and then by modulating their emotional-affective responses through sound. In asking listeners to wear their masks at shows, to take care of their mental health, and otherwise look out for one another, De Souza creates a space of trust that allows listeners to experience catharsis—to surrender their sovereign control over their own emotional states and feel the resonance of shared traumatic experience.

Hailing young and marginalized subjects, "Real Pain" exemplifies and literalizes this collective invitation by featuring the layered screams of De Souza's fans, who sent recordings of themselves at the artist's request. These recordings are stacked on top of one another in order to build a collective scream-space that sits at the heavy heart of this track. Signifying by sonifying, De Souza conflates all painful experiences into one general expression, allowing listeners to vibrate alongside the band and experience catharsis as a sonic form of care. A little less than halfway through the song, the groove, which, though deeply melancholic, had been bouncing along at around 90 beats per minute (BPM), suddenly falls apart, grinding down to around 60 BPM within the span of just two bars. As the new beat establishes itself (30 clicks slower, and now maintained by the flat insistence of bass and bass drum), the loss of any guitar chords leaves a sizable sonic gap that is at first filled only by De Souza's haunting repetition of the word "going." Soon, though, it becomes clear that this isn't a moment of reprieve so much as complete recentering of focus; as the bass oscillates between F-sharp and B (I and IV!), De Souza's voice maneuvers above a scene that is becoming dramatically overfilled by escalating distortion and the layered overlapping of so many screams. This metastasizing horror lasts for nearly two minutes, longer than any other section of the song.

There is yet a third act to come—but the middle part of this song, its chaotic center, is clearly the heart of what makes "Real Pain" work the way that it does. In spite of the fact that a few narrative clues in the early moments suggest that this is a song about heartbreak ("And love might go, but is not gone / I still know you, I still know you"), the idea that "Real Pain" could be considered predominantly a breakup song is belied by the fact that the screams we are hearing have been recorded by De Souza's listening community; even the idea that breakups are both painful and universal does not account for the noise that occurs here, which absolutely breaks open any boundary on what kind of trauma is being referenced. The inchoate, brutal catharsis that takes place by wearing out one's vocal cords does not know, cannot hold any distinctions because all pain is always already experienced as "real." Here sounded by the simultaneity of any number of stories, causes, or experiences, the narratives are rendered immaterial: the content matters infinitely less than the form; put another way, that one feels moved enough to scream into a recording is proof enough that it is necessary to do so. We don't need the backstory here to justify the expression.

Because of the sheer overwhelming force of this dense noisescape, it feels as though this black hole in the middle of an otherwise coherent, gut-wrenching song has been created in order to become dense enough to hold any particular pain—ambiguous enough to plausibly reference an infinite number of harms, challenges, or struggles, yet earnestly articulated enough to allow fans to feel seen and literally heard as they struggle through whatever issue this song becomes about *for them*. The music swells until it's big enough to hold all of it.[5]

Given the above discussion of De Souza's comportment both online and in performance, it becomes more plausible than not to feel that she is expressing something here that she knows other people feel—to read "Real Pain" as if this song is less about whatever pain De Souza has personally experienced, and more about creating a space of catharsis for people who have felt similar genres of pain, genres that feel implicitly understood and shared between

5. I hear a similar approach in Wednesday's unbelievable single "Bull Believer," an eight-and-a-half-minute builder in which screaming plays a central role. I say unbelievable in part because this is the opening track from their 2023 LP *Rat Saw God*. After such a physically and emotionally taxing release, the feeling I am left with as a listener is, "What could possible follow that?" The answer, apparently, is an entire record: the catharsis is just the beginning here, the precondition for what's to come.

listener and performer. If one is familiar with De Souza's fan community, perhaps via its self-presentation in her music videos (see "Hold U" for example), or else by attending her shows, it is also easy to sense why this might feel necessary or even urgent for the kinds of communities to which De Souza belongs: the young, diverse, queer listeners who gravitate toward her music are exactly those listenerships who feel traumas as a result of who and how they are in the world. The pandemic, climate grief, the inability to afford rent or save for a future, the renewed and relentless assault on LGBTQ+ people in the form of anti-trans bills and the overturning of *Roe*, the violences of white heterosexist patriarchy, perpetual fear of gun violence—plus whatever specific personal struggles any listener might bring to the record, which we don't know but might well imagine—*all* of these fit within the scream-space "Real Pain" creates.

Continuing to follow writers who read trauma as encompassing the painful effects of social conditions enfolded into everyday life, experiences of pain and the mental/emotional struggles that result are generalized enough to become assumed as shared among communities with similar histories (Cvetkovich 2003; Fisher 2009; Holmes 2023). We see here a clear example of Cvetkovich's formulation of trauma as "a window onto the study of how historical experience is embedded in sensational experience and how affective experience can form the basis for culture" (2003, 285). Furthermore, "When culture takes over from the clinic . . . it continues to perform therapeutic functions" that are "embedded within collective and public practices" (286). In the context of musical performance, "Real Pain" collaboratively stages trauma between performers and audiences, creating a context for therapeutic catharsis and identification—again, rendering listener subjectivities and personal difficulties visible, audible, perceptible, and material.

Music's capacity to stage such therapeutic performances has been long understood. But for my argument, it is also critical that such performances can "make an emotion public without narrative or storytelling; *the performance might just be a scream, a noise, or a gesture without a sound*" (Cvetkovich 2003, 286, my emphasis). In this way, "Real Pain" functions as something of a stacked signifier—not empty or floating, but nevertheless deferring particularity enough to allow any generalized trauma to feel relevant and represented. Lyrically, this is not a song about abortion or rape culture or toxic masculinity; but at the same time, it is a song about all of those things and more—*plus* the heartbreak that she might be singing about. The difference is that the location of this "about" is less in the lyrics and more in the creation of sonic space that affects listeners' sentiments.

Feelings, Care, and the Politics of a "Good Non-Sovereignty"

If the common experiences tying listeners together are informed by pain, it is the response to that pain by Big Feelings that is queer: an insistence on taking care of one another in community in a culture that mercilessly assails any notion of collectivity or substantive well-being—an insistence on the importance of feelings both as indices of our values and orientations as well as aspects of our health that need to be attended to, processed, and collectively held. I suggest that this experience of queer care is communicated affectively, and can therefore be experienced—albeit differently—by people of diverse experiences and orientations. Following Kara Keeling, "'queer' involves how one signifies or how groups of living beings as are made to signify within a given set of significations. It may include what one does, how one does it, and where those actions place one in relationship to the maintenance of the present organization of things . . . 'Queer' is palpable, felt as affect" (2019, 17–18). *Queer is palpable, felt as affect*. I have heard this claim borne out anecdotally in my interviews, where fans gravitate towards Big Feelings artists through vibration and sense, perceiving variegated shades of queerness before, in excess of, or in spite of statements by the band on matters of identity and desire. I have heard this claim borne out by self-identified queer fans and their "beloved straight dude friends" who attend shows and sing together, both differently experiencing something of the same vibration, who "walk away crying."

In closing, I turn back to my interview with Katie, whose insights help me connect the therapeutic experience of music performance to the notion of a "good non-sovereignty." Near the end of our interview, I asked her,

DD: What would you say feels important for people to know about this music? What would you want people to know about it, how would you want to talk about it, if it were you?

KM: . . . I think [artists like Indigo de Souza] show you—for like four bars at a time—that they can like . . . blow your fucking mind. They can . . . swell you with sounds and feelings that you're not prepared for—and then they just take it back and they go back to some other dynamic. . . . They just use it exactly when they want to and no other times. . . . There's something that I would like to say about, like . . . she's completely in control of every feeling in the room, somehow. (Katie M. 2022)

This is a description of De Souza's musical virtuosity as affect modulator. And in this formulation, *she's* completely in control; you are not. When you attend a concert by an artist whose music moves you, you are willingly placing yourself in a situation where you risk a loss of control over your own emotional state. Such a move resonates directly with Lauren Berlant's description of both traumatic experiences as well as the promise of politics. Speaking breathlessly in a 2011 roundtable, they put it as follows:

> Optimism and trauma do the same kind of thing: [it] lights up a part of the brain that makes you non-sovereign. And so the thing that really interests me is the ways that people desire and don't desire to become non-sovereign, people desire and don't desire to become attached in a way that makes them lose control. And those forms of losing control are the forms of belonging to the social—because I want to actually be involved with people I don't know in order to build a world that I can't see yet. That's the political. That's my attachment to the political. . . . That's what the political holds out: it holds out the possibility of a good non-sovereignty. (Berlant 2011, 46:16)

Good non-sovereignty happens when you can afford to relinquish control over yourself, or more precisely, your fantasy of control—it takes the interdependence that constitutes human life and embraces it, rather than remaining inside the enclosures that so much of daily life demands in order to protect ourselves from harm. The kind of concert experience that Katie describes, the kind that I experienced and that I watched others experience, places our fantasy of control over our own emotional states into the hands of an artist—or more precisely, a *song*—with the capacity to move us through something, collectively. It models a political community insofar as it has established a trusting space wherein the outcomes aren't foreseeable or guaranteed, but which we have decided is worth the risk. We give up control because we desire to be attached—to the music, to the feelings elicited by it, to one another.

Trauma, the kind of pain I've been concerned with in this chapter, lights up your brain. Taking "brain" to also mean "body,"[6] this is also what music

6. The actual inseparability of the entities categorized by Western thought as "body" and "mind" is a position well-established across not only non-Western epistemologies, but also recent academic work, from theories of embodied and situated cognition to divergent affect theories for which "bodies *and* thoughts—in their inseparability—are simultaneously immersed in their own particular worlds *and* in the wider world" (Seigworth and Pedwell 2023, 12). Here, I mean to invoke those works while also foregrounding Margaret Price's discussion of the term "bodymind" (2015). Working in feminist disability studies, Price asks to what extent "the turn towards desire in [disability studies] moves too quickly past the question of undesirability? Of pain?" (8), arguing that caring for bodyminds "must incorporate

does—perhaps particularly the kinds of music that deliberately provide opportunities for raising and then feeling through the pain that caused the initial non-sovereignty in the first place. So the loss happens on both ends of the equation: young listeners are affected by acute trauma or else the low-key hum of chronic anxiety that attends any awareness of our crisis conditions, or both. Then, in performance, that trauma becomes mapped onto affective-cathartic musical forces that induce a loss of control that is intentionally pursued and desired as a means of redress, as a means of soothing pain by virtue of invoking the very experience that allows one to resonate with the feelings being performed on stage. This kind of good non-sovereignty probably isn't sustainable, but it's also not metaphorical; in the moment of performance, people who don't know one another place themselves in relation in part but precisely in order to participate in something collective. In contrast to political discourse that offers the promise of more sovereignty, "belonging is all about the possibility of having a world that you could trust with your non-sovereignty, with your dependence on other people and with the way that you have to be in the world with them in order to build a life" (Berlant 2011, 47:00).

The concert setting does not fully mirror the kinds of everyday situations that Berlant invokes in the above quote, where we build our lives out of the "inconvenience of other people"; the show will disperse, the moment will end. But for however long it lasts, strangers create a space of belonging together, suspending their fantasy of control in order to experience a pleasurable loss of responsibility over oneself, a release of that effort. When music hails listeners into a physical and collective space, it evinces their "desire to become attached in a way that makes them lose control," holding open the potential that this loss will occur if emotions run high. Artists like Indigo De Souza can use their music and actions to cultivate crowds in which this might be more possible than others, affectively orienting people with shared investments and common experiences.

More so than they re-scramble existing modes of perceiving and identifying within the social, I hear the queer-feminist affects generated by Big Feelings artists hailing those communities who are already orientated toward

---

serious and specific attention to pain as well as desire" (11). While Price is most concerned with "limit cases" involving "exceptional experiences of disability" (10), her focus on mental disability, her helpful tracing of overlaps between queer theory and disability studies, as well as her focus on care practices, resonates with the above discussion, suggesting that music studies likewise could benefit from attending to the composite experiences of pleasure and pain, experienced and evocatively described by the kinds of listeners I have spoken with for this project.

that direction, bringing them into a space where safety and community can be practiced outside of the individualized demands of neoliberal "self-care" as surface balm, outside the white-cis-hetero-patriarchal public that makes it increasingly difficult to locate spaces of refuge. This is a critical kind of political work, but it is, as Barry Shank describes via Berlant, "juxtapolitical," a term for that "sphere of people attached to each other by a *sense* that there is a common emotional world available to those individuals who have been marked by the historical burden of being harshly treated in a generic way and who have more than survived social negativity by making an aesthetic and spiritual scene that generates *relief from the political*" (Berlant 2008, 10). I raise this argument in order to be clear that I don't view music's affective catharsis as a mechanism for increasing political awareness or forming a constituency that is united in its approach to politics. It's true, as Shank writes, that "music is one of the central cultural processes through which the abstract concept of the polis comes into bodily experience" (2014, 16); but at the same time, as he also attests, this bodily experience constitutes a sense of belonging that is pre-political—which may "lay the affective groundwork necessary" for more focused political action, but is not, in and of itself, sufficient (260).

Avoiding narrowly political discourse, Big Feelings is quintessentially juxtapolitical, which is neither apolitical nor anti-political. Rather, it builds potential, preceding politics through what is understood to be-in-common, even or especially when it's pain. Such experiences don't necessarily, but *can* become the basis for a shared sense of belonging, as well as a deeper understanding about what we're up against. As Shank puts it, "the sentimental attachment to the equality of ordinary feelings produces a soft but necessary commitment to all who feel this way" (49). That commitment is where politics begins.

"All of This Will End"

In this chapter, I have suggested that music staging experiences of the kind of mental health fallout that can result from the pain of patriarchal capitalism might resonate in multiple ways with young listeners both burdened by the world and aware of their place in it. This is another way in which Big Feelings artists indirectly produce queer-feminist affects, which are not instructive but bind together sentiments commonly felt by those in community—even if said communities arise (in part) as a result of shared and painful social experiences. While Big Feelings *may* fit the kinds of sad-girl cultures that Goldfine and Thelandersson suggest help facilitate "precarity-focused consciousness raising" that ties feelings of anxiety to the structural/political conditions informing them, I don't necessarily hear consciousness-raising as the primary social outcome of Big Feelings music. Rather, while political consciousness does often accompany the music (because it attracts certain kinds of listeners), I suggest that the music primarily functions to consolidate affects-in-common, helping listeners to find community and to process grief—all of which may have a variety of complex relationships with any political consciousness, ideological positions, and levels of engagement.

Experiences of collective catharsis are important for healing or processing. The collectivity involved in live performance can be a critical factor in this process, insofar as feeling isolated exacerbates trauma, whereas feeling recognized in others does the opposite. This catharsis provides an alternative model to the individualized and ultimately profitable kind of "care" advocated by neoliberal self-help culture and girl-boss triumphalism; it also differs from the kinds of consciousness-raising efforts that center sociopolitical questions in the processing of pain. "The pain of trauma can split the body from language," writes Eleanor Paynter (2024, 44)—here we might also think about music's capacity to split our bodies, or to make them go through something that we can't make sense of linguistically. Precisely for this reason, it is not guaranteed that experiencing collective care in concert will lead listeners to questions about politics. But that doesn't render either listeners' pain or their care for one another any less political; fans of Indigo De Souza and Soccer Mommy orient toward the music out of a shared sense of belonging, a feeling, however vague, of inhabiting a common experience of the world. To recognize a world in common is to organize around a shared set of values and a rejection of others. In this way, musical aesthetics are never just about style, but rather advance an argument about the right way to fit things together—and the "right way" is always a judgment with political implications.

4 • "Lipstick Stains"

Asian Diasporic Musicians and Queer of Color Critique

Tenderness is all I've got.
—Jay Som[1]

Asked in 2019 what it feels like to be a part of "the wave of queer Asian women shaping the indie rock landscape right now," Melina Duterte (Jay Som) responded by talking about a joint tour, on which she was joined by Michelle Zauner (Japanese Breakfast) and Mitski Miyawaki (Mitski):

> It's pretty insane. I never thought that it would happen in my lifetime, let alone that I'd be part of it. It's humbling and exciting and I'm just so grateful that I got to step into that tour in 2016 with Japanese Breakfast and Mitski. That was crazy because I was huge fans of them beforehand and really looked up to them. Especially since during that time, in 2015 and 2016, I began to see women become more prevalent in indie rock. It was just so game-changing to see someone who looks like you in videos and on stages. And it was also cool to be on that tour because everyone was queer, like literally everyone in the crew for both bands—that was really amazing. (quoted in Factora 2019)

Both James Factora's question and Duterte's response place equal emphasis on the Asian American and queer identities shared among musicians and collaborators, reflecting an intersectional understanding of community-building and its important role in lifting up and caring for folks too often left out of indie rock cultures. Such perspectives are absolutely central for under-

1. From "Tenderness," track 6 on *Anak Ko* (2019).

standing the intervention that Big Feelings artists are staging. But the exchange also indicates that some of this work has already been successful, reflecting a shift in indie rock that has seen more room in the conversation around both queerness and expressions of Asian diasporic solidarity in the form of tours like the one mentioned above. In 2022, for instance, Karen O (Yeah Yeah Yeahs) was joined on stage at the Hollywood Bowl by Japanese Breakfast and the Linda Lindas, a group of Asian American and Latinx musicians between eleven and seventeen years old whose song "Racist, Sexist Boy" had unexpectedly gone viral in 2021, touching a nerve amid COVID-19 lockdowns and a corresponding rise in visible instances of anti-Asian violence. Together performing "Kids in America"—a song firmly ensconced in the United States zeitgeist—the performance sees three generations of Asian American rock musicians celebrating their place in rock history and by extension, American culture generally. It also comes in the wake of what Shelina Brown (2023) has termed a kind of "Yoko Ono revivalism" that has seen widespread and belated recognition for Ono's singular legacy after decades of marginalization informed by white supremacist and patriarchal epistemologies prevalent across US media.

A critical precedent for feminist performances of (post-)punk fury, Ono's vocal techniques bridge at least three distinct traditions: classical Japanese musical techniques (in particular, from Kabuki performance traditions); singular modernist avant-gardism (developed out of her Western classical training and her pioneering work in the Fluxus scene); and rock music's unique capacity to create with and from overloaded feedback. Although far from alone in linking high performance art and vernacular music across the 1960s, Ono worked simultaneously from a more marginalized position (compared with, for example, the Velvet Underground or Theater of Eternal Music) as well as more expansively, introducing both Japanese cultural practices and feminist political perspectives to her groundbreaking solo work (the collected works in *Grapefruit*, the performance art landmark *Cut Piece*) and prolific collaborations (with John Cage, Ornette Coleman, and John Lennon, among many others). Although frequently overlooked in mainstream criticism, modernist musicology, and rock history alike, musicians and scholars have more recently helped to slowly carve out a place for recognizing and theorizing Ono's contributions across disciplines—including (feminist) rock music (Gaar 2002; Shank 2014; S. Brown 2018).

Turning back to indie rock more specifically, recent scholarship from Toru Momii, Summer Kim Lee, and Runchao Liu has focused on contemporary Asian American indie musicians, noting that despite the long and even foundational contributions of musicians like Ono, academic discussions of identity formation and subcultural politics "significantly overlook how Asian cultures have had a constitutive, and not just symbolic, role in complicating the trajectory of Western rock music" (Liu 2019, 108). In part, then, this chapter is concerned with joining such discussions, with giving space to contemporary Asian diasporic musicians and the queer-feminist perspectives that together mount a serious challenge to the persistence of ostensibly "common sense" characterizations of indie rock as a white musical genre. While it has always been essential to identify the ways in which indie rock has been overdetermined by white men (performers, critics, industry leaders, et al.), it is also equally critical to recognize that overdetermination as a situation achieved through the co-option of work that was all along being done by a diverse group of musicians—as I argue throughout this book, periodic reassertions of white-masculine dominance have repeatedly occurred across rock subgenres precisely because white men were never the only ones making the music.

Similarly, despite deserved criticisms of the riot grrrl movement's prevalent whiteness (Nguyen 2012), women of color were nevertheless active in the movement, particularly in places like the Bay Area (Cateforis and Humphreys 1997; Liu 2021). As Liu shows, zines like *Bamboo Girl* specifically address issues facing Asian Americans, even as Liu finds such work marginalized, "on the fringe of, outside of, and between" queercore and riot grrrl countercultures (2021, 157).[2] Liu also writes extensively about Dianne Chai (the Alley Cats), Leslie Shixiu Mah (Tribe 8), Janis Tanaka (various), and more, joining work in Jen Larson's book *Hit Girls* that documents musicians such as Caroline and Jane Fujimoto (the Welders) and Reck, née Kawashima Akiyoshi (Teenage Jesus & the Jerks).

Further back, the widely influential, all-women band Fanny was formed in 1969 by June and Jean Millington, biracial Filipina American musicians who have had a multifaceted influence on generations of artists, and who continue to help girls fight for space in rock music through their educational initiatives long after the height of their popularity (Powers 2015; Liu 2021). Fanny has been cited as direct influences on the Bangles, the Go-Go's, and David Bowie, among others; moreover, June Millington is known as a "godmother of women's music" (J. Taylor 2012, 158) for her involvement in the New York scene, participation in Cris Williamson's definitive *The Changer and the Changed*, and subsequent headlining of women's music festivals. Her

2. See also, for just some examples, *Hermana, Resist, Hey Mexican!*, and *Mamasita!* in the Riot Grrrl zine and music collection, #8125, Division of Rare and Manuscript Collections, Cornell University Library.

pioneering work as a queer, feminist, Asian American rock musician is therefore a direct precedent for the music I discuss in this chapter.

Despite the ways in which Asian American indie rockers have been generally invisibilized in rock history, the 1990s and early 2000s did witness moments of heightened notoriety for some bands, albeit often enough with predictably problematic framings. Boredoms, for example, is a long-running noise-influenced rock collective from Japan, who built steady avant-garde cred by working with Sonic Youth, John Zorn, and Nirvana during the late 1980s and early '90s. Additionally, Cibo Matto and Shonen Knife were two Japanese punk bands who, Gayle Wald demonstrates, "had to negotiate the terrain of U.S. youth and music cultures differently than have their (primarily white) Riot Grrrl counterparts" owing to the ways in which Asian women's visibility in the United States is "often predicated on their acquiescence to orientalist stereotypes" (1998, 599). Like Boredoms, Shonen Knife, in particular, achieved more widespread fame after being championed by Thurston Moore and Kurt Cobain alike, even joining Nirvana on a brief tour. But despite Cobain's earnest feelings about these bands, and the clear ways in which his efforts to champion less mainstream groups served as one aspect of his queer-feminist interventions into the alternative rock zeitgeist of the 1990s,[3] bands with ties to East Asia infrequently amounted to more than novelty acts in the eyes of the press, again demonstrating Liu's point about their simultaneous centrality to and marginalization within rock culture.

Other important Asian diasporic musicians in this period include Kazu Makino of Blonde Redhead; Toko Yasuda of Enon; Satomi Matsuzaki of Deerhoof; James Lo of Chavez; Richard, Edward, and James Baluyut of Versus; Karen O of the Yeah Yeah Yeahs; Miki Berenyi of Lush; Ashley Hideyo

3. I'm thinking here of Cobain's famous lists of favorite albums and how the presence of bands like Beat Happening, the Slits, Marine Girls, the Raincoats, PJ Harvey, the Breeders, the Pixies, as well as Shonen Knife, seem so clearly to stand both as authentic testaments to Cobain's listening life as well as polemics for those rock bros Cobain knew were also listening to his records, how his simply expressing his preferences could be read as a provocation toward those fans except for the fact that Cobain really did love those records, really did live as a rockstar trying to push toward a better and less sexist culture. Beyond his well-known entreaty, in the liner notes for *Incesticide* ("At this point I have a request for our fans. If any of you in any way hate homosexuals, people of different color, or women, please do this one favor for us—leave us the fuck alone! Don't come to our shows and don't buy our records."), Sasha Geffen notes, "[Cobain] wore dresses not just in the safe enclosures of video shoots and television interviews, but to Nirvana's early concerts on college campuses, before they broke big" (2020, 194). In this way, Cobain's attire, his record collection, and his life choices work in concert to demonstrate the extent to which the music he made and championed wasn't just for "loud, obnoxious boys."

Bowie of Helium and Polvo; John Lee of aMiniature; Yuki Chikudate of Asobi Seksu; Hiro D. Yamamoto of Soundgarden; as well as David Pajo, a uniquely prolific and influential Filipino-American guitarist who rose to prominence with the indie band Slint before working with Tortoise, Stereolab, Zwan, Interpol, the Yeah Yeah Yeahs, and now Gang of Four—among many others and a slew of solo projects. This incomplete list nevertheless outlines a diverse array of indie bands: groups like aMiniature and Slint released a few studio records that seemed to capture and distill a kind of late '80s/early '90s indie sound into its most concentrated form, becoming influential and emblematic despite remaining mostly underground.[4] Bands like Blonde Redhead, Deerhoof, and the Yeah Yeah Yeahs remain active and hugely influential, releasing albums as recently as 2022 or 2023 and continuing to build their already deep legacies by bridging indie rock, dream pop, shoegaze, and noise music.

Notable for its overlaps with the British indie pop scene is Lush (1987–1996), fronted by Asian-European musician Miki Berenyi, and who, along with their sometimes collaborators Cocteau Twins, were early pioneers of what became known as "shoegaze" in the English press, an indie subgenre that I see as connected to the feminized discourses attributed to the kinds of lo-fi indie music discussed in chapter 1. With shoegaze, dialing up atmospheric reverb on indie pop's clangy guitars became a means of shielding the performers from personal scrutiny; combined with a diminished vocal presence that was described by Berenyi herself as an effort to hide (Wills 2001), bands like Lush center the performance of insecurity indicative of daily experience for women in patriarchal spaces, further foregrounding feminized perspectives already associated with indie and dream pop sounds.

Finally, of course, the success of the Smashing Pumpkins saw James Iha, a second-generation Japanese American musician, vaulted into the heights of rock and roll fame in the '90s. Despite rock media's perpetual fascination with Corgan's role as a kind of dictatorial egoist, micromanager, and musical polymath, it is incontrovertible (even by Corgan's account) that Iha played a foundational and fundamental role in what was, for a time, one of the biggest bands on the planet.

Following such essential but overlooked musicians, in this chapter, I argue that today, Asian diasporic musicians—beabadoobee (Beatrice Kristi Ilejay Laus), Fazerdaze (Amelia Rahayu Murray), Hana Vu, Jay Som (Melina

---

4. Slint's *Spiderland* and Helium's *The Magic City / No Guitars / Ends With And / The Dirt of Luck*, for example, each received glowing reviews as a part of *Pitchfork*'s "Best New Reissue" series in 2014 and 2017, respectively.

Mae Cortez Duterte), Japanese Breakfast (Michelle Zauner), Juliet Ivy, Mei Semones, Mitski (Mitski Miyawaki), Pictoria Vark (Victoria Park), Tanukichan (Hannah Junghwa van Loon), SASAMI (Sasami Ashworth), yeule (Nat Ćmiel), and more—have been pivotal in the development of Big Feelings, and by extension, contemporary indie rock writ large. More to the point, many of these musicians also push beyond the core sound of Big Feelings, expanding into other genres in ways that I suggest have to do with (queer) diasporic aesthetics, in part a resistance to the social and logistical confines of a traditionally white indie rock sphere.

While I focus here on Mitski, Jay Som, and SASAMI, I hear their work resonating in the larger context created by all the bands listed above, and more. Treating intersectional identity constructions as both critical and insufficient, I attempt to think through this musical work not through a reductive grouping that would understand them as inherently linked on account of a static understanding of identity, but rather via shared social conditions and discursive frameworks through which their work is refracted.

As I noted above, it is equally critical to consider that each of the artists I discuss in this chapter is not only Asian but also queer. Their music is central to Big Feelings for how comprehensively it embodies the affective orientations I have been concerned with tracing in this book—and as I have been suggesting from the beginning, that aesthetico-political approach to indie rock is in no small way caught up in queerness as a worldly orientation, as a mode of relationality that involves but is not limited to questions of desire. Relatedly, this chapter's subtitle mentions queer of color critique because I aim to foreground how the lived experiences and aesthetic expressions of queer musicians of color have long been understood (in the tradition of critical race theory) as scholarship of its own kind, constituting its own theoretical work, producing its own critiques.

In this chapter I study the texts these musicians provide by focusing specifically on music videos from Mitski, Jay Som, and SASAMI. Throughout, I also consider discursive frameworks through which their music has been interpreted, in addition to drawing on extant scholarship that helps to contextualize their work. In all cases, academic work, pop-cultural productions, and the lived experiences of queer musicians of color insists on the inseparability of identity categories to the point where it is—or should be—impossible to think about identity categories in isolation, for example, to consider queerness without also understanding its co-constitution and imbrication with racial constructions in a given context. Ultimately, then, this chapter is concerned with the co-production of queer-feminist and Asian diasporic sensibilities together, tracking how the Big Feelings aesthetic that these musicians have helped pioneer can be utilized in service of forging a common world.

Mitski: Vulnerability, Asociality, Agency

As I write, I am watching Mitski's Tiny Desk concert from 2015. The performance here is raw and direct: Mitski appears as a person rather than a star, for though the video proves how accomplished she already is at her craft, she is also young—twenty-five when the video was made—singing in a plain black tank top and not much adornment. The performance feels stripped down for other reasons, too, not least of which is that she doesn't have a band; here she sings alone, accompanying herself with an electric guitar that she strums with negotiated punk energy, or screams into, so that it feeds back into her precisely-pitched and straining vocal chords, reciprocally resonating, amplifying what about Mitski is already self-evidently and quintessentially a rockstar, the casual performance of virtuosity.

This performance has been praised by critics for its direct forcefulness, powerful enough to help a brilliant songwriter like Karly Hartzman (Wednesday) start a band and already by this time leave a mark. Since 2015, that is, we've already come a long way: Mitski has already influenced a younger group of musicians, who have in turn contributed to a transformation in rock music. As for Mitski herself, even the briefest comparison will suggest that she has also been through a lot in the intervening years. Her music, for one thing, has expanded beyond its initial indie rock underpinnings, becoming more grandiose, polished, and multivocal. In this, Mitski joins Fazerdaze, Japanese Breakfast, SASAMI, and, as I discuss in chapter 6, Vagabon—particularly insofar as each of these artists has moved from quintessential Big Feelings indie rock records toward subsequent projects foregrounding synth/pop sounds. I point this out here to emphasize that even as they are reforging what indie rock is all about, these artists of color can also be heard departing from a narrowly indie rock palette in ways that I consider less than accidental.

Genres are tightly linked to scenes and industries; and while it's too simplistic to suggest that the general whiteness of the indie rock industry is the *reason* that we have seen indie artists of color move beyond guitar-based rock music, I see it as at least a relevant factor for at least two reasons: first, we know that the indie rock industry has continued to feel alienating for women and people of color—including musicians and fans—even as they struggle to and have succeeded in building their own networks of support therein. Second, as scholars like Gayatri Gopinath have theorized, "aesthetic practices of queer diaspora" (2018) often take on capacious and unruly qualities, resting uneasily in one place and instead wandering promiscuously, ultimately refusing to stay restricted to the times and spaces deemed "appropriate" by majoritarian culture. Discussing queer Asian diasporic indie music more broadly is therefore essential here not only because these musicians have been so central to the Big Feelings affect, but also because they help outline its contours. In other words, thinking through the ways in which Mitski both exemplifies and departs from Big Feelings aesthetics helps us consider the musical/social dynamics revealed by her navigation of genre and identity as one of indie music's most visibly successful artists. Ultimately, while this kind of genre-play is not exclusive to minority groups in the indie rock space, I suggest that these artists variously demonstrate diasporic aesthetic sensibilities that can't be contained by restrictive understandings of indie-as-genre, which has been gatekept as white and male, which continues to be associated in a broader public discourse against which Mitski, for one, has variously struggled.

In part reflective of such dynamics, Mitski's music often explores feelings of isolation produced by a larger situation that is either alienating or hostile to the protagonist. One of her most discussed videos, "Your Best American Girl," has been noted by journalists and scholars for how it stages and reflects on the kinds of normative standards of desirability in white society, and Mitski's complex efforts to navigate them while also exploring her own identity (Goldfine 2017; J. Zhang 2017; Lee 2019; Liu 2021). "It's the perfect antidote to the indie rock tradition of rarely acknowledging its own whiteness" Jenny Zhang writes, "but it's also a song of pure heartbreak—the POC kind" (2017). Two years later, "Nobody," a single from *Be the Cowboy*, exploded in popularity, and although it doesn't explore similarly political subject matter, it nevertheless allows for the same kind of powerful identification that Zhang identifies, a particular alienation or loneliness that listeners from similar communities understand intuitively, a question of somatics.

On one level, "Nobody" fits perfectly with the themes explored throughout this book: "My God, I'm so lonely," it begins, opening up a space of vulnerability and intimacy both universally experienced at the same time that they are increasingly central to the emotional lives of young people. Against the backdrop of an expertly crafted and deeply fun disco groove, Mitski continues to speak about love through the languages of both astrology and casualized disaster, a kind of lingua franca for millennials and Gen-Zers that conflates personal heartbreak with the context of environmental collapse and thus reflects the structuring effect of that collapse on our thinking, on our being:[5]

5. "When I'm feeling optimistic, I see [Mitski's] broad appeal as an example of cross-generational solidarity in times that can feel apocalyptic" (Zoladz 2022).

Venus, planet of love
Was destroyed by global warming
Did its people want too much, too?
Did its people want too much?

Already, then, there is clearly much that links Mitski's music with the central concerns of Big Feelings, even if "Nobody" is situated outside of rock music, a dark pop jam. But on another level, the video in particular raises a kind of depressed affect that hasn't been explored yet in this book, a specific shade of loneliness that Summer Kim Lee sees as uniquely reflective of Asian American experiences: "To be an Asian American woman," she writes, "is to have and cultivate a certain relation to one's aloneness" (Lee 2019, 28). Viewers understand the surreal and totalizing nature of this loneliness from the earliest moments of the video, the opening shot of which zooms out to reveal Mitski sharing a milkshake with another version of herself, seated across from her in a restaurant booth—but actually, the milkshake is an hourglass filled with white sand. As the camera continues its movement, we sense more than see people dancing in the restaurant (just torsos, really) as Mitski continues to stare into her own eyes, undisturbed by any others on the periphery of her intent gaze. Throughout the video, Mitski continues to navigate an uncanny wonderland in which she is the only character: mail shows up with no indicated sender, people's phone numbers melt into strings of zeroes, and an effort to track down a friend results in a horrifying encounter with someone wearing Mitski's face on a glitching tablet screen. No matter where she turns, Mitski only ever sees herself in the video, a degree of repetition that threatens to dissolve her subjectivity: in this hall of mirrors, endless repetition renders sight and sound both meaningless, so that loneliness becomes the same as nothingness.

Notwithstanding the truly impeccable songwriting and the intricately catchy hook "Nobody" produces, the song's subject matter clues us into the reasons why Mitski has become, for some, the quintessential "sad girl," a "patron saint of introverts" (Bell 2022). Like many Big Feelings artists, Mitski stages a wide range of emotional experiences that resonate with her fans in multifaceted and often intensely personal ways. What might differ, however, is the degree to which fans have come to expect or even demand performances of radical vulnerability from the artist, and the ways in which such expectations are caught up in a press apparatus eager to hold Mitski up as an example of Asian American excellence in white spaces.

Before the start of her career in journalism, Jael Goldfine's excellent undergraduate thesis analyzed the promises and limitations of sad-girl indie rock culture, which she wrote was not a nihilistic embrace of negativity as much as a refusal to acquiesce to emotional hegemony by performing resilience in the face of recurrent structural harms. Written in 2017, Goldfine's thesis spends a significant portion of its analysis on Mitski's Twitter profile, which had by then become a central platform through which emotions circulated through the consolidation of fan communities speaking both about and to Mitski. Goldfine suggests that Mitski's Twitter personality "perform[ed] an identity that is darkly self-deprecating, excruciatingly vulnerable, and humorously introspective" (2017, 100), and that this performance makes space for discussions of women's pain outside of the fetishized glare of media treatments, standing in contrast, as I see it, to celebrated streaming programs like *Girls* or *Fleabag*.[6] Moreover, and in the same way as Indigo De Souza, Mitski at this time was particularly transparent about her efforts to ensure that her live shows created "soft and open" spaces for fans, in spite of recurring challenges staged by male indie rock fans and white people in general, who have in the past disrupted spaces intended to support vulnerable populations. Thus, for Goldfine, spaces of emotional safety and tenderness are understood as precious, rare, and worth pursuing, difficult as they might be to establish and maintain. But as Mitski became increasingly known for creating such spaces, it is clear that at least a faction of her fanbase valued them so highly that they began to expect or even demand certain kinds of special, intimate experiences from the artist, an expectation that extended beyond the concert venue and into Mitski's own life, assumed to be transpicuous and genuinely available for fans at any time.

It is at this conjuncture where sad-girl indie rock intersects with deeply ingrained and widespread cultural expectations in the United States around the ostensible "inscrutability" of East Asian women (Huang 2018): in this context, exacerbated by queer theory's valorization of the social, Asian American and other minoritized subjects have been burdened with what Summer Kim Lee calls "compulsory sociability and relatability" (2019, 29) in which one must bear the responsibility of "representing and standing in for the totality of the community to which they belong" and must be "accessibly and accommodatingly" transparent in doing so. That is, the stereotype associating Asian women, in particular, with "reticence" and "withholding" produces a kind of trap whereby musicians like Mitski either fall into the stereotype or must evade it spectacularly, even if they don't feel like sharing—particularly in a music genre in which one of the only available roles for women has been that of the "authentic" "confessional."

Invoking the tarot, Lindsay Zoladz writes that "Mitski's most vocal fans

6. On the cultural politics of women's trauma as a subject of streaming programs, see Clein 2020.

treat her as a kind of high priestess of modern-day sadness," adding that the role "makes her uncomfortable" (2022). In turn, Mitski said "she wished she 'didn't have to perform pain and struggle to be valued.'" In the same piece, Zoladz describes how "fans often expect more from Mitski than she is willing to give, or push back when she tries to establish perfectly reasonable boundaries." One of these boundaries has been erected around social media: in 2019, Mitski deleted her Twitter account, returning only after securing a management company to run it. The kind of personal, relatable, and available Twitter personality Goldfine wrote about is no longer a part of Mitski's public performances, reflecting a consequence of listeners' intense identification transforming into a kind of emotional entitlement. Far from a benign mismatch of expectations between performer and audience, coverage of Mitski's difficulties in this arena portray at times abusive dynamics, a kind of dark underside to indie's capacity to foster intimacy and catharsis of the kind discussed in chapter 3 (Beaumont-Thomas 2022).

Thinking through this transition, Toru Momii has pointed out the ways in which Mitski has become "more selective with how and where" to engage personal questions—particularly those having to do with race, identity, or her background—in order to argue for her strategic deployment of opacity, following Édouard Glissant (Momii 2021). Similarly, Stacey Anderson writes in *ELLE* that she "admire[s]" how Mitski answers "leading questions about her biracial, Japanese heritage": namely, "She doesn't" (2022). Where Mitski continues to talk more openly with select individuals in her life, she has adopted a reserved posture toward mainstream press outlets by deliberately taking steps to control her own narrative. Seemingly either unaware of or insensitive to the pressurized dynamics informing Mitski's mindful navigation of the press's spotlight, music journalists can (as of this writing) still be heard, if not bemoaning, then at least struggling with Mitski's more careful posture, characterizing her as selectively guarded, deeply private, and overly sensitive to ostensibly normal interview questions (Caramanica 2022).

It is true, as I sketched above, that Mitski has adjusted her approach to both the press and to fans, which one imagines would be particularly necessary given her increased popularity following the release of *Be the Cowboy*. But rather than considering Mitski's orientations as reflections of an idiosyncratic individual grappling with newfound levels of fame, several scholars have made efforts to situate Mitski's work in larger cultural contexts, tracing connections that show how her actions reflect longstanding social tensions. Critical for this chapter is Summer Kim Lee's theorization of Mitski's work through the notion of *staying in*.

For Lee, staying in is an "Asian American aesthetic practice" that "rearranges what constitutes the social" in order to critique and navigate the Western construction of Asian Americans as a problem or vexation in the social fabric (2019). Staying in can look like declining to go out (with friends, to a show) or else going out alone, in order to experience something while still scrambling normative expectations for what a social experience looks like (2019). When Mitski protects herself from demands for transparency whether by the press or by fans, she resists the myriad and racialized ways in which US culture demonstrates entitlement to an indie artist of color's interior life. But for Lee, this is not an *anti*social posture; it is instead one that preserves the possibility for *different* modes of sociality on reimagined and more equitable terms, terms that are opened up in part through the energy reserved by refusing the initial, exhausting arrangement. It is certainly uncanny when, in "Nobody," Mitski finds herself trapped in a world comprising only herself; but these potentially frightening encounters also empower her to explore her own thoughts and fears in new depth—she pores over her diary, for example, makes music, and, thinking back to the opening shot, takes herself on a date. Ultimately, Mitski ends the video by sitting in a director's chair, surveying a scene over which we now understand she has been in charge all along.[7]

In resisting demands for transparency and vulnerability, Mitski finds more space to navigate the lonely realities of a destabilizing world on her own terms, ultimately performing a "divestment from normative, well-behaved, likable, socialized forms of subjectivity that both refuse and are refused by Asian American subjects" (Lee 2019, 42). By declining a certain type of accommodating performance, Mitski chooses to redirect energy in ways that might sustain "a different kind of desire for oneself and others, the desire to relate differently, in order to live through what and who comes to pass" (45). Thus for Lee, Mitski's asociality appears not as an endpoint or a collapse into non-signification, but rather as an opening that allows for the possibility of new, still emerging forms of sociality outside of white-normative expectations—forms that Mitski's fellow young, queer musicians are helping to imagine into being.

Jay Som: Yearning as Queer Indeterminacy

Jay Som's music presents a full spectrum of queer life, portraying heartbreak, joy, camaraderie, and the dramas of the quotidian. From the kind of

7. In this, "Nobody" echoes "Your Best American Girl," in which Mitski walks off set when the video ends, showing the audience how crafted and intentional the ostensibly confessional feelings in her music have always been (see Moss 2016).

unresolved yearning that can feel singular and totalizing to the everyday aimlessness of hanging out with friends, most of Jay Som's music inhabits the ambivalent in-between where emotions are always refracting themselves into nuanced shades. Whether performing as Jay Som, Bachelor (her supergroup with Palehound's Ellen Kempner), or as a bassist for boygenius, Melina Duterte's queer anthems and "gay horny songs" are no less fun to rock out with for their being affectively complex, interlaced with the kind of deep foreboding that can accompany strong feelings of desire. "I think every queer person can relate to that feeling of doom that comes along with a crush," Ellen Kempner says of one such anthem, Bachelor's "Anything at All"—another song organized around major-seventh tonalities. "At least early on, where you're like, 'No, I'm not supposed to feel this,' or, 'I don't even know if this person's gay.' It's so many feelings, but it also was a lot of fun" (in Velasquez 2021).

"So many feelings" but also "a lot of fun" is a descriptor equally applicable to "The Bus Song," a Jay Som single from 2017. Directed by Michelle Zauner and further evincing Big Feelings' comprehensive approach to collaboration,[8] the music video in particular brings a colorful levity to the performance that renders "The Bus Song" as delightful and charming as it is melancholic. The melancholy can be heard from its first moments, where the movement of the guitar circulates a quiet energy around a major-ninth sound-world. Through the timbre of the guitar/vocal combination, through the circular slide of the chord pattern, through the soft but somehow pointed placement of that opening melody note, together the song immediately places listeners in an ambivalent affective space: the narrator is in love—but something is wrong.

And yet, where the song on its own might remain for listeners mostly inside this kind of complex wistfulness, the video immediately introduces a contrasting current: Duterte is not alone while she's exploring the difficult emotional landscape conjured by the music. She is instead joined by a whole community of kind friends, eager to hold space for what's hard as a means of helping Duterte's character move through it. This subdued musical undercurrent is revealed in the video early and constantly: eight bars in, when the band explodes onto the scene to accompany Duterte's solo opening, the video cuts to a smooth montage shot along a sunny San Francisco street. Duterte's character, in the house with several bandmates, suddenly emerges to greet more friends waiting outside. Everybody is waving and beaming here, a most welcome surprise, and literally jumping as they get together in single file to march their music across the neighborhood. "Why don't we take

8. In addition to Zauner's involvement, many of the friends featured in this video are actually musicians Jay Som knows from the area (e.g., Future Shapes, No Vacation, Plush).

the bus?" Duterte sings once they're off. Back in the house, but this time bobbing heads along in grinning unison with the band, she follows up, "You say you don't like the smell / BUT I LIKE THE BUS!" On this last line, bandmates pop out into the frame to shout in unison, lending the sentiment a kind of anthemic treatment. It's a point of pride, for Duterte, and perhaps one sticking point in the relationship being explored in the tune—if not the reason for its stress, then a reflection of it. The subject of Duterte's address isn't down with public transportation, and although this disagreement clearly indexes something painful flaring up in the relationship (perhaps emblematic of larger philosophical or class differences) Duterte's character isn't alone in managing her feelings; no matter what happens, the song and especially the video portray a community that has her back.

It is perhaps this community that helps Duterte feel buoyed enough to level with her person, to offer kind permission instead of demanding compromise: "Take time to figure it out," she sings in the chorus, "I'll be the one who sticks around." Clearly sad, but also coming to the conversation transparently and non-defensively, Duterte finishes the chorus with an ascendant melody on the lines "And I just want you to need me / And I just want you to lead me." We don't know how the conversation will resolve, how the relationship that earlier was metaphorized as a breaking-down car, will fare. But by the end of the video, two dozen friends have gathered outside another house to serenade triumphantly, finding joy in the situation.

Like the major sonority around which it is organized, "The Bus Song" contains both sadness and joyful tenderness together, simultaneously. The video adds yet a third affect to the mix, which is a warm humor: as the video closes, all its energy seems to culminate squarely at the feet of a friendly sheepdog, seemingly the object of Duterte's affection all along. While the song's complex semiotics do contain traces of such whimsy, the music video uses friends, neighbors, and affable pets to help draw out ambivalent strands in what otherwise might pass for a more straightforward breakup song. Taken together, there is rather nothing plain about "The Bus Song," which offers a complicated mosaic of emotional experience: love, friendship, heartbreak, joy, hope for the future, unguarded sharing, and the navigation of everyday life according to what makes one feel right. It is a brave song that's also normal, a scene from ordinary life that captures what's magic about it, what's hard.

Ultimately, "The Bus Song" showcases a musical dynamic that is common among Big Feelings artists, but which simultaneously helps Jay Som's music stand out as distinct from both Mitski's and SASAMI's: namely, it performs an intentional and expansive kind of *softness*, an active, intentional refusal of competitive/aggressive subjectivities rewarded by neoliberalism, in favor of traditionally devalued qualities such as openness, gentle acceptance, and care. Thinking with Andi Schwartz's theorization of soft femmeness as "a combination of emotionality, vulnerability, relationality, and hyperfemininity" (2020), I see Jay Som as exemplifying the gentle radicality of Big Feelings' queer affects: tender in its approach to both positive and negative emotions, the music prioritizes kindness towards oneself irrespective of the circumstances that have made us feel however we do. I read this in line with an artist like Mei Semones, for example, whose *kawaii*-informed physical presentations overlap with intricate guitar technique to produce music as comforting as it is deft—sophisticated craftwork belied by easy, inviting, and explicitly feminized gestures.[9] This is music that insists on tenderness, and is all the more powerful for it—like Indigo De Souza's performances of feminized care, performances of softness are juxtapolitical insofar as they explicitly resist "neoliberal and masculinist ideals," (A. Schwartz 2020, 5) as they have since the riot grrrl era's embrace of selective markers of girlhood (e.g., flowers, bows, and pigtails). The difference here is that where riot grrrl used such signifiers ironically, soft femme aesthetics rely on performances of sincerity for their affective pull.

In an article about Jay Som's "quietly revolutionary" music, writer James Factora poses the following question to Duterte: "My friend and I have this theory that there's something inherently kind of gay about songs about cars and traveling and transit. What are your thoughts on that?" Duterte responds by saying,

> You're not the first person to suggest that. Someone who suggested it to me also made up their own reasons, and it was because gay people can't drive. There's always that one designated gay that has a car and picks everyone up. I feel like that's a common thing with queer people. Everyone uses transit, but I feel like a lot of people I know, they're biking or taking the train or buses, they don't have cars. We need scientific facts to back this up. Hopefully there'll be a study soon about why there's so many gay transit songs. (quoted in Factora 2019)

---

9. "No more cool people 🤢🙅♀🧊❄️/Only warm people 🙂🤷♀❤️🔥" Semones collaborator John Roseboro writes via Instagram, while announcing a new joint music video and inviting fans to "say something nice" (@john.roseboro 2023). Semones, meanwhile, can often be found on Instagram casually gliding across blistering arrangements of jazz standards, bossa nova rhythms, and new indie rock material while wearing crocheted bunny ears, "My Melody" slippers, and bows of all sorts (@mei_semones).

"The Bus Song" is, admittedly, only tangentially about public transportation. But I love how this quote captures the kind of playfulness that Jay Som brings to topics that can rightly feel quite heavy. Here, queerness isn't an evident matter of object desire, and less about the kind of difficulty that comes from navigating a world that is not organized to accommodate you; rather, this quote discusses the kind of queerness that is presented in "The Bus Song," which turns on everyday life and the ways that queer folks might perceive and navigate it in ways that are subtly different from the norm.[10] This is not about sociological proof, as Duterte's tongue-in-cheek response implies; the point is more about a perception that's held in common and used to organize community.

Another reason I quote this exchange at length is because "The Bus Song" is not the only "transit song" that Duterte has produced; Bachelor's first single, "Stay in the Car," is a song about transportation that also works as a "detailed soundtrack for queer desire" (Thilesen 2021).[11] In a statement, Kempner describes a striking encounter that occurred when visiting Florida for her partner's top surgery:

> I had run out one afternoon, post-op, while he was healing to grab lunch for us and as I was gathering my stuff in the parking lot, a big car pulled up and this absolutely beautiful woman got out. She was dressed all in red, dripping with jewelry and had the most wild fiery mane I'd ever seen. She was yelling at the man behind the wheel asking him what he wanted from the store and I wished I was that man. I

---

10. I am also reminded here of Karen Tongson's suburban-focused rendering of queer world-building as liminal aimlessness, a formulation that resonates with my discussion of the queer Midwest (see chapter 5). "So much of queer suburban sociability transpires in cars," Tongson writes, "driving around, looking for something (or someone) to do. While queer cosmopolitans are likely to find such searching and confined listening abject, I would argue that there is something tremendously generative in the acts of imaginative transformation that can turn a freeway or parking lot into a social- and soundscape, without needing the crutch of cool" (Tongson 2011, 26).

11. Also in this category are "Superbike" (the opening of which was informed by Third Eye Blind's quintessential '90s hit "Semi-Charmed Life"); "Nighttime Drive" ("Been watching hours pass / Inside cars with no glass"); "Peace Out" ("You're driving no control / Wanna crack the window / Toss your phone"); as well as Bachelor's "Sick of Spiraling" ("Driving on to the next town / Keeping the rubber side down"); boygenius' "$20" and "Leonard Cohen," which both include lyrics about transit; illuminati hotties' "Truck"; Why Bonnie's "Hot Car," and more. Again following points of resonance, it seems significant too that Sarah Records—so often celebrated for its foregrounding of soft, anti-macho aesthetics—numbered its compilations after the bus routes in Bristol "because we were celebrating public transport," as cofounder Clare Wadd put it (in Dawkins 2015).

> wanted to be a part of her life, her best friend, her driver, whatever she wanted me to be. I was completely mesmerized. (quoted in Thilesen 2021)

There is perhaps nothing inherently queer about this scene of desire and identification, a moment where Kempner is starstruck in everyday life; but at the same time, there is everything queer about it, insofar as the anecdote and subsequently the song itself organize sentiments that are reflective of and resonant with queer life—with others who have experienced similar events and who have preexisting language for the kind of social genre where top surgery and femme desire can coexist in easy and inspiring ways.

Trying again, desire isn't quite the right word here, or if it is, it's a particular kind of queer desire that's always already given permission to identify with/crush on another person, to be starstruck by the fierceness of someone else's fire, the way they move unapologetically, fantastically, gorgeously through a world more content with their silence and invisibility, because the question of (non)monogamy is beside the point here, the point that heteronormativity denies but which nevertheless refuses that denial: that we are human, that we desire capaciously, that we need to be dumbfounded by others in order to find our own way forward, modeling ourselves on those who have previously knocked us flat, and sometimes, if we're lucky, also loving them. As with the examples of feminist affect in Soccer Mommy and Indigo De Souza, here queer-feminist affects are not present because "Stay in the Car" or "The Bus Song" go out of their way to name queerness itself, or the ways that Duterte and Kempner live their lives. Instead, these orientations are perceptible for how they cohere around objects, scenes, and modes of relating to everyday life that are not necessarily exclusive to this or that identity position, this or that political posture—but which will be resonant with those folks looking for attestations of their own experiences in sound.

That being said, I began this section by noting that Jay Som's music furnishes a full spectrum of queer life—and this sometimes includes more explicit invocations of queerness alongside the implicit vibrational scenes I have been describing. "Lipstick Stains," for example, is about as straightforward a disclosure of queer affection as you can get. The first stanza, unfolding ever so gradually, reveals, "I like the way your lipstick stains / The corner of my smile / How you brush my hair aside." Presaged by the swelling and receding of ethereal chord clusters, by the time Duterte sings this initial stanza, the song is already nearly over. The second stanza starts with repetition: "I like the way your lipstick stains / The corner of my smile," Duterte continues, but this time the final line has changed: "I pray it lasts a while,"

Duterte sings, just as all sound disappears. The song is completely over some five seconds after we hear the word "while," suggesting or more accurately performing the very ephemerality of the sweet moment that Duterte's narrator struggles to retain. At under two minutes and with little to no development, "Lipstick Stains" paints a discrete moment in time, which Duterte recognizes on some level, even as it's happening, as fleeting—the most fragile kind of beauty. The loss inherent to the moment of reverie is its deeply human underside, the kind of tinged scene of romance that Big Feelings stages, where any radiant happiness is always already complicated by the nature of life itself.

In this sense, "Lipstick Stains" undermines both US hetero- *and* homonormativity by deferring a performance of "successful" partnering, charting a different expression of romance than the dominant neoliberal model that is, whether straight or otherwise, organized around financial capital, commodity fetishism, and marketable beauty standards. Instead, Jay Som lingers on queerness through its affective embrace of yearning, which has to be understood as inherently unresolved—that is, it stages queerness as non-terminus or suspension, something "not yet here," as José Esteban Muñoz famously put it (2009, 1). Yearning presupposes an ongoing process that might yet let you down, that might not have the outlet or opportunity it needs to continue, that is constructed out of questions for which there are no readily available answers. "Take time to figure it out / I'll be the one who sticks around." Unsure of what result might yet lie at the end of her waiting, Duterte insists on staying open to what's possible, even in the face of potential disappointment. Inherently sutured to our evaporating present, it is in the space of indeterminacy that the good music lives.

SASAMI: Water Sign

To close this chapter, I turn to SASAMI, a multilayered artist who performs everything critical about Big Feelings in ways that are perhaps more direct than others, including its dramatic melancholy, its feminist energy, its queer orientations toward both desire and community. Sasami Ashworth's multifaceted approach to both music and affect is clear in the video for "Not the Time," a single from her eponymous, 2019 debut. Shot in the kind of '90s VHS filter common to so many Big Feelings videos, the song follows Ashworth as she wanders in Los Angeles (via the Gold Line or bike) looking for a place to play her French horn. Dressed in a red marching band uniform—complete with a cape and sporting a curlicue mustache drawn in marker—

Ashworth's character draws blank stares from fellow Angelinos (one of whom opens the video by asking "Like, do you know a Rihanna song?"). There is a quiet humor threaded throughout the video (e.g., the tip jar Ashworth carries around, which reads "Horny but Wholesome," the "o" in "horny" spooling out as the body of a French horn); but at the same time, the first half of the video reads to me as deeply melancholic, in large part because, for however delightful Ashworth's character, when combined with the music being played, it is clear that she is out of place, aimless, and searching. Backed by the kinds of bittersweet, emotional chords I've discussed throughout this book, Ashworth's character keeps moving, unmoored. No matter where she performs throughout the city, she can't seem to find a place where her gifts are appreciated.

Lyrically, "Not the Time" is (once again) evidently a breakup song.[12] But that it might also bear on some deeper themes in Ashworth's life is first suggested by the throughline of the French horn in the video. Unlike the band uniform, for example, the horn itself is not merely a device for humor but reflects Ashworth's real life: she is an accomplished horn player and, after graduating from the Eastman School of Music, scored and arranged professionally before turning to indie rock full time. Second, it becomes clear that the video for "Not the Time" is about something beyond the song's subject matter when Ashworth's character bikes into an elementary school where the Linda Lindas are playing.

In 2018, their L.A. Public Library performance of "Racist, Sexist Boy" had not yet gone viral, and their youngest member, Mila de la Garza, would have been about eight years old. In SASAMI's video, the Linda Lindas are dressed in matching school uniforms, relative unknowns themselves, who enthusiastically wave for SASAMI to join them onstage when she shows up unexpectedly, pointing hopefully to her French horn. From that moment in the video, as the band plays triumphantly for dancing grade-schoolers, Ashworth is ebullient: she takes a triumphant horn (read *guitar*) solo, rolls around on stage, and hangs out as other kids perform various talents. The scene culminates in a huge group photo in which everyone is beaming, but perhaps no one quite like Ashworth, standing on a drum throne, holding her flowers.

Ultimately, the video for "Not the Time" tells a story about a misfit kid who finds a home. Thus it is especially significant that she does so with the help of a band of young punk girls, "half Asian and half Latinx," who would

12. A potential topic for further study is the feminist reappropriation of breakup narratives as both valid in and of themselves (against cultural dismissals of women's relationship narratives as trivial) and simultaneously vehicles for covert social critique.

Figure 9. SASAMI, "Not the Time," screenshot from the music video

soon go on to national fame on the reputation of a performance calling out the kind of reactionary, xenophobic hatred that swelled in the United States during the height of the COVID lockdowns and which was specifically directed at Asian Americans. I see their inclusion in this video as one means of community-building, helping to signal acceptance and a wider world out there, where misfit kids might find each other. In other words, the video establishes SASAMI and the Linda Lindas as fellow travelers, part of a shared project of musical belonging.

Zooming out from the single, consider the album cover for *SASAMI*, which shows Ashworth precariously balanced on the Matanuska glacier, permanently disappearing due to climate change. Again consistent with Big Feelings' overriding social orientation—which does not tackle politics directly as much as it reflects a kind of not-totally-nihilistic resignation that assumes those with the capacity to help will not do so—the cover contextualizes Ashworth's debut in the general context of "political depression" that Ann Cvetkovich describes as "the sense that customary forms of political response, including direct action and critical analysis, are no longer working either to change the world or to make us feel better" (2012, 1). Thus, the lines "It's not the time or place for us / Even though we tried to make it work" can be read in multiple ways: first as a breakup narrative; second, as indictment of the adult world in which SASAMI can't find a home (in the video, she instead finds her value recognized only by young people, a kind of riff on riot grrrl's privileging of adolescence); and finally, as a lament about the generational condition of millennials and younger people, who have been born in a time not made for them, who have not known life without experiencing the steady degradation of the environment and the promises of further disaster on the horizon. Combined with the wistful harmonic vocabulary and crystalline melody, this track represents the absolute core of Big Feelings as an idea.

At the same time, and like Mitski (among others), I think it is important to also consider the ways that SASAMI has stretched this approach into other areas, carrying explorations of feeling and queer-feminist affect beyond narrow indie rock genre markers. To think more about how SASAMI both exemplifies and stretches the Big Feelings concept to a limit, I turn now to her second album, *Squeeze*, which differs from *SASAMI* in its exploration of glam rock vocabulary and more monstrous, heavy metal influenced visual presentations. On this new direction, Ashworth told *Rolling Stone*, "I've always toured with an all-femme band, and that can be this physical battle of convincing the sound people you're worthy of their care and attention. You're constantly being told to turn your amps down. So it's this very literal manifestation of, like, the more I feel I'm made to be small, I just turn the amp up and my voice gets more aggressive" (quoted in Blistein 2022). *Squeeze* is not always straightforwardly metal, though live performances can bend more in that direction; the album itself incorporates elements from the metal's sonic vocabulary into Ashworth's ambitious musical vision rather selectively. "Sorry Entertainer" features shredding guitar solos and double bass-drumming, and "Skin a Rat" is similarly built from chugging harmonic minor riffs. "Say It" comes from a more industrial direction, but doesn't stay there; all the while, songs like "The Greatest" foreground Ashworth's serene, soaring vocals in a way that's not at all unrelated to her earlier work. "Feminine Water Trouble" and the closer "Not a Love Song" are ambitiously scored, but together with Ashworth's apparently effortless vocals, in what sound to me the most easeful part of her range, maintain an intimate indie sensibility. In other words, *Squeeze* can't be easily reduced to a "metal album," even as Ashworth made several concrete decisions that helped to explore the heavier side of her vision—for example, by hiring Megadeth drummer Dirk Verbeuren, or by incorporating stereotypically masculine shredding (a virtually unheard-of departure for a Big Feelings artist!) from guitarist Graham Brooks. The real difference here seems to me a matter of emphasis, which turns up the energy in certain directions in order to make use of heavy metal's vocabulary—both sonic and visual.

And it is absolutely critical to consider the visual elements of the record, which take the kind of demonic imagery that has long been a hallmark of metal genres and turn them toward Ashworth's own life. Ashworth is from a Zainichi family, a term for Koreans living in Japan who are often discriminated against as a minority group. This lends a particular significance to the album cover, specifically, which features Ashworth in the form of a Nure-onna, a Japanese yōkai (demon) that is part beautiful woman and part man-eating snake. Of the traditional folktales in which the Nure-onna appears, Ashworth said, "I love that she's this unassuming, beautiful woman washing her hair in the water, and these aggressive, presumptuous sailors will come across her, and she will destroy them. She's a really good symbol for the energy of the songs, which is like, feeling hot and being violent. I'm also a Cancer sign, so the fact that she's a water bitch, I'm like, 'Yes, this is my bitch right here! This fucking water snake, yes!' (quoted in Blistein 2022).[13] It is clearly meaningful that Ashworth here embraces a figure considered demonic in a Japanese context in order to explore and self-fashion aspects of her identity. But additionally, the gendered dimensions of the Nure-onna, who often appears holding a baby, are key to Ashworth's feminist disruption of Japanese folklore. As Raechel Dumas writes, "monstrous configurations of femininity have long occupied a place in the Japanese cultural imaginary, routinely emerging as sites for modeling deviant (and reinforcing) normative moral behaviors and social norms" (2018, 3). Building on Barbara Creed's work, Dumas shows how the "monstrous feminine" in contemporary Japanese popular culture updates longstanding tropes inherited from Buddhism's "pragmatic hostility towards women"—as well as its visual manifestations "across a spectrum of [other] medieval and early modern Japanese literary, visual, and performance arts" as a means of "negatively reinforcing the virtues of female sexual propriety, maternal devotion, and spiritual practice" (3). In part, the Nure-onna functions as a metonym for the ways in which women's sexuality can lure men to their doom, a cautionary tale intended to revalorize patriarchal modesty.

Taking a step back, the gendered implications of the Nure-onna also link up

13. In Western astrology, the twelve signs are grouped according to four elements: fire, earth, air, and water (the same as the four suits of the tarot). Ashworth's sun sign, Cancer, is considered the "cardinal" water sign, meaning the energy's initial manifestation. The other two water signs are Scorpio (water's "fixed," sign, meaning fully embodied, or determined) and Pisces (water's "mutable," sign, more fluid and anticipating change). It is worth noting how often water shows up in these discussions, whether in Ashworth's own chart (as Cancer), Soccer Mommy's "Scorpio Rising," or boygenius' references to the Three of Cups (see the outro). In all cases, water represents emotional currents, thus linking directly to the idea of Big Feelings.

Figure 10. SASAMI, *Squeeze* album cover

with critical feminist interpretations of both horror (which, as a genre, is closely linked with heavy metal in a way that Ashworth explicitly exploits)[14] and of Yoko Ono (who again stands as a foundational precursor for the artists discussed in this chapter). The connection lies in feminist psychoanalyst Julia Kristeva's influential theorizations of *abjection*. For Kristeva (1982), Creed (1993), and Dumas (2018), the abject is a key theme across cultural explorations of horror, helping to construct the figure of the "monstrous feminine" that

14. Beyond this, there is also a long tradition of queer identification with "monstrous" figures, particularly in horror genres. As one respondent told me, "I always identified with the monsters in movies right, and so did a lot of my queer friends, who then when they came out as queer they went 'ohhhh.' . . . So I wonder if maybe that's part of it, that supernatural element being 'I feel so othered and alien that I relate to this imagery'" (Sam H. 2023). See also Benshoff 1997; Brintnall 2007; Godin 2022; Petras 2019; Stryker 2024; Vallese 2022.

Creed first theorized in 1993. The abject is a category of human experience that we radically repudiate, the horrifically animalistic irruption that we must reject in order to "secure and reinforce the boundaries of culture" (Dumas 2018, 2), a reflection of the psychological need to tame and disavow the primal body in order to shore up the functional fiction of coherent subjectivity. But this disavowal is fundamentally and from the beginning gendered: a category that Kristeva theorizes as based on the infant's need to reject the maternal body in order to construct its own self-identity, the abject manifests in patriarchal culture in the nexus of the horrific and the feminized, often appearing (per Creed) through the tropes of pregnancy, motherhood, menstrual blood (and other fluids), corpses, and especially any iteration of the preceding that transgresses a fundamental boundary (life/death, human/inhuman, good/evil, et al.). Simultaneously threatening to and essential for life, the abject occupies a radical exteriority for the self-contained rationality of stable, idealized, and masculine identity constructions. Though Dumas focuses on the "monstrous feminine" in contemporary Japanese culture, her analyses are predicated on the enduring cultural debates around (in)appropriate gender roles indexed by feminized yōkai like the Nure-onna.

Relatedly, it is instructive to consider Yoko Ono's vocal technique, which, while not necessarily reproduced by Ashworth's heavy metal explorations, has nevertheless been established as essential precedent for women's reappropriated deployments of ostensibly masculinized rage in the punk rock mold. In *The Political Force of Musical Beauty*, Barry Shank theorizes the Japanese concept of *sawari* as an essential theme of Yoko Ono's oeuvre. Sawari refers to the intrusion of a sounding body's material properties into the "pure" aesthetic space of a musical tone—for example, the slide of a hand as it changes chords on an acoustic guitar. Shank cites Toru Takemitsu's use of the "loose bridge of the biwa" as an example that illustrates sawari as "an intentional inconvenience that creates a part of the expressiveness of the sound" (in Shank 2014, 99). More than intentional or inconvenient, sawari is *necessary*—it is evidence of the essential, generative, and ultimately creative materiality of the instrument in question, the form required to achieve sound. Thus, "if music is heard properly, one always hears the necessary sawari, the physicality of the sound, the disturbance in the air" (Shank 2014, 99). Critically, however, Shank also notes that one of sawari's many connotations, per Takemitsu, is "the monthly biological function in women," a "potentially creative" "inconvenience." To claim that Ono centers sawari—that she "consistently, perhaps obsessively, interrupted [her] performances through the apparatus of an obstacle" (102)—is also to claim that she obsessively centered her own subjectivity, social position, and identity as a woman.

"Quite probably Ono's most firm insistence on a noisy obstacle . . . is her use of Kabuki vocal techniques" (Shank 104)—a significant fact in and of itself given that in Japan, women were barred from Kabuki performances in 1629 (this despite the fact that the art form was invented by Izumo no Okuni and inaugurated with all-female troupes). Necessitating precision, control, and power, such vocal techniques often produce sounds that Western listeners hear as screams, utilizing the material folds of the vocal chords to achieve complex overtones and abrasive timbres. Thus sawari is invoked merely in Ono's deployment and manipulation of such sounds, linking Ono's vocal performances with connotations of menstruation—connotations with which she would be quite familiar—and therefore abjection, that which mainstream society must reject in order to keep its conception of itself intact.

Published in 2014, the same year as Shank's *Musical Beauty*, Shelina Brown's "Scream from the Heart" connects Ono's abrasive provocations even more directly to the abject: skirting the question of sawari altogether, Brown uses Western perceptions of Ono as screaming to claim that her performances (perhaps particularly in collaboration with rock musicians and their instruments) constitute examples of sonic abjection in their rupture of bodily interiority, in their invocations of horror. Linking the expulsion of bodily fluids to the expulsion of sound from Ono's body, Brown writes that Ono's scream:

> Points to a violent abjection that conjures the pangs of birth. . . . The horror of the scream thus alerts us to a body in crisis, a body being ruptured, fragmented—a pre-verbal, transformative body that resists co-optation within the symbolic order. . . . Given the fear of the feminine that comes to be ascribed to the abject, Ono's vocal performances can be interpreted as a direct sonic challenge to the boundaries that anxiously prescribe and reinforce patriarchal order. (S. Brown 2014, 179)[15]

When Ashworth deploys the horrific imagery of the Nure-onna, she reclaims the power of gendered/demonic iconography, using a figure that has been traditionally used to reinforce patriarchal norms to instead disrupt those same norms, celebrating, in her quote above, the ostensibly tragic death of so many anonymous men and identifying with (not against) the yōkai through queer-coded and Western astrological practices. When she dons glam makeup, fishnets, six-inch heels, and devil horns before ripping a sick metal riff and scream-

15. See also Elizabeth Lindau's 2016 article on motherhood and Ono's work, where she also cites Kristeva and writes that "Ono's trademark vocal style began as an imitation of a reversed imitation of an imitation of a woman in labor" (69).

ing in front of a band of long-haired dudes, equally thrashing, SASAMI performs an unapologetic catharsis that is not identical to, but shares affinities with, Yoko Ono's immanent critique of patriarchal normativity and rock masculinity alike. Both Ono and Ashworth reference traditional, patriarchal social codes, utilizing references to normative Japanese culture as a means of intervening in and refuting those same norms. Where Ono utilizes sawari to reference the abject, Ashworth repurposes demonic imagery from Japanese folklore—a different means of achieving the same critique. Together, Ashworth links Ono's aural performance of abjection to a visual representation of the monstrous feminine through an embrace and reappropriation of that which society refuses; her high-femme interventions into heavy metal ask what would happen if all of the genre's traditional homoeroticism was embraced rather than rejected, was performed in the service of inclusivity and group catharsis rather than exclusion and oppression. On *Squeeze*, Ashworth uses heavy metal's embrace of dark fantasy and orientalism to explore her own identity on the interconnected axis of race, gender, sexuality, ethnicity, and more. Embracing femme-coded demons becomes a way of queering both heavy metal and traditional Japanese folklore and has allowed Ashworth to continue exploring different "monstrous" personalities at the nexus of genre and identity. *Squeeze*, "which focuses on catharsis, is an open invitation to femmes, people of color, queer folks and anyone else to revel in pent-up frustration and disillusionment" (McCammon and Wang 2022).

In conjunction with the album, her recent covers of System of a Down's "Toxicity" further intervene in metal history: performed live, Ashworth will often dig into the song, performing it at full volume and high energy, as System of a Down would. Such performances revise heavy metal discourse by inserting an Asian American femme at the head of the band—though System of a Down are Armenian American, and critique US imperialism, their sometimes nu metal aesthetics still connote mainstream/aggressively male signifiers, particularly for those who are only passingly familiar with their work. Where US culture is trained to expect only demure, docile, or overachieving stereotypes of Asian femininity, Ashworth uses metal's masculine bravado for her own devices. On the other hand, Ashworth's recorded version of "Toxicity," which appears on the *Soccer Mommy and Friends* singles series, completely deconstructs the song, transforming it from a propulsive lambast to a haunting dirge rendered in solo acoustic guitar. When she reaches into the metal genre to turn it inside out, her intervention becomes about much more than "representation." While representation is important—especially in terms of getting artists paid for their labor—it can also be problematic since it "can look and sound a lot like ideas of assimilation and normalization that shore up liberal multicultural logics undergirding the state, the academy, and capital" (Lee 2020, 9). Instead (and along with the other artists discussed in this chapter), SASAMI's music evinces a sensibility that Summer Kim Lee calls "minoritarian listening practices," which "stubbornly move against the grain" of harmful majoritarian expectations.

What I hear across Ashworth's humorous deployment of the French horn (culturally coded as "fitting" for the model minority stereotype) in the context of an indie rock anthem featuring up-and-coming punk icons the Linda Lindas is the same movement I hear in her deconstruction of System of a Down: a subtle inversion of expectations no matter where or how they adhere. SASAMI manipulates sound, sight, and genre in order to produce the feeling of a strange fit, a just-so subversion of heavy metal, classical music, indie rock, or synth-pop that manifests minoritarian listening practices' "insistence on one's creative capacity to hear, see, and feel oneself in pop cultural sites in the *wrong way*" (Lee 2020, 8; my emphasis). Finally, they do so through Ashworth's aesthetic range—what we might call a kind of genre promiscuity—which then directly links to Gayatri Gopinath's understanding of "aesthetic practices of queer diaspora." For Gopinath, queer diasporic aesthetics "disrupt the normative ways of seeing and knowing that have been so central to the production, containment, and disciplining of sexual, racial, and gendered bodies; they do so, crucially, through a particular deployment of queer desire and identification that renders apparent the promiscuous intimacies of our past histories as they continue to structure our everyday present, and determine our futures" (2018, 7).

Drawing on the very promiscuity and queer identification that Gopinath suggests imbues the present with past histories, SASAMI's recoding of historical Japanese imagery links with both her musical promiscuity and with her capacious approach to gender presentation to subvert normative Asian American identity expectations in the present moment. Smashing together glam rock, metal, and indie pop sensibilities, Ashworth critiques ostensibly white-male genres even as she makes use of them.

But for all that's seemingly changed between *SASAMI* and *Squeeze*, at least one throughline strings together 2019's lo-fi shoegaze introspection and 2022's genderqueer glam rock: both see Ashworth embracing different versions of herself. And I mean this nearly literally—for example, the music video for one of SASAMI's most tender tracks, "Take Care" (2019), culminates in a hazy sunset scene showing Ashworth pulling herself out of the water, apparently rescuing herself from drowning before embracing herself with a huge smile. Whether we interpret "Sasami double" Kasarlina Wang (whose body Ashworth pulls from the water) as literally representing Ashworth—or as merely a kindred spirit—the image is mirrored three years later in the video for "Make It Right" (2022), a driving classic rock treatment somewhere in between the Go-Go's and St. Vincent. The final shot in the video ends with Ashworth embracing her mirror image, unquestionably herself on both sides of the hug. While this chapter has stretched and at times ways even abandoned the Big Feelings concept, SASAMI's music always generates queer-feminist affects in multiple ways, sonic and visual. In "Make It Right," we feel these affects through the interplay between her voice, the guitar, and the drums; through her makeup (what a blue![16]); her harness and trench coat; but most of all in the insistence intimated by her holding her own double, an insistence on taking care of oneself, of championing, nurturing, and pushing oneself. These acts may not in themselves constitute politics; but when practiced by a queer, Asian American woman, they become radical in the context of US white supremacist patriarchy, in the context of a hegemonic capitalism that makes no space for care that can't be monetized. In the "Make it Right" video's closing shot, as music fades and the camera zooms out from Ashworth, she does not grin for it, instead tracking its movements as it goes, unflinching and protective of the woman in her arms.

16. This is another example of a shared language (see Nico 2024).

5 • "Open Sky"

Liminality and Fragility in a Queer Midwest

Who would I be without you,
Without them?
—boygenius[1]

Long before the idea for this book organized itself into anything remotely coherent, I was trying to write about the Ophelias, a four-piece band originally from Cincinnati, Ohio, and connected to what singer Spencer Peppet wryly described to me as the "boygenius cinematic universe." I've been listening to the Ophelias since at least 2016, when one of my advisors mentioned that his student was in a band. Since then, their music has become, for me, variously a comfort and a challenge, a crepuscular fairy tale within which I found myself cocooned during times of heightened emotional intensity: as I defended my dissertation, for example, or rounded the corner on a difficult period in my relationship, as I packed boxes, slowly and alone, in a place I didn't want to leave. Like the greatest bands, the Ophelias have a sound both instantly recognizable and necessarily singular. But more so than any music I have discussed in this book, that sound has from the beginning felt so threaded to the folds of my life that I have never known how to talk about it, how to discuss what feels important to me about their music without also talking about myself in ways that threaten to overshadow the magic they make with my own story of its working. Here too, I have been unable to disentangle myself from what they do, and I have not tried to hide this fact. Instead I hope to render what feels special about their music not in spite of but through my own experience. Any attempt to do so is, for my part, necessarily caught up in questions of place, and not just because the Ophelias

1. From "Without You Without Them," track 1 on *The Record* (2023).

intentionally and often discuss Ohio; it's also because the moments when I came to know their music were also those moments in which my heart was breaking because of that same state, synonymous with the Three of Swords experience that floods my nervous system every time I leave it.[2] And because any discussion of place is really a discussion about the people who live there, trying to tell you about Ohio requires detours around how I see the vibrant and queer and joyful communities who raised me reflected in the Ophelias' worldview, how their approach to music partially performs what it's felt like to live there, in or alongside a margin.

Thriving/Hurting | Leaving/Returning

Mic Adams (drums), Andrea Gutmann Fuentes (violin), Spencer Peppet (vox/guitar), and Jo Shaffer (bass) have been making beguiling indie records since their high school days, when they found in each other relief from traditional boy-rock musical cultures. In March 2023, the Ophelias were poised to release an EP of covers and had just headlined a sold-out show in Brooklyn. We talked the next day around my brother's dinner table, Peppet sporting a Frankie Cosmos hat, and the rest of the band Zooming in.[3] Among other things, I was grateful for the opportunity to finally get some help articulating what I loved about their gorgeous and perplexing music—and that's what I asked about first.

"I feel like the best way to describe our band is in images," Peppet told me, before rattling a few off: "Midwest; gas station slushie; sunset through a window; blue hour." These pictures immediately made sense to me when I heard them, because they felt sentimental in a way that ties directly to a sense of place, or a way of living there. But if it is easier to describe the band's inscrutable approach with such effervescent imagery, they have nevertheless honed

---

2. Where boygenius is a Three of Cups band, the Ophelias are a Three of Swords band, and that iconography appears on T-shirts, stickers, and other, often handmade merch. Indicating a heart pierced straight through by three long blades, the Three of Swords tarot card invites us to face squarely whatever heartbreak or acute hurt we are experiencing, rather than running from, ignoring, or downplaying that pain. It suggests that healing can only come through sitting with, acknowledging, and respecting our feelings, through honest and open engagement with what we are experiencing, however difficult. In this way, we might think of the Three of Swords as the card most succinctly representing the kind of concert experience I described in chapter 3, where musicians and listeners collaborate in staging difficult experiences precisely in order to move through them.

3. Unless marked otherwise, all of the band's quotes in this chapter come from Ophelias 2023.

their sound into something that feels solid. Ever self-aware, the band's term for it has been "Midwest moth music," a combination of whimsical cottagecore and a darker, gothic melancholia.

"I remember we'd have to find spaces to put on shows," Peppet said of the band's early Cincinnati days. "A lot of times we'd end up in warehouses, community buildings, stuff like that. We would have to go to Michael's and get stuff to decorate the stage." For the Ophelias, this way of making one's own fun is deeply tied to a sense of home, of the Midwest in general and Ohio specifically. It's not like New York or L.A., they told me, where a young band might try to hop on a friends' bill at the next show; these are spaces and scenes that have to be built.

Like their previous records, their latest—*Spring Grove*—is at least in part about this kind of peripheral geography. Named after a Cincinnati cemetery (the third largest in the nation), the album creates mystical sonic atmospheres while dropping hints about its origins along the way. "We all stan the Midwest," Gutmann Fuentes said amid laughing agreement. "I think that growing up in the Midwest—it does something to you," Peppet continued. "It's just a very specific set of experiences and I feel very protective of it." As I myself have experienced, Peppet told me that in her view, "People love to shit on Ohio. People love to be like 'Oh my God you live in New York now that's amazing, good for you.' People love to act like escaping Ohio is the best thing you could possibly do and I think that they just don't understand. They don't get it."

• • •

And I have to pause here to explain that if you grew up in Ohio during the '90s, and likely other times besides, the feeling of an unspoken expectation to "get out" pervaded your consciousness before you were aware of why or where it came from, like a middle school rumor that everyone suddenly whispers. "It bears mentioning that I come from a place people leave," Hanif Abdurraqib writes (2024, 224), and while there are probably a lot of places in the United States where it's expected that if you want to "do something" with your life, you'll have to move on, the feeling that I know is the one that's particular to Ohio, which calcifies a fierce and righteous underdog mentality in everyone who chooses to stay or return. After years of conversations with strangers who admit they "actually liked" that one time they passed through; after the accumulation of a series of national jokes ("The mistake on the lake," "the fumble," "the drive") that embedded themselves in public consciousness before I was even born; after years of media narratives overrepresenting the region through the figure of the "white working class" that purportedly propelled a racist sexual predator to the presidency;[4] after learning that young people use "Ohio" as slang for "anything weird, cringey, or random" (Alcántara 2024); after coming to understand that the two symbols attributed to life in Ohio are rural flyover country and urban rust-belt decay;[5] the formation of an entire identity is necessary in order to move through the world while loving this place on purpose.

Which is not to say that there aren't good reasons to leave Ohio; it's just that they're not the reasons people usually assume. It's not as much that

---

4. Such dominant media narratives are perhaps most forcefully represented by my father's hometown of Youngstown, symbolic because of how thoroughly its economy collapsed when the steel mills closed. Having worked in one his entire career, my grandfather was in some ways indicative of the demographic understood to vote for Trump out of feelings of abandonment. But such coverage tends to defer discussions about how he (and folks like him) immigrated here after the war, speaking not much English at all, and it seems to miss the fact that it was unionized, poor immigrants running those mills, seems to miss the fact that Trump's base is actually on the whole more well-off than working class, the fact that white people of certain income levels remains an unbelievably obtuse category of analysis in a world where financial precarity is endemic to mere existence in this country. And this isn't even mentioning the "disproportionate and specific consequences of deindustrialization, population loss, and economic decline" for people of color generally and Black Midwesterners specifically—many of whom *live in Youngstown*, composing some 40 percent of its population—all of which remains "conspicuously unaddressed" in any mainstream coverage of the region (Williamson 2020, 15).

5. Something of this dichotomy is also reflected in scholarship, where on the one hand, queer theory has, for example, overwhelmingly focused on life in big cities like San Francisco, New York, Chicago, and DC. On the other hand, accounts of queer Midwestern life, already in the minority, have tended to focus on either rural contexts or else Chicago, creating a kind of rural/urban binary that excludes the many other sizeable cities housed within the large and amorphous idea of the Midwest, an extension of the old framework that equates cities with progressive (queer-inclusive) life and rurality with conservative (queer-exclusive) life (Manalansan et al. 2014). In other words, when people talk about the queer Midwest, they tend to treat the region (outside of Chicago) as a metonym for rurality, as if an urban Midwest is contradictory. It's true that post-industrial cities like Cleveland continue to shed their populations; but as of this writing, Columbus is the fourteenth most populous city in the country. Indianapolis, with more people than San Francisco, toggles between fifteenth and sixteenth. Detroit, Kansas City, Milwaukee, Minneapolis, and Omaha all sit in the top fifty, above New Orleans, Orlando, and Newark (New Jersey). Certainly, these statistics don't capture larger contexts and metro areas; but they nevertheless help me to identify the deficiencies in a persistent imaginary about the Midwest—in tandem, it must be said, with their often radically conservative governments— that flattens the contradictions emergent within such spaces, the diversity of the people who live there. Part of this likely has to do with the unique imprecision attached to the word "Midwest," which claims both rust-belt cities like Detroit along with Great Plains regions like the Dakotas. Precious little can be found in common across such expanses, making any effort to theorize the Midwest difficult from the beginning.

Figure 11. An Ohio Landmark, I-71 in between Columbus and Cincinnati (photo credit Devin Copfer, Ellen Connors, and Rose McKibben)

there's nothing to do here, for example, especially in what have been and are still, after all, big cities. In my estimation, it's more to do with the fact that since I've been alive, the state has been doing everything in its power to make life as miserable as possible for everyone who isn't a middle-class white man, efforts that have lent an ironic literality to one of Ohio's most infamous landmarks.

Increasingly right-wing and insulated by partisan gerrymandering, the state government has moved in recent years to follow the kinds of reactionary legislative attacks on gender-affirming care, the book bans, the anti-DEI and anti-abortion measures sweeping red states post-2020. As I sit here listening to the Ophelias, trying to find the language that would do justice to the queer beauty of Ohio, organizations like the Human Rights Campaign mark 2023 as the "Worst Year On Record for Anti-LGBTQ+ Legislation" (HRC Staff 2023; Factora 2024). Arrested at protests, afraid in the classroom, targeted by laws or harassed on the street, my queer and trans friends, my nonwhite friends, my educator friends, as well as those marginalized in multiple ways at once, feel mere existence becoming fraught in the state where they have built their lives. It is difficult not to imagine this as the ultimate point of such bills, to imagine that banning books about queer/non-white identity or policing bathroom stalls could be anything other than an effort to force us out, one way or another, to make us unwelcome in the place we love.

• • •

Which is to say a few things that might need to be said, depending on how you come to this, first of all that, yes, Ohio is diverse, in spite of what one might assume based on a Republican supermajority in government, in spite of the rurality surrounding our cities and the stereotypical white rage to which it is not reducible, but which, we must be clear, does exist there. And because Ohio is diverse, this is also to say that it is paradoxical, that it exists for people like us as a matter of cracked glass, both institutionally normative and socially fantastical at once. The violence of the state coexists, in other words, with the music we make, as florid and devastating as anything anywhere, and in part a reaction to our circumstances. For those of us who grew up loving Ohio's cities and the people who increasingly find it difficult to live in them, the state therefore feels a destabilizing duality, caught between the beauty we have witnessed and the nightmares it visits. Hence the question of leaving is never altogether absent, even if temporary, or at least it feels present for me, sitting now in another Midwestern city characterized by these same paradoxes, listening to "Soft and Tame" again, over again, a song from 2024's *Ribbon* EP, a song that exemplifies everything dusk and October about Peppet's guitar tone, which here opens the track in a heart-wrenching 13 arrangement, sounding alone[6] before the full progression begins—and that sequence is itself an ascendant longing that builds steadily into a sweeping and gentle explosion before Peppet delivers one final, fading verse:

> You tell me it's not my home after all
> I don't belong, I'll make my own
> Giving up love in the south of Ohio
> I hate it here, in the in between

6. For me, the chord quality and strumming pattern evoke Wye Oak's "Siamese," a song that was formative for me in the year of its release, when I ran around Bexley neighborhoods and wondered what to do with my life, with the way I felt about finishing school, the possibility of leaving.

I wanna feel safe, I wanna feel seen
The curve of the hills when the sun is gone
A knot in my throat, another fucking song

Woven together tightly in this stanza is a pair of twin heartbreaks: an ambiguous split inflected with implied long-distance complications, and the feeling of being told that you don't belong in the place that you thought was your home.

To my ear, this is a doubly and quintessentially Midwestern sentiment, especially insofar as Big Feelings teaches us to hear the word "love" capaciously, to include all manner of intimacies, some without names; but while anyone here can come to feel alienated from what they had once taken for granted, it is notably some external other who's telling Peppet's character that she doesn't belong, somebody *else* making her feel unseen and unsafe. Thus, the feeling of needing to get out of Ohio that any resident may at points feel takes on a particular urgency for Peppet's character, who is being actively rejected. It is the kind of alienation that might resonate especially for those who have been similarly ostracized from their communities, for the kinds of women and queer people who see themselves in the Ophelias' music, made to feel unwelcome whether by individual bigots or the implications of state policy. It is an example of the subtle but unmistakable ways in which this band creates queer-feminist affects that draw in and consolidate listenerships similarly caught "in between." Vibrating with my own life and the profound, precious time I spend in Ohio, the Ophelias use imagery, text, and sound to render a distinctly queer Midwest, both a reflection of actually existing communities and a fantastical imaginary of the not-yet-here, the contingent ephemerality of the worlds that come into being only in spaces where queer lives are allowed to thrive. The fact that queer folks do thrive in Ohio and in the broader Midwest coexists with the fact that queer life is still an irruption into the here and now, a disruptive force that must be constantly reimagined as the world variously maintains its apathy or acts on its antipathy. "Queerness is a longing that propels us onward," says, José Esteban Muñoz (2009, 1), because queerness is, in his formulation, never quite here yet. What matters is our capacity to glimpse it, most often through art, and how we then act to bring that dream into reality. Queer is potential beauty that flitters across the inadequate present; in this way, it is not unlike the Midwest, where we have to build worlds that don't exist but could, perceiving a better version of this place in the very reality of what's already here.

This contradiction also gives birth to another, necessarily entwined: because of the particular ways that the Midwest produces beautiful communities as well as structural violence against them, because of the ways that the

Midwestern imaginary is in part constituted by the act of leaving it behind, the thriving/hurting that we do here produces a leaving/returning contradiction from which we will never escape. And this is precisely where my own experiences come to overdetermine how I hear the Ophelias: there is no way for me to hear Peppet sing those lines in "Soft and Tame" and not remember what it felt like to be alone in Los Angeles, standing on a hill at twenty-four years old and realizing with first finality that I had indeed given up love in the south of Ohio, that I couldn't go back even if I physically returned. One of many ways in which this chapter tries to raise contradictions that persist without collapsing is this: *Big Feelings* is an academic book that has been subjected to a rigorous peer-review process, yet it is also personal, and nowhere more so than this chapter, about this music, which sounds hitherto nonexistent shades of bittersweet and evokes Ohio at the very moment when I have left it, again (again!), after multiple returns. And I don't mind telling you that I'm mourning it, not just the leaving but also what I perceive to be lost potential, the fact or the sense that I never stayed long enough in one place to see the rewards of what I put into it, that I was always catching glimpses before starting over somewhere, or trying to pick up where I left off. It is in fact essential to confess that I hear each leaving in the way that Peppet's guitar crunches its chords together, in Shaffer's note selection, plucked out one at a time like so many stars.

In allowing myself these sentimental digressions, I am trying nevertheless to advance an argument: first, that there is a both-at-once experience of living in the Midwest, home to the most beautiful people I know and the site of radical violence upon those same people. This, I want to suggest, has something to do with, is perhaps uniquely expressive of, the way that some of its most important theorists have formulated the condition of queerness itself, which is to say (second) that I am positing some kind of a connection between queerness and the Midwest, certainly not homological, but resonant insofar as "attention, desire, and action are structured by the material conditions of place" (Kopcienski 2023, 32). Third, there is the dialectical leaving/returning that the first two points engender, even if you never leave, even if you never return: both somehow haunt us, I want to say, imperceptibly imprinting our psyches in the way that all geography does, but which in this case specifically is about a certain type of yearning that you're doomed to be caught within, unresolved, so much given up by either choice.[7] Something

7. And this is what Midwest emo—that namesake subgenre—is all about. Riffing on the houses that appear on so many album covers and the housing of cassette tapes, Sean Peters (in process) writes that Midwest emo bands have preferred cassettes not just for their perceived

about the particular poignancy in the Ophelias' intricate arrangements evokes these feelings, straddling multiple lines/borders/liminalities. It is impossible to leave and it is impossible to stay, because your life is here, because it won't have you; because you carry it, because it's fragile.

• • •

SP: I still feel very deeply connected to Ohio and very deeply connected to all of the kind of emotional ties and images and sounds associated with it. I feel like I will never not be a Midwestern person, regardless of where I am in actual literal location.

Midwest Moth Music

How can I propose a connection between queerness and the Midwest beyond assertions that queerness does exist here (as in the ostensible contradiction "the queer Midwest")? And what does it mean to claim that the Ophelias *produce* queer Midwestern spatialities? Let me back up now and touch on some other themes that are important for thinking through this band, in their own words again, which they will often and with any excuse use to describe an originary enchantment that continues to animate their music: falling in love with your bandmates.

SP: I feel like one of the best things about our band is how collaborative it is and how it is four very distinct people with four very distinct musical languages and tendencies working together.

MA: In my experience being in bands led by cis men, they'll ask a woman

---

DIY credibility, but in part because they capture something of Jacques Derrida's notion of hauntology: "the sense of being haunted by lost futures," which, in my reading, invokes not just the post-industrial collapse of manufacturing in the region but also the possibilities foreclosed by choosing to leave or choosing to remain there. The Midwestern homes featured on so many covers in this subgenre (paradigmatically, American Football's 1999 record) are nostalgic and intimate because we so often leave them behind during formative years, or which, if we stay, are tied to uncertain futures amid systemic disinvestment. Cassette tapes, which house their own nostalgic memories, symbolize and reify lost futures in their anachronistic materiality. It is this sense of loss and liminality that contributes to the affective register of the genre, whose lyrics often concern the fracturing of relationships across long distances. While internet articles like *Vox*'s "It Shouldn't Be So Hard to Live Near Your Friends" (Bernard 2024) testify to the fact that alienation and isolation are increasingly universal, I suggest that feeling forced to leave home is particularly fraught in a region with fewer opportunities to begin with, with much greater physical distance (and likely no trains) between you and the next city.

or a femme to join, but then micromanage their parts to the point where it's just what they would be playing if they had extra arms. . . . I think when we first formed, we had our first practice in high school and we wrote nine songs like immediately. Being in that space of women allowed us just enough creative freedom to write our own parts without hesitation.

AGF: I just really want to emphasize that. I think Spencer, Grace [Weir][8] and I were eighteen, and Mic was sixteen. We all went to Mic's house for our first band practice in the spring of 2015, and we sat there for like . . . I think it was two and a half hours and just hammered out nine songs all recorded on Spencer's phone as like a voice memo. That turned out to be our first album.

SP: I remember leaving and being like, "That's not normal . . . right? That's not what happens every time, right?" I just remember I would play you guys something and you'd be like, "I have an idea"—and then you'd play it and I'd be like, "Wait that's perfect. How did you do that?" And then you kept doing it.

As the Ophelias relayed this "core band memory" (as they put it) to me, each of them beaming, I felt for a moment that I was privy to the kind of rush they must have felt in that first rehearsal, the kind of exhilarating thing that can happen when you recognize something of yourself in someone else. As we've seen throughout this book, it is a kind of love, an emphasis on community and care, that has long been marginalized in rock and American popular culture writ large. Though the success of boygenius has seen conversations about queer/feminist friendship celebrated by venerable rock institutions like *Rolling Stone*, it's still a radical model of music-making in the context of an individualist, competitive culture. And even if "movement" is too strong a word, it's a model that is being lived by a growing network of young musicians, finding ways to connect to each other online and on tour.

SP: I think you kind of hit the nail on the head, where it's like, there's a long history of women and musicians of color and queer folks making music, and that I think the main difference now is just what kind of resources people are getting. I do personally feel very much in community with people, especially other women and queer people. . . . But I feel like that kind of community is maybe the thing that has existed for a long time. The community aspect might be the

8. Grace Weir is the original bassist in the group.

thing that goes back the farthest, rather than the kind of attention economy or whatever you want to call it—who is actually getting the funding because . . . capitalism, you know.

MA: I think for me . . . since we grew up in the Midwest, at the beginning we were with white-dude indie rock bands so it's like this new thing for me where I feel kind of held and there's a kind of safety net of queer artists, of women artists, artists of color—that I know that there's enough of us now where we feel empowered to support each other. It's like there's somewhere to go, and I know that there are other people out there—not that it wasn't there before, but I'm more familiar with it now.

JS: I would also add I've been surprised by how developed some of the smaller cities' queer scenes seem to be, and I wonder about the role of the internet. I grew up really desperately wanting to be part of one of those scenes. I wonder how that sort of environment changes when you don't need to be in one place to have access to a scene like that.

If this book's premise has been caught in between a celebration of what can feel like a new flourishing of diversity in indie rock and the fact that indie rock has always been diverse, the Ophelias' responses here help me to understand how that distinction shows up in their lives—they reflect on how what's new might be access, visibility, and in some cases, even resources. But beyond that, I hear in this reflection something more about the relationship between the Midwest and queerness—without conflating them, I want to linger on this adjacency, this relationship between two different ways of being peripheral to something: if that's a resonance that's meaningful, what might it sound like?

• • •

When I broached the topic of how identity connects with musical expression, Peppet talked about how one learns to play music in the first place: "I think for a lot of male musicians there's encouragement to start guitar really young and have lessons," she told me. People tell young boys, "You can be a rockstar; be a rockstar! And here are the records you should listen to, and here's all the different things you should do, and when you turn eighteen we'll give you a record deal."[9]

9. This is, of course, an exaggeration, but one that accurately captures dynamics that see easy encouragement unevenly distributed. For me, it echoes Donna Dresch, writing in 1989:

By contrast, it is less likely for women, queer musicians, and musicians of color to be as easily helped along into preexisting support networks, long lines of indie rock bros all too ready to pass along their tradition. But for as long as that patriarchal lineage has existed, there have also been those making their own way in the music. Especially in places like the Midwest, musicians on the outside of normative rock culture have made their own spaces, searching for like-minded people just as they search for the right sounds on a guitar neck, in the absence of any mentorship. While this kind of alternative musicality isn't strictly about gender, it's also true that many women, nonbinary, and otherwise queer artists have developed deeply personal sounds out of nonconventional tuning systems and chord structures—in part, I suspect, because of the way that sounds become associated with people, with social connotations that can start to sound like a worldview.[10] It is perhaps more than coincidental, then, that Peppet told me, "I don't think I have a single song where I play just like a normal chord. Maybe one." On the other hand, "There's one song [on *Creature Native*] where I have the capo on the eleventh fret. I used to play it like this," she demonstrated, pointing to the ground, "and slide my finger up. All these fucking high school guys would make fun of me like, 'What are you doing?' . . . I thought it was cool, so."

From these kinds of personal explorations, the Ophelias have created a sound that communicates something—if not everything—about who they

---

"I was trying to tell Ed that I think that most girls aren't given an instrument for Christmas and don't usually have parents who say, 'Here, honey, we bought you this drum set you've been wanting, now go play in that loud rock band'" (Dresch 1995).

10. Joni Mitchell's alternative tunings, for example, are well-known and much discussed. But additionally, Land of Talk's Elizabeth Powell has also made alternative guitar technique a cornerstone of their music—importantly, the way they talk about it has nothing to do with music theoretical concerns, but rather with free play, exploration, and following sounds where they want to go. Similarly, Shelina Brown writes that "guitarists such as China Burg and Lydia Lunch avoided learning conventional guitar technique. . . . Rebelling against the notion of 'three chord rock' and western tonal harmony. . . . Lunch claims proudly that to this day, she has never learned a single guitar chord" (2018, 174). Given both "three chord rock" and Western tonality's overdetermined associations with white men, it is fair to read Lunch's refusal of guitar technique as a rejection of masculine-oriented rock music. In this vein, it's also worth considering Thurston Moore and Sonic Youth, given their challenges to normative rock culture across several decades. Finally, Peppet is not alone among her contemporaries in the Big Feelings universe: Laetitia Tamko (Vagabon, discussed in chapter 6), "despite years of longing for more formal training," now considers "her musical naïveté as an advantage," telling *NPR*, "If I try to cover a song, I'll play it so wrong that I'll write a song. If I learn a fifth of an African song on guitar, I will learn it the wrong way and I'll make my own thing. That's what I'm protective of'" (quoted in Gathright 2019).

are and where they come from. It is a feminist sound, a queer sound, a fantastical, explorative, creative approach to indie that blends different styles and maps out different ways of living. The notes, chords, and scales out of which songs are built carry social meanings as much as any finished product, and the Ophelias are sensitive to these dynamics.

JS: I think in particular . . . like in dude blues rock with the shredding and the pentatonic scales . . . it has a very specific connotation, and I always find myself . . . I don't know, I get sheepish if I notice that I'm using a pentatonic scale too much [laughing].

SP: I feel like we're a band of fourths.

JS: That's what you told me when I first joined, Spencer! You were like, "We're a fourths band."

AGF: And we're very averse to guitar solos.

SP: That's a great point—that's another thing that feels very gendered.

AGF: We always joke about the pedal bros. . . . Any dude will come up and be like "oh what pedal are you using?" I have this one little pedal that I bring with me on tour and it's just a harmonizer . . . but we've started to dabble into pedal stuff, so we're growing, you know. . . . We're coming to embrace some of these things that at first we were . . . being a little defiant about.

MA: I'm trying to defend the guitar solo I have to say. I think we can do it.

SP: Well Mic, you're a *dude* now, so it makes sense that you're into guitar solos! [everyone laughing]

MA: But I think we can still do it ironically!

At this point in the interview, Peppet leaned over to the laptop and asked a question of her own. I note this because I think it speaks to the band's working relationships. In part, I think, because she's the singer (traditionally the subject of the press/male gaze), Peppet was keen to emphasize just how integral all four members are to the magic that makes the Ophelias work, pausing frequently to loop in other voices—"I don't know, what do y'all think?"; "Jo you looked like you were about to say something"—and asking several questions of her own, as she did here. I was grateful for how she pushed the conversation into compelling directions, but I was also moved by how much respect everyone demonstrated for one other.

"Actually Mic, can I ask you a question?" Peppet asked, while still on the topic of guitar bros.

SP: I'm really interested to know do you feel like your taste or like tendency and playing has changed since you transitioned.

MA: That's a good question . . . I definitely feel like . . . guys used to always [ask] me during soundcheck "Is that the loudest you're going to play?" You know, that kind of thing, like they thought I was playing too light. And maybe I was, I don't know. That could be a reality, cause I was scared. But no one has said that to me [lately], and I think I also play harder. I have more confidence just playing loudly—that's the only difference. I feel like I have permission to, and also because . . . I feel like . . . if I were a woman doing that people would think "Oh she's playing loud to compensate" or "Oh she's playing loud to assert herself," whereas if a guy's playing it's like "Oh he's—yep, another loud guy!" I don't know, it just feels like every move I made as a woman was perceived as very premeditated, do you know what I mean? Whereas I can just do anything now and people just take it at face value. I don't think my taste in music has changed at all, just like how I play has.

SP: That's really interesting. Thanks Mic, thanks for letting me ask.

Both at the Same Time: Queer Musical Iconographies

Like other Big Feelings bands, the Ophelias communicate their queer-feminist orientations in a variety of ways that are not limited to harmonic vocabulary, timbre, or other sound considerations: social media posts, for example, represent the band both as they are (joyful, whimsical, young, queer) as well as in more stylized settings (dressed fantastically for a music video, say, or captured rocking out at a show). Likewise, they have also in the past been explicit and vocal about their support of trans rights and Palestinian liberation, and their disdain for the Supreme Court. They have also talked about their personal lives, how they identify in terms of gender and sexual orientation, and have otherwise shared, albeit selectively, details about who and how they are in the world.

That being said, like other Big Feelings artists, their band-oriented work (lyrics, videos, merch) most often communicates not "about" but *from* a certain outlook on the world, for example, with T-shirts featuring the Three of Swords, or text reading "I WENT TO THE OPHELIAS SHOW AND ALL I GOT WAS THIS OVERWHELMING SENSE OF DREAD." Including everything from knit figures to hand-painted "cursed amulets," the Ophelias' often-homemade merch is a meaningful aspect of their constellated iconography, appearing across lyrics, music videos, performance attire, and beyond, helping to construct a world that listeners inhabit while experiencing their music. Such physical and digital statements work in tandem with musical devices that have historically held more appeal for women and feminist indie rock bands than not: alternate tunings, chord extensions, lush textures, and looping, irregular phrases, less linear development than cyclic accumulation and its unexpected drop-off.

Of the respondents with whom I spoke for this book, Sam was the most familiar with the Ophelias' music. After I asked her what about it resonated with her, our conversation moved into the visual elements attached to their records—as well as other artists in the Big Feelings universe. Sam's consistent framing of the music as "sitting in the middle" or doing "both things" echoed again and again, whether talking about feminine/masculine imagery or else light/dark musical affects. Speaking to me from a different part of the Midwest, Sam's language also indirectly invokes the middle of the country, where queer life flourishes even as it is under attack, both literally and metaphorically in-between. "It speaks to certain people going through a bunch of different stuff," she told me:

> Like, maybe there are people who are totally fine with their gender who'd be like, "What the hell are you talking about?" if they heard me be like, "Well you can be a girl and not a girl at the same time when you're listening!" . . . There's something about the imagery that they use too that I think a lot of people love aesthetically. . . . Like "moon" is such a big word. . . . All the Instagram girlies would just be like "the moon, yes, obviously, duh, I know her I love her she's my best friend." But teeth and dogs are also ones that I notice in . . . Mitski, boygenius, Soccer Mommy . . . there's so many very specific images—flowers, too: Mitski talks about the flowers in her hair, Soccer Mommy has the wildflowers, and then the Ophelias have *Crocus*, that's a whole album. (Sam H. 2023)

For Sam, these images are directly connected to questions of queerness and girlhood, specifically. In another moment, she put it this way:

> Not to be like "oh kids today have it easy"—cause that's not at all true—but there's something to be said for how mental illness and neurodivergence was treated when I was much younger versus how it's treated now. . . . It was very "you can't talk about this"—on top of being a female presenting person where it was like, "If you're crying,

> you're being hysterical, it's time to go sit in the corner." . . . There was also this real big push when I was younger . . . against girlhood . . . I remember having to be like, "Oh pink, I hate pink, I don't look at this pink stuff that I have, don't look at these flowers that I enjoy."
>
> But I also liked darker stuff too, like I have a squirrel vertebra in a little, you know [glass]. . . . I enjoy and embrace both, but because you do you feel kind of on a precipice of something. Having music that kind of sits in the middle of everything, where they're not afraid to talk about things that are dirty, they're not afraid to talk about things that make them upset, and in a way that *is* poetic. . . . It just seems to mirror the ways that I have felt and a lot of the imagery that I have enjoyed but was not allowed to—but now I can unabashedly love. And I will say too I think there's something about queerness that falls into that space as well. So for me, I happen to be bisexual . . . there's something about the yearning there and feeling this extra bit of alienation that I think women in particular are good at articulating. (Sam H. 2023)

Sam's compelling description links queerness, femininity/girlhood, and neurodivergence together with certain images, themes, and moods that are evoked by bands like the Ophelias, suggesting that she feels hailed by the ways that they tap into shared languages that signal acceptance and validation to listeners without ever being didactic. The Ophelias' particular approach pairs queer-coded iconography with obviously DIY modes of production to reinforce the queer-feminist affects of their music, amplifying their worldly orientations. The band's homemade dioramas and painted amulets not only invoke a feminist DIY ethos, but are also explicitly rendered via the aesthetics of crafting, which Ann Cvetkovich shows works in a feminist register that "combines art, politics, and everyday life to rework debates about domesticity" (2012, 159). Considered in this way, crafting is "a model for creative ways of living in a depressive culture" that in my reading overlaps with tarot and astrology as "ordinary form[s] of spiritual practice" (159). In so doing, crafting expands beyond its own feminist history to include queer and disability cultures invested in exploring new ways of grounding themselves in somatic practices of self-care, ways of being "more 'in the body' and less in the head" (168).

Sam's reflections help show how the Ophelias create queer-feminist affects that are related but not reducible to their musical content: using sight and sound, music and merch, vibe and inclination, the band orients listeners toward a sensibility held in common. And while this sensibility has always

Figure 12. Clockwise from upper left: The Ophelias, *Almost* album cover; hand-painted cursed amulets ("Yes, they come pre-cursed. Only good curses though :)"; "Rind" cover (diorama art by Spencer Peppet & Jo Shaffer, photo by @mikkocastano, VFX by @jojshaffer); Three of Swords T-shirt.

been feminist and queer, the band has also changed since first rehearsing at Mic's house, growing and putting experience under their fingers. Unreleased at the time of this writing, the Ophelias' upcoming *Spring Grove* demonstrates this growth as a full-throated articulation of the queer Midwest.

Fantasy/Reality | Midwestern/Queer

Spring Grove begins with "Open Sky," counted off in quintessentially Ophelias fashion: acoustic guitar strumming in two-beat harmonic rhythm (G, A, E, B), violin swirling a four-note loop, Peppet's low vocal range narrating a straight shot through the whirlwind, telling a story of nostalgia, power dynamics, and ambivalence about growing apart. But unlike past records, there is a muscular drive here that simultaneously preserves everything quirky about the band's music while also resting it on a sure foundation. Produced by Julien Baker and further evincing the centrality of queer support networks to this scene, *Spring Grove* sees the Ophelias' creative vision met and matched by a producer with shared sensibilities and mutual respect.

Compared to their previous efforts, the band spent much more time in the "demo" phase, working with Baker to choose the best tracks from a folder of ideas. "By the time we got to the studio it felt like we knew exactly what we wanted," said Peppet. "We still got to add a bunch of fun stuff and find new things there, but the base was solid." This kind of extensive collaboration demonstrates a kind of trust and creative synergy that the band hadn't experienced in the past; although everyone involved in the conversation was careful to avoid simplistic reductions, the band feels the different ways that men and not-men have interacted with them across the music industry. Whereas earlier projects were frustrated by the obtuse, domineering approach of male sound engineers, working with Baker seems to have been more reciprocal and creatively generative—it's had a profound and positive impact on the band.

SP: Not to be like "ohh men and women are *so different*!" But you know, working with Julien was like a completely different experience. She is just super thoughtful, super aware—almost like hyper-aware—and also is a queer woman from the South and she *knows what she's talking about.*

MA: Yeah, and I'm sure it's happened to her! So she just knows what to avoid. And it's also just the kind of person she is. She was very careful

> not to overstep, but wasn't reluctant to jump in and give her opinion. I think it just comes down to respect, honestly. I think she respects us and we respect her.

The result of this collaboration and these social dynamics is clear from the full-throated confidence of *Spring Grove.* At thirteen tight tracks, it retains all the whimsy of past efforts (the 3/4 lilt of "Parade," for example), but with more cohesive integration between the parts. Tracks like "Salome" and "Sharpshooter" are particularly gratifying for how they showcase the guitar, more forward in the mix, and with the kind of driving distortion only teased in the past. On "Open Sky" and "Spring Grove," tinted, sweeping melodies loop in irregular cycles, swept along by strings and held in paradoxical place by Adams's disjunct approach to the kit, here tuned lower, deep enough to hold everything. To my ear, Adams's drum parts always sound improvised, demonstrating a musical approach to the instrument that is all the more compelling for the fact that (apparently) they aren't. Such thoughtful complexities play with and against Shaffer's bass parts brilliantly, which often make beautiful tension out of extended chord tones and double stops, but also take turns in a more traditional role, anchoring the band when they really need to hit something. Throughout, the consistent presence of Gutmann Fuentes's violin both places the Ophelias in a lineage with other great feminist rock bands while also demonstrating new sonic possibilities: rather than jump in for a flashy solo (like that dog.), or grind away irreverently in order to invert the instrument's Western classical semiotics (like the Raincoats), Gutmann Fuentes takes an approach simultaneously more structural and more lyrical. Listen to how she swirls energy upward, in "Cicada," for example, or else widens the band's sound from below, stretching. Often, as here, the violin is the height of what makes a climax soar, an aching and unapologetic slide into that upper register for which the instrument is best known, but which is, with this band, kept in reserve.

While the Ophelias have always arranged their songs intricately, stitching together unlikely lattice, here they also groove in a way that feels new to me: "Salome," for example, begins with a distorted, off-beat riff that skips the energy onward, while Adams simply rocks on downbeats, creating an interlocking synergy. But while the track is structured around this ostensibly "straightforward" approach to riff-based rock music, it's full of clever and unexpected details, including the metric ambiguity created by the absence of the drumbeat at the very beginning, as well as Peppet's manipulation of both timbre and rhythm in the vocal line, which unpredictably and irregularly punctuates space only every two bars or so. In other words, it's not that distorted guitars or rock and roll drumbeats represent a departure in the band's approach to songwriting, but rather that the band has widened their range of sonic palettes and textures in both directions: the deep and driving on the one hand, and the ethereal floating on the other, both thicker and richer than I've heard before. In total, *Spring Grove* is a dark, tender, bittersweet, smart, and catchy album about how to make a world from feelings. It is by turns cinematic and delicate, fabulously groovy and subtly strange.

Despite its forceful stride, *Spring Grove* doesn't give way to one energy, instead remaining gorgeously caught in between worlds: fantasy and reality, adolescent exploration and wizened reverence for an old way of doing things. "The Ophelias definitely try to ride the line between the everyday, the mundane and the otherworldly and how those two cross over, how you can see yourself in all of those things," Peppet explained to Elysia Scholl in 2022. Years later, I see this imagery on the cover for *Spring Grove*, which features a gas station at twilight, the band all out of the car and lingering before whatever comes next, the banal and the dreamy merging into one. I read this description of "the mundane and the otherworldly" and think of Sam talking about experiencing both genders at the same time, which in turn reminds me of Sara Ahmed's "queer phenomenology," a term for describing how queerness manifests in part through the experience of feeling diagonal in the world, sideways in heteronormative space, moved to navigate this reality by the terms of another—and thus caught in between. This is all about liminality and contradiction, multiple worlds folding into a single experience.

That a Marathon station can glow with romance is perhaps uniquely intuitive for fellow Midwesterners, for those of us whose sense of romance is itself shaped by the kind of liminality evoked here, on the way somewhere else. And it is again that doubled sense of fantasy-in-reality that I think ultimately links the Midwest and the idea of queerness together, because to be peripheral is to see the border between one world and another. For queer theorists like Sara Ahmed, José Esteban Muñoz, and Kara Keeling, being queer in a heteronormative world means inhabiting two realities at once. It is the cross-eyed experience of navigating this world while also walking paths toward something different, another time, another place, but one which is somehow also the underside of this very moment. Neither fully imaginary nor present in our here and now, "we can glimpse the worlds proposed and promised by queerness in the realm of the aesthetic" (Muñoz 2009, 1), in the imaginings and world-buildings that come with finding our ways forward even as those paths themselves must be created. "Queer is, after all, a spatial term" (Ahmed 2006, 67), which is not to say that it is distinct from ourselves or exists somehow apart from us; rather, Ahmed's notion of queer phenomenology theorizes how "the orientations we have toward others shape the contours of space" (2006, 3), tracing queerness along the diagonal lines we follow when directed by desires oblique from the vertical alignment of compulsory heterosexuality. "Orientations shape not only how we inhabit space, but how we apprehend this world of shared inhabitance, as well as 'who' or 'what' we direct our energy and attention toward" (Ahmed 2006, 3). This work therefore theorizes the split-screen experience of queerness across spatial terms, where Muñoz does the same thing in temporal ones. Bringing the two together, Keeling writes, "A temporal mode 'always in the horizon,' 'queerness' also spatializes, even if only through the imagination of or the desire for it. Queerness produces horizons and, as Sara Ahmed points out . . . other spatial orientations" (Keeling 2019, 86). When I read this work, I think about the infrastructure of Ohio, which does not belong to its moment, abandoned, unsupported, and thus necessitating imaginative ways of going without. I also think about Midwestern psychogeography, on the periphery of something, askance from what we are constantly told to value. And while I don't want to suggest that the Midwest is inherently queer, there is a vibration between the kinds of non-normativities produced by Midwesternness and queerness for those of us who are sensitive to those overlaps, for those of us who might want to follow such sideways trajectories in order to imagine a different way to live—to "love what has been deemed unlovable."[11]

The Ophelias consistently plumb this zone of resonance. The music videos for "General Electric" and "Neil Young on High," for example, explore quotidian and spectacular Midwestern spaces, the first filmed at a high school football field (where the band subverts its function) and the second at the American Sign Museum (the weirdness of which, for anyone who's shopped at Jungle Jim's, somehow makes sense for Cincinnati). Fantastical spaces ("the black house," "the void," "the glow") merge with real locations in Cincinnati ("The Summit," "The Comet," "Wooster Pike") across lyrical evocations that combine with cinematic song structures to produce a world of feeling, a universe both real and imaginary at once. This both/and construction, as I have been suggesting, directly mirrors an experience of queer phenomenology, born from the inadequacy of the actually existing world, yet in the act of recognition fracturing it, providing a glimpse, a promise, a hint at a life lived otherwise, should you try to pursue it. This happens in particular ways in the Midwest, which requires dreaming, in the margins of experience,

11. Although I can't remember who precisely spoke it, this beautiful phrasing is how panelists formulated resonances between queer and Midwestern life in a session on the Black Midwest (Ervin et al. 2023).

when the conditions are just right. That kind of queer liminality can be disorienting, painful, and even violent. But it is also a vision out of which beautiful sounds emerge.

• • •

This is resonance: a synchronous sonority between "Midwest" and "queer" where the terms don't conflate but amplify one another's frequencies, if we know how to listen, over and against the common sense that understands them as opposed. To be in the Midwest is to fantasize so diligently that it becomes real, majesty blooming not in spite but because of the inadequacies of what's here. This is also what it means to live and to love queerly, insofar as the world's hostility requires dreaming as necessary for anything at all: fantasy in reality, both at the same time. Just one trouble in this formulation is how to sustain it, how to make a life without the infrastructure that would support it, how to fortify when the state or the "ruins of neoliberalism" encroach (W. Brown 2019), how to abandon love when you've decided that it's impossible to stay. Another increasingly universal dynamic to which the queer Midwest directs our attention might be the fragility of everything it makes, the many reasons why we might be forced to leave behind what we've built.

Final and Mostly Unapologetic Aside Having to do with My Life

And is it too indulgent now if I tell you that I grew up in a Cleveland suburb, spending an idyllic, lucky childhood in the unlikely but magnificent forests of its Metroparks? That some of my earliest memories already perceive the antiquated grandeur of its public institutions, and the dignity and kindness of the folks who keep them running today, in an era for which they were not built? Because I know there to be a certain tenuousness involved in building something beautiful here, a gossamer translucence that raises the dialectical problem of leaving-and-returning that always remains, and which Hanif Abdurraqib has written so overwhelmingly about, this writer who must be mentioned in any writing about Ohio from now on, whose work and thinking and kindness and community care I admire so deeply, a hero to all of us and someone in whom I see something of myself, though our stories are different.

My Ohio started in a radically privileged Cleveland, where I learned to love music and found friends to play it with, in basements or recital halls. Because I'm writing here about margins and peripheries, it feels important to tell you that it was in those early suburban days that I came to feel how liminal, anonymous spaces could be made magical as sites for hanging out: the most meaningful places in my memories are often empty golf courses, rooftops, parking lots, suburban sidewalks, strip malls, or patches of woods, still warm from our lingering there. It was thrilling to drive to University Circle and play in an orchestra or study percussion, to feel a part of something beyond the universe of high school, to feel like we were going places. But it is largely those empty, foggy roads I see when I think back to my time there, a serene stillness we filled with our laughter.

I spent my undergraduate years in Columbus, where I forged the kinds of strong and deep friendships that can be made under pressure. In the rare moments when my friends and I weren't practicing our instruments (or taking breaks from practicing), we tried on adulthood in fits and starts—first dates, downtown jam sessions, and the experience of what it means to know a city for the first time, to be able to compare it to where you've come from and to understand its cultural topography, different and the same, to know where to go or not go for pizza or music or stillness. Everything I studied at conservatory seemed to bottle itself up and come pouring out just as I finished. In the year after graduation, I started to feel what I might be like as a musician, what I might be interested in doing, though I imagined I had known all along.

I left, then, for a little while, and grieved in October, when the smell of Los Angeles air didn't change as I'd expected it to, as I'd experienced every October of every year of my life until then. I spent three years in California, which significantly influenced my life. I love and admire so many people I met during that time, but it's not quite an exaggeration to say that I raced back to Ohio as quickly as I was able—and I was just in time. When I returned to Cleveland, it was just a month after Hannah had also moved there, into the other side of a duplex I shared with some of my oldest friends. We overlapped in the city for around seven months—so dramatic and eventful, so overloaded with change—before she returned to Philadelphia and her PhD program. But it was long enough for us to find each other.

The next year, I returned to Columbus to start my own PhD. I stayed in the city for another five-year stint that deepened everything I had missed about it the first time through and simultaneously added an entirely new dimension on top. I began playing music again, which I had quit entirely from 2013 to 2014. The impression that I'd gotten from my time away—that my friends were doing big, exciting things—wasn't misguided at all; they were indeed growing up, building scenes, making art and music and love and infrastructure and attracting new, younger people in their wake. I was desperate to be a part of it, even as I was compelled forward in my academic work, pulled in two happy directions by people who cared about me and work that made me feel like my real and actual self.

In 2019, I accepted a job and defended my dissertation, each event within a week of the other. I moved to Cincinnati, which I had only visited during the summer of 2016, when Hannah worked at the Museum of Art. It was, as I intimated in the third chapter, a lonely seven months, what should have been a two-year gig curtailed not as much by COVID as by the rapacious, short-term thinking of the administration at Miami University. But I will never regret time spent absorbing the culture of Ohio's third great city, utterly distinct (as they all are),[12] and which helped me to know in yet further relief how geography can shape a sense of self. I made a record that year, and wrote a book, everything made possible by my communities, which grew as I added new friends. I was by turns deeply depressed and ebulliently joyful, held in such knowing by the people in my life, in my state, who were getting married and buying houses and sometimes having kids, but always in ways that shirked normative models of the good life and what Jane Ward calls the "tragedy of heterosexuality" (2020), their spaces oozing instead with their own idiosyncratic weirdness, their big-hearted, space-making refusal to give up their individuality or ambitions, their dreams just getting bigger or their own rooms in which to ferment.

I spent the debilitating uncertainty of lockdowns in Canton and then

12. As I have written elsewhere and about which I have opined incessantly to the annoyance of my friends, Ohio's three great cities represent three distinct cultural climates. In Cleveland, where a popular chain of soft serve shops is called "East Coast Custard," we don't tend to think of ourselves as a part of the Midwest at all. I remember how shocked I was when my L.A. friends laughed at this suggestion, how sincerely I had voiced it. But if it's a stretch to consider Cleveland of a piece with Pittsburgh (and by extension, at least technically, Philadelphia), then we at least feel more connected to Chicago, Detroit, and Minneapolis than we do Omaha, Des Moines, or Kansas City. It's a question of Great Lakes vs Great Plains, in my mind, but whether organized around the idea of the Rust Belt or topography or weather, Clevelanders often identify more with cities outside of Ohio than cities within it. Columbus, by contrast, is a quintessentially Midwestern city, so obviously indicative of middle America that chains like Burger King test new products there before anywhere. Long home of The Limited brands (Bath and Body Works, Victoria's Secret, et al.), Columbus's football culture and agrarian history position it as white and normative while the second or third largest university in America continues to help ensure a growing population—a feature unique among the three cities. Cincinnati, finally, is in the South. Its airport is literally in Kentucky, and many people commute to work from below that border. It takes less time to drive from Cincinnati to Louisville than to Columbus, and the culture reflects that fact, even as it insists on its own synthesis, its own blending of Appalachia, Midwest, and South in a way not dissimilar, come to think of it, to Pittsburgh.

upstate New York, with no clear way to return. But because someone looked out for me, by 2021 I was back in Columbus to see everything for myself, to huddle around fires in February, when roads were encased in ice for two weeks straight (but we lived close enough to walk over). Later, as the city blinked back on, Hannah and I landed full time work there, together, for the first time. We found a half of a small house in German Village with a porch swing and a busted-up patio. We moved all our things together for the first time in years, with new bookshelves or benches we had each bought ourselves while living apart, new to the other. We talked to the neighbors about my practicing in the basement and set aside time in the afternoon. We saw therapists to talk to about the academic and curatorial job markets, about the impossibility of continuing to try and the impossibility of quitting. We wrote and worked and went to our friends' exhibitions, in museums or galleries or houses or coffee shops. We traveled and returned, hosted parties with the front and back doors open. We went back to Pigeon Roost and Lynd's for pumpkins and apples, cooking them both down into goop for our freezer or someone else's. After nine years of on and off long-distance, we had carved out a little corner of a city in which I'd long dreamed of staying. I am still furious with Ohio for not finding a way to keep us.

I guess what I'm trying to tell you is that I didn't grow up with an inherited pride in this place but also that I have it anyway, because of the people who live there, because of the spaces that hold them and the imprints they leave. It's not buckeyes or Polish boys or chili dogs; it's not disdain for the coasts; it's definitely not a sports team, or whatever else is supposed to define life in the Midwest—especially not if it has anything to do with a particular version of nationalism; it's the people and the work, the accident of their doing it there and the reciprocality of staying somewhere that shows marks left in both directions: you in the place and the place in you. I'm saying that it could have been hot dish, but for me it's casserole, that I might have learned what intimacy means from walking the same route to school every day and knowing just what my friends would say when I told them what I saw along the way. I'm trying to tell you that I know the beauty of that place, and carry it, because perception is the same thing as embodiment. I have felt and studied and lived it. I have drunk enough Great Lakes Christmas Ale, spurting out of a keg, to make myself unable to eat for two days following. In better health, I have returned again and again for ebidon at Diaspora and ramen at Meshikou. I have waxed poetic outside the Bottle Shop, arms spread wider for each additional and serendipitous encounter. I have seen Vaughn at the Music Hall *and* the Women's Club. I have revisited favorite trees outside of what used to be International High School, have moved through exhaustion with Sahara's coffee and hookah. I have marched to the statehouse and occupied John Glenn International. I have spun out on icy freeways in the winter, driving from Columbus to Cleveland to ironically catch a train, which you cannot do in the *capital city* of the fucking state. I have taken first dates to Mama Santa's, talking of cavatelli while walking down the hill. I have played music with Pat Benatar at Cleveland State and with my friends at Severance Hall. I have lost tires to potholes and seen it hail in July. I have wept watching my oldest friend, a queer, Brown, socialist organizer, testify in front of the Cleveland City Council, imploring them to stand against the genocide of Palestinians in Gaza, knowing they were surrounded by comrades, who burst into applause as soon as time ran out, showing everyone in that chamber how radical and kind our communities are and directly refuting the fearmongering local news, who, instead of airing my friend's beautiful words, only talked about the council member who felt unsafe during peaceful demonstrations.

I have sat uncomprehending in Youngstown garages, listening in a circle of lawn chairs to Italian American dialect derived from Abruzzese and now so cured, so deeply rooted in this particular neighborhood, that no one else anywhere could know its meaning. I have befriended the mushroom foragers at the West Side Market, spent whole days walking across Cleveland's bridges out of sheer joy to be there, above the construction and the hollowed-out flats. I have vomited from the cold. I have heard folk music at the Barking Spider and grunge at the Happy Dog. Like Raechel Anne Jolie (2020), I first glimpsed a different way of living on Coventry, where I was old enough to be left there with my friends, but too young to understand why I was enchanted and romantic about it—or more accurately *pulled*, intoxicated by a possibility I couldn't articulate, the punk music spilling out of the Grog Shop, the "lesbian witches" at City Buddha, the world that existed between Mac's Backs and Record Revolution. I was too young in those days to see the original Pumpkins, but I was seventeen when Zwan came to the Agora, so swept up by it that I crowd-surfed that night, that one night, buoyed in multiple ways by my dear friend Tom, who introduced me to more music than anyone. When he came down from his turn above, one of his shoes had disappeared forever, an offering.

I have closed coffee shops in Cleveland and opened bakeries in Columbus. I have sampled spectacularly at Grandpa's Cheese Barn. I have shoveled snow for hours. I have scratched the beer cats at the 14–0 and stuck my face in the branches of trees as they glowed in autumnal luminescence, all up and down the residential streets of Clintonville, with its spookiest decorations up. I have heard beautiful, raw music played in a laundromat with giant holes in its walls, pipes for backdrops. I have had my mind changed about sweet pizza sauce by the Plank's on Sycamore. I have gladly dropped cash at Parable for transcendent coffee and fair wages. I have seen the most incongruous crowds of boomer regulars, Gen X misanthropes, and young, intimidated musicians alike, all bobbing their heads in Dick's Den to bluegrass or jazz standards or pop music or experimental noise, because the point is to be there in that place, to be cradled by wood turned black from decades, to be where you've been since *you* were that intimidated musician in the corner, following every note the most well-known or most obscure musician in town is playing and happy to pay $4 for a cover because that's also the most a drink is going to cost you—all night and a decade from now. I was not there on the impossibly tragic night that Max Williams was paralyzed by a bullet, but I have sat many times where he sat that night, and I cried for him.

I have heard radical poetry at Two Dollar Radio and Ace of Cups,[13] seen independent films at the Wex and the Gateway, bought academic books at Downbound and science fiction at Prologue. I have watched as my friends became the first-call musicians in their respective scenes, the institutions that once ignored them instead offering invitations, however self-serving. I have witnessed some survive what they should never have had to, becoming newly radiant. I have of course seen the Ophelias both at home and farther afield, their tours growing with time. I have felt their music connect me with people more intimately, like the sharing of a secret: my advisers, certainly, and my partner, friends I already knew (but grew closer to) and friends I only got to know because of how talking about bands can serve as a way into someone's life. I have shivered under chills reading Hanif or Raechel or Saeed Jones or Ruth Awad or for that matter Toni Morrison, each of whom knows how diverse Ohio is despite how it shows up in our media, how queer and radical, how aspirational and undeterred. I have so often paused to look around and marvel at the unlikely connections and divergent communities gathered in its backyards or breweries or markets. I have cried at the unlikeliness of it all, the fragility.

• • •

And this isn't to say that I have some kind of privileged insight about the state, and what I mean by invoking these experiences is the opposite of an appeal to authority. I am trying instead to describe my particular process of study, which I consider a synonym for love—to name some of the beauty I

13. Another connection between queer-feminist indie and tarot: Marcy Mays of Columbus's own all-woman punk band Scrawl opened Ace of Cups in 2011. It continues to host tons of indie bands who come through town, including, with some good regularity, the Ophelias.

have experienced and to call out to those who were there with me, who see the world like I do and who care about me. It is to say that I know the feeling of seeing us under attack and nevertheless living well. That I can say anything at all about the doubled existence of life in the Midwest is only by virtue of the fact that I have received the gift of community and have known its care, have tried to learn how to be worthy of it, and have come to know how that very care takes place within and sometimes directly through institutions that would sooner see us disappear, depending.

• • •

Spring Grove has its own themes, patterns, rhythms. It is not an album about the Midwest, or about any one thing at all; the band can tell you more directly than I can what it is—and they will. In my limited way, what I'm trying to do is reflect a bit on what the album does, for me personally, in the context of years of listening to this band, in the context of uprooting my life. I am hoping that this reflection also helps you listen for the wayward geography that the Ophelias' music helps bring into existence and makes me feel I belong to, the kind of Midwest I have lived and loved in, but which can also feel imaginary, as if I dreamed it. This is a place that can unspool itself anywhere, connecting people together at a fish fry, at a market, on a porch—and it does, it does this even now, linking me to a home that's as affective as it is material. I am hoping that in some ways my sense of belonging in that place might help to further think through the musical force of contemporary queer-feminist indie, even filtered through my narrow lens. In the end, maybe it was right all along that this book should be complicated by my own big feelings.

• • •

This chapter is about how the Ophelias perform the liminality and longing that characterizes a queer-Midwestern musical sensibility; it's also about the life experiences that help me become sensitive to those qualities, about what it feels like to catch something beautiful and to try to hold it, like a trick of light. Such moments make a kind of fragile floating, an ephemeral possibility that we might spend a lifetime following because in the experience of its recognition is voiced our longing for something beyond the place we have been put. A margin is an edge, a both-at-once possibility wherein the state of being ostracized also sharpens our boundary enough to cut through the fabric of normative space-time into some outside. A margin is a threshold.

• • •

In the end, I'm thinking again about fragility, how balancing on an edge becomes more difficult as time goes on. I'm thinking about the etymology of the word "periphery," from the Greek stems "bher" ("to carry") and "peri" ("around, about, beyond"), how our inability to maintain balance might be relieved by friends who can help take us where we want to go. I'm thinking about how the very moment when indie rock has made enough room for diverse artists so that Mic Adams, for example, can reflect on the feeling of being held in "a kind of safety net of queer artists, of women artists, artists of color"—how this is also exactly the moment when it has become all but impossible to sustain a career in a music industry utterly wrecked by algorithmic extraction, with bands absolutely wrung dry of any financial value and left to starve. I'm thinking about how Spotify's decision to demonetize 86 percent of its music coincides with Ticketmaster's full consolidation of the live performance industry, and how all this takes place in the context of a historic housing and cost-of-living crisis driven by those same predatory interests of asset managers, of shareholder value and finance capital, how scholars and musicians from Robin James (2023a) to Miki Berenyi (in Eastaugh 2022) have attested that what music needs to thrive is cheap rent and cheap shows, enough financial stability to try something out, to take a risk, how all of this music might disappear if we can't force our institutions to take care of people's basic needs.

I'm also thinking about fragility in my own life, so much of which is lived out on the road, between the two cities where I live and the third where I still play. Across so many of these trips I have wondered how much longer I'll be able to sustain a schedule that has me careening ten hours just to play one show, to stay two days in Columbus before heading back, which is stupid but which I will continuously do because I can't tell you what a privilege it is to play music with friends you first played with fifteen or twenty years ago, can't explain what it feels like to see them come into their own voices—the same as ever, but finally and fully realized after all manner of transitions and survival and growth—to be able to communicate on that level with them because of the history that we've shared. Or how it's a different version of the same thing when I sit up aimless until dawn with the same people I've known since I was twelve years old, having a new version of an old conversation strictly for the pleasure involved in being reminded of things about your own self you had long forgotten, of seeing someone see you that well. It's true that splitting time across disparate locations can make me feel unmoored and disjointed. But as I've loosely attempted to show in this chapter, holding onto what matters always requires living in multiple worlds at once.

• • •

After living in Columbus for something like a dozen years, when I finally heard Hanif read, it was ironically in Lawrence, Kansas. I was too nervous afterward to say much of anything, but I did get out that I had just moved to the area and was having a hard time with it. I later regretted the expectation I had raised, that he might have felt, to comfort me in that moment, wishing instead that we could have bonded over something and laughed, an impossible expectation to place on an interaction as one of 200 people in a line for autographs. But even though I imagine that he is buffeted constantly by such unvoiced wishes on the part of perhaps too-eager readers, he did of course oblige, signing the two books I carried "Ohio against the world" and "To Dan, with hope."

6 • *Infinite Worlds*

Vagabon's Kaleidoscopic Opacity

My folks get older every day
And my friends got bills they cannot pay
—NNAMDÏ[1]

Laetitia Tamko is a Cameroonian American multi-instrumentalist and producer performing under the name Vagabon. Of her debut LP, Father/Daughter records writes that "within the songs of Laetitia Tamko there are infinite worlds: emotional spaces that grow wider with time, songs within songs that reveal themselves on each listen," priming listeners to hear in Vagabon's music sonic explorations of the ways that emotions can extend outward, how feelings can grow so large as to become a world. This description of Vagabon's music stands out to me for how it mirrors many arguments made by affect theorists who are specifically interested in emotions. For writers like Sara Ahmed, emotions are not internally incubated as much as they are caught up in the influences of the outside world, entangled with and emerging through all sorts of life-stuff, whether material or ephemeral (Ahmed 2014). Likewise, Vagabon's music often meditates on the ways that everyday things elicit strong emotional responses, becoming imbued with the magic of another person, regardless of how blissful or devastating our encounters with them might be. The music video for "Cold Apartment," for example, shows sketched images of objects divided into three categories: "Things That Are Yours *(That I need to Give Back)*"; "Things That Are Mine *(But Remind Me of You)*"; and "Things That We Shared *(And I Still Have)*." A lamp, sneaker, iPhone cable, tea cup, set of keys, book (Octavia Butler's *Parable of the Sower*), and toothbrush take on both specificity in the context of the song's narrative, as well as universality, insofar as love may be the most common means by

1. From "Sudafed," track 15 on *Please Have a Seat (Deluxe)* (2023).

which we come to know how innocuous materials can become imbued with affective force, which is to say sentiment. Carrots, perhaps improbably included, testify to the freshness of the break, the immediacy or suddenness with which it must have struck the song's protagonist, left holding the physical metonyms of a relationship abandoned mid-stride.

In this chapter, I want to think about how Vagabon takes up space, sonic and otherwise. I speculate about how this space-making matters both aesthetically and politically, particularly to the degree that her music insists on prioritizing Tamko's exploration of emotional experience in a cultural context that has traditionally reserved public space for white feelings. Beyond the fact that certain songs in her oeuvre powerfully embody the Big Feelings aesthetic, Tamko's example helps to think through critical questions of genre, identity, and feminism in indie rock because, on the one hand, her example contributes a Black feminist perspective to the genre, still associated with whiteness in spite of critical historical contributions by people of color. On the other hand, Tamko also steps outside of that genre quite deliberately, challenging even tacit efforts to identify and categorize the music she makes. Connecting directly to chapter 4's discussion of queer diasporic aesthetics, I want to suggest that Vagabon utilizes what I call *kaleidoscopic opacity* to frustrate efforts to pinpoint what she does—including efforts invested in praising her for excelling as a symbol of diversity in an ostensibly homogeneous genre. But rather than attributing Vagabon's stylistic multiplicity to the current "postgenre" consensus, I suggest that Vagabon mobilizes genre out of a keen sense of its deeply entrenched status in American popular music, how tightly those notions remain sutured to social constructions of identity. Like "postrace" and "postqueer" politics, "postgenre" frameworks act out a fantasy of diversity and inclusion that only ever takes place through the (profitable) terms laid out by white neoliberal capitalism. Critiquing both genre and postgenre, I ultimately read Vagabon's work in conversation with Kapwani Kiwanga, a visual artist informed by Afrofuturism and postcolonial theory. Kiwanga's work raises questions of diaspora, indigenous knowledge production, and the spatiotemporal interval of queerness in ways that I suggest are directly invoked by Vagabon's music video for "Every Woman," from 2019.

"The Embers" and Black Queer Feminism

Before we arrive there, I want to linger with *Infinite Worlds* in order to better appreciate Tamko's subsequent movements. One of the tracks I hear as most directly performing the core Big Feelings sound, Tamko's 2017 single "The

Embers" is a powerful, expansive anthem with a slow tempo, creating all the more space to be filled in by feeling. "I feel so small," Tamko begins, as if to belie the explosion of sound, the big feelings to come—and they don't take their time, either; by the end of the first line, a scant eight bars long, the bedroom indie sensibility we first hear gives way to a full breakdown, unflinching eighth-note triplets hammered out by multiple guitars, overlapping and building. Right away, it is notable that the chords being hit so cathartically are merely two: Amaj7 and E, a back-and-forth vacillation that builds the entire song. Of course, given this book's emphasis on the major-seventh sonority, the central presence of A maj7 is significant here, a critical affective aspect of how "The Embers" swells into a sound-world. The centrality of this chord is further reinforced by the bass line, which not only consistently runs down a riff that includes the seventh but also introduces itself into the mix by landing pointedly—and then lingering—on that seventh. This cheeky introduction situates listeners immediately in an ambivalent affective zone: before any further developments help us to hear longing, nostalgia, heartbreak, or sweetness, we somehow perceive all options at once.

Once the song starts moving in earnest, its momentum never really abates. But this isn't to say that "The Embers" tells a story; instead, narrative drive is almost entirely avoided in both the lyrics and the harmonic progression, which totally eschews the standard (masculine) linearity inherent to the Western harmonic musical tradition. Rock music has long undermined the "standard" functional tendencies of tonal harmony; but particularly when combined with the other aspects of Tamko's performance, the circular movement between two chords—like Soccer Mommy's "Cool"—resonates with and exemplifies Big Feelings' rendering of non-masculine sensibilities, taking the time and interest to get inside a single feeling and in so doing rejecting the masculinist criticism of femininity as overly dramatic, making mountains out of molehills. In other words, to treat "small" feelings seriously—to give them their own space—is itself to critique masculine epistemologies organized around what is ostensibly rational, but what is actually an inability to intelligently navigate the world. On "The Embers," Tamko builds a sound-world big enough to hold the contents of her inner experience, spilling out in performance.

On the level of form, what narrative remains in the song is produced almost exclusively through the "soft/loud" dichotomy that Theo Cateforis has identified as central to '90s alternative (2022), a technique that further places "The Embers" in a lineage with the kinds of rock histories explored throughout this book. The nostalgic lean of the song is reinforced by the music video's low-fi haze, its subtle invocation of DIY, homemade signifiers.

At the same time, "The Embers" presents a story that is comparatively more ambiguous than many feminist rock precedents. "You're a shark that hates everything / You're a shark that eats every fish," Tamko sings. But how should listeners interpret these figures? How should we understand the "you" that is being characterized as a shark, in contrast to Tamko's description of the narrator—if not herself—as a fish?

Visually, "The Embers" oscillates around two kinds of scenes: the second we see is the more straightforward, where Tamko is seen singing in front of various aquatic locations (what looks like a pet store, a closed seafood restaurant, large aquarium tanks, and so on). The first scene viewers see is more enigmatic, and also undergoes slight variations each time it appears. Here, the visual framing is key: at these points in the video, Tamko appears situated in the middle of two rows of white men wearing only bathing suits and sleeping masks. This moment in the video happens almost right away, as Tamko sings, "I feel so small / My feet can barely touch the floor / On the bus where everybody is tall." On one level, then, this is a song about feeling out of place on public transportation, a context where it is notoriously commonplace for men to take up more space than they should. But the composition here is rather more striking than the general hostility of public spaces for women, queer folks, and people of color: the four men present on the bus literally frame Tamko, drawing attention to the space that she takes up in the center of the shot.

Beyond the obvious fact that we are listening to *her* music, Tamko's centrality is further reinforced when these same men, in a later scene, carry her on a kind of water rescue board—she is up on their shoulders, very casually held as the four men stand in a knee-deep pool. This kind of arrangement is familiar enough through popular culture depictions of royalty, where a queen is carried through the labor of her subjects. But I also think here about the extended music video for Kendrick Lamar's Black Lives Matter–era anthem, "Alright," where four white police officers carrying Lamar and company on their shoulders in a kind of reversal and pivotal turning point from the opening of the video, which foregrounds racialized police violence (1:55–2:36).

I'm not suggesting here that "The Embers" presents a vision nearly so stark or pointed as Lamar's; but I do see a limited parallel insofar as both music videos place their protagonists in the "unlikely" position of royalty, explicitly reversing the hegemonic relationship between (in the case of Lamar) Black people vis-à-vis the state, and (in the case of Tamko) Black people vis-à-vis indie rock—it is this formal similarity, rather than the actual stakes of the imagery, that I want to connect. Furthermore, it is notable that

Figure 13. Vagabon, "The Embers," screenshot from the video

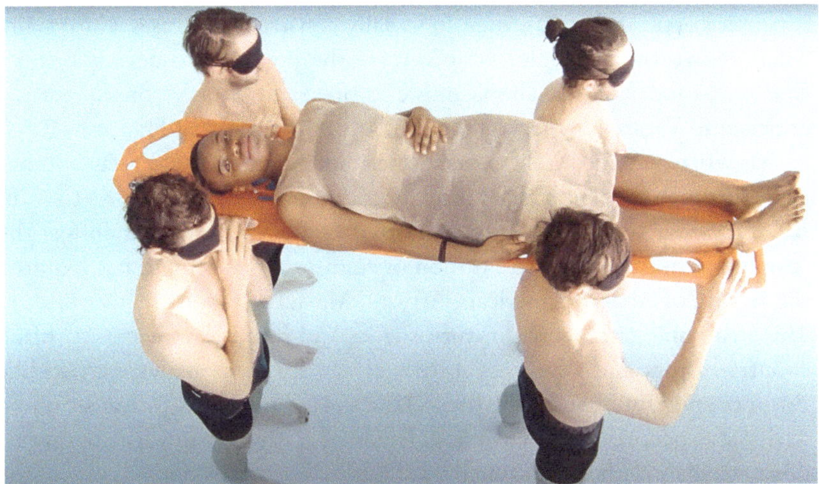

Figure 14. Vagabon, "The Embers," screenshot from the video

swimming pools and buses stand out as particularly fraught and historically meaningful sites of contestation around desegregation in the United States. If this helps us entertain the idea that "The Embers" is at least in part making a statement about race and identity, about genre and belonging, then it is easier to understand "the shark" and "the fish" on both interpersonal and broadly social levels. In keeping with the long tradition of Black cultural production—particularly from (queer) Black women—in which personal relationship narratives are also often metonymic for larger social relationships (Davis 1998), we can read lyrics about betrayal or hope as both love stories and as metaphors for Black resilience in the wake of ongoing systemic racism, with all its attendant consequences. On this view, while "the shark" might not literally stand in for white supremacy in the indie rock space, Vagabon's identity, career, and self-presentation in "The Embers" invite us to consider the work that she performs as a "small fish" intervening in a genre whose dominant representation in popular discourse still does not make space for people like her.[2]

As I wrote in the introduction, my suggestion that indie rock is "white" is meant to emphasize—rather than elide—the foundational, essential contributions of Black people and Black women specifically to rock music from its earliest moments. In other words, that rock remains white in public consciousness is not due to the actual history of the music, but rather to ongoing efforts that uphold and reinforce associations between rock music sounds and whiteness in ways that are arbitrary, contingent, and contested. Yet, if it is people's actions that continue to socially construct rock as a white genre when it isn't, other people's actions carry the potential to decouple those concepts—and I see Vagabon's music as one such effort. Consequently, I understand Vagabon's intervention similarly to the way that Francesca Royster has written about Black artists in the country music space, (yet) another genre in which the centrality of Black musicians has been erased over time. In *Black Country Music*, Royster writes that "creating and maintaining" the "commonsense and pervasive notion of country's white sound has required the erasure of African American, African, Mexican, and other histories. . . . This structural gatekeeping in turn shapes and limits fans' access to Black country history and awareness" (2022, 13). In Royster's analysis, artists like Beyoncé and Our Native Daughters claim a place in country by transforming what we expect of it, interweaving details of everyday life with sounds we don't associate with those same lives. And because music remains one of the key sites through which our understandings of identity are shaped, recentering Black people in country music or indie rock is never only about correcting the historical record: "Rather than simply asking for a place at the table, the artists in [*Black Country Music*] are using country music as a way of exploring a more complex Black identity" (175).

I suggest that we read Tamko's powerful indie rock music in the same

2. Connecting her experience as an engineering student to that of being an indie rock star, Tamko tells Katherine Cusumano, "Being the only one in the room doesn't freak me out. I also thrive off of proving people wrong. I'm a Scorpio." Cusumano continues, "So Brooklyn's insular music scene, which also tends to skew quite male (and quite white), didn't faze her at all. 'I was ready for it,' Tamko said" (in Cusumano 2017).

way: taken together, *Infinite Worlds* performs everything about how Tamko—and musicians like her—are reshaping rock into something other than what it has been since its appropriation and recoding as a paragon of white masculinity, claiming a right to the sonic, emotional, and professional space in the face of mainstream expectations that would deny or contradict that right. This space-making is inherently political, not only because Tamko is Black, but also because she is a woman, because she is queer, because she writes from her perspective in a way that bears on shared experiences of people like her. Furthermore, Tamko suggests that her experiences are connected to others', that there is something shared among marginalized groups—however limited and conditional—that can serve as a basis for community. Whether "trans or non-binary, immigrant, refugee, whatever . . . everybody who has been disenfranchised, or everybody who is oppressed and feels marginalised" shares a certain understanding about how power works, a certain feeling of alienation in which Tamko's careful, captivating music resounds (Tamko, quoted in Finn 2019).

The feminist affects generated by Vagabon's music are always already Black- and queer-feminist affects, resonating in ways that obviously overlap with the overall tenor of Big Feelings, while remaining at once distinct. It is important not to lose track of this distinction, for as I have been suggesting, Vagabon joins other Black women in indie (rock) spaces in demonstrating the political stakes of emotional vulnerability, challenging indie's implicit and explicit whiteness simply by virtue of making music. As Daphne Brooks, Angela Davis, Francesca Royster, and many others have shown, it can be radical for Black women to make music about their lives when that music sounds in a world that so systematically attempts to foreclose any such opportunities for self-expression. While Tamko's music does not explicitly foreground feminist politics, or even social struggle, her work as a musician is made political by the context in which it occurs.[3]

Returning to "The Embers," I want to think briefly through the climactic chorus to which the song eventually builds: here, a kind of refrain emerges, repeated in some form more than half a dozen times. The whole line—"Run and tell everybody that Laetitia is a small fish"—gets variously broken up and reiterated, so that the chorus ends up sounding:

Run and tell everybody
Run and tell everybody
Run and tell everybody that Laetitia is
Run and tell everybody

3. "Which is cool if they didn't make us talk about it" (Tamko, quoted in Coscarelli 2017).

Run and tell everybody
Run and tell everybody that Laetitia is
A small fish
A small fish
I'm just a small fish

These lines are compelling to me in part through the apparent contradiction between the exhortation to "run and tell everybody"—an excited, eager, loud prospect that seems to prepare listeners for big news—and the message being relayed, "that Laetitia is a small fish." This ostensibly pejorative descriptor stands at odds with the energetic affect conveyed with the message, frustrating straightforward interpretation with a counterintuitive construction.

Ultimately, two factors help me hear this whimsical message as one of defiance and space-making, rather than resignation and disappointment: first is the line's phrasing, which initially pauses just after the word "is," so that the line sounds like (and in the first two instances *is*) "Run and tell everybody / That Laetitia is." In this line, the "is" hangs, unresolved, apparently the end of a statement that simply asserts Tamko's existence, her identity, her being, and in that assertion claims space. This feels reminiscent to me of the kind of insistence Emily Lordi describes as central to soul (2020), where unapologetic pride in Black identity often took the form of repeated acts of self-assertion, resolutely drawing attention to the existence and value of the performers and the communities to whom they spoke.

Additionally, when, on its third iteration, the line extends itself to its full conclusion, the exuberant tone of Tamko's disclosure ("Laetitia is a small fish!!!!!") reads to me, against the backdrop of ascendant vocals and exultant guitars, as a kind of final casting-off of any preoccupations or anxieties around being who or what she is—in other words, it sounds to me that Tamko's (newfound?) sense of self-awareness has unburdened her, left her free to embrace what may be perceived as smallness by others, but which has ceased to bother her one way or another. There might even be a reclamation at play here, a reappropriation of past critiques, whereby Tamko's character identifies with the traits once used to diminish her, and which can therefore be held onto, nurtured, turned into a source of strength.

Vagabon, Genre, and Black Rock Aesthetics

Tamko's 2019 follow-up is a departure from *Infinite Worlds* insofar as it is much more consistently organized around synth sounds. In fact, only two songs foreground guitars of any kind: "In a Bind," which also features a violin, and "Every Woman," which I discuss below. Much more indicative of the record's energy is the single "Water Me Down," structured on top of a gentle four-on-the-flour kick, a lilting synth bass, and warbling, haunting echoes that indeed sound as if they're submerged. I am interested in this departure because of the ways in which the press hailed *Infinite Worlds* as a kind of announcement, a rare, even landmark entry from a Black woman onto the rock scene.[4] For this reason, in addition to being praised as a kind of avatar, Tamko also gets compared to other artists of color in the scene. "I get Tracy Chapman all the time," Tamko told Natty Bakhita Kasambala in 2017. "I get Nina Simone because I'm dark-skinned with a shaved head. I get Mitski because I'm a woman of colour and I must sound like her because why would we be two separate people?!"

As I read it, this quote is not about any effort on Tamko's part to distance herself from her contemporaries. Far from it, Tamko is proud of and deeply invested in her relationships with artists like Mitski, telling *NPR*'s Jenny Gathright that her group text with Miyawaki and Ashworth has "saved [her] life so many times" (2019). Further, "In the liner notes for *Vagabon*, Tamko credits them for being part of the 'chosen family' that made the record possible." I take this wording to be precise in its invocation of queer kinship networks. I also read it as indirectly referencing a different kind of queerness, which is the presence and in many ways ascendance of people of color in an indie rock space that continues to be dominated by white industry leaders.

Indeed, I don't think that any comparisons to other important artists of color are either wholly inappropriate or else the precise issue that Tamko raises in the above quote; what I think it suggests is exasperation with accumulated comparisons over time, some of which are undoubtedly reflexive and unthoughtful. An uncharitable reading of the Chapman comparison occurs when commentators simply link two (ostensibly rare) Black women who play guitar. More charitably, Chapman's work is often concerned with everyday and interior life in a way that resonates with Tamko's. But as if in part to prevent this easy reading, *Vagabon*—the album—takes a conscious step outside of the rock idiom. To think about this departure or deferral, I want to situate Tamko's records in a larger conversation about Black rock aesthetics, in part through a comparison with Tamko's contemporary, NNAMDÏ.

---

4. "That a black woman dares to create, especially in the #SoWhite world of indie rock, is revolutionary. But the revolution lies not just in Tamko's mere existence in the scene, but in her artistic intervention there: *Infinite Worlds* is the most powerful meditation on the politics of space I've heard since Solange's *A Seat at the Table*" (Gathright 2017).

Like Tamko, Nnamdï Ogbonnaya is a first-generation polymath straddling genre spaces. Like Tamko, Ogbonnaya studied engineering in college and has been subsequently involved in the music industry as composer, performer, and producer.[5] That is to say that while both musicians are impressive for how thoroughly they have seemingly mastered multiple genre styles, they are also impressive for how they produce their musical visions on both sides of the mixing board. For a quick introduction to Ogbonnaya's capacious approach to songwriting, let's briefly engage the first two tracks from his 2020 record, *BRAT*.

The first, "Flowers to My Demons" (FTMD), is structured around a shimmering and dexterous acoustic guitar riff over which Ogbonnaya develops haunting melodies across three octaves, at points oscillating between a low baritone and a high falsetto. The guitar here sits at the nexus of Midwest emo tonality and the math rock complexity from which it was inspired—filtered through Ogbonnaya's idiosyncratic and promiscuous musical background. Listeners may recognize something of the pained and hard-driving "Art School Crush" (2013), in a polished and subdued form; those less familiar might hear echoes of Dirty Projectors in the way that Ogbonnaya intercuts chords with rapidly moving connective lines. In any case, before it's possible to fully ground our ears in what's happening, the beat that Ogbonnaya introduced on the drums at around 1:30 has begun winding the song upwards, escalating in intensity with Dave Grohl–like bombast that the production choices have contained, just barely. The song reaches a high point just at the second before a final downbeat ends it—it feels premature on purpose, because this opening track is really part of an extended statement that the second track continues, elaborating through contrast.

The second track, "Gimme Gimme," begins *immediately* after the final harmonic in FTMD sounds, and following Ogbonnaya's live performances (NNAMDÏ 2022), should be understood as a kind of second movement, an extension of the record's opening statement. But as second movements go, "Gimme Gimme" seems designed to explicitly dash any listener expectations that FTMD may have established. Where FTMD unrolls a quirky and emotional guitar riff, "Gimme Gimme" immediately drops a trap beat, one of those weird ones that's played on a synth bass and can therefore slide around in between pitches, a kind of intergalactic sound that can be heard from St.

5. Insofar as we can still consider indie music bound up in the culture around college campuses, it seems notable that many of the artists performing contemporary Black rock come from immigrant families, which often (and stereotypically) place a strong emphasis on higher education; this was indeed the case for both Ogbonnaya and Tamko, who have each expressed appreciation for it in interviews.

Vincent ("Surgeon") to Jamila Woods ("GIOVANNI") to Vagabon herself ("Water Me Down"). What I'm trying to suggest by thinking about the transition between these two tracks is that they encapsulate something of Ogbonnaya's overall record, as well as his career: the stark and abrupt shift from emo-adjacent indie rock to psychedelic hip hop is indicative of Ogbonnaya's voluminous interests, his musical virtuosity, his ambition to excel in every part of the music-making process. I am positing a connection, in other words, between the fact that Ogbonnaya wrote all the music for *BRAT*, played nearly all of the instruments, and produced the record (on the one hand), and (on the other hand) the fact that the album itself spans multiple genres, creates magic out of more than one musical lineage. Connecting these ideas is an evident aspiration to do anything and everything and to do it damn well, which is to say, convincingly, in a style that feels hyper-authentic to the artist.

Another track that in itself exemplifies Ogbonnaya's omnivorous musical appetite is "Sudafed," from the deluxe edition of 2023's *Please Have a Seat*, a song about someone having a really hard day. Structured by a quirky synth riff that reminds me of Vampire Weekend, Ogbonnaya's pentatonic melody is filtered through a kind of auto-tune styling more indicative of hip hop from Lil Nas X. This latter association is further reinforced when the beat drops—it's a groovy, digital hip hop treatment that feels compelling at the same time that it's a strange fit for a song that's *so sad*. With a confident rhythm, Ogbonnaya narrates having an emotional breakdown on a train in a way that feels so intimate and real it's disorienting. But after just one verse with the drumbeat present, the entire song changes: the digital drums are replaced by a full acoustic kit, and the synth gives way to doubled, ascendant guitars in the style of Queen. Ogbonnaya doesn't sing during this classic rock breakdown; instead we get just two cycles through this apparently brand new song before the entire thing ends, two minutes and seventeen seconds with no resolution. What Ogbonnaya does in the space of this single, discrete track is the same thing he does with the entire *BRAT* record: it's a synthesis of ostensibly disjunct musical styles that cohere organically because of a specific life in music.

The connection I'm trying to make here is this: NNAMDÏ's approach to rock music—one that is both virtuosic and stylistically omnivorous—is exactly the kind of "Black rock aesthetic" formulated by Maureen Mahon in her 2004 book *Right to Rock: The Black Rock Coalition and the Cultural Politics of Race*. Building on the writing and music of Greg Tate, Mahon frames Black rock as an emphatic and polystylistic effort, in part, to speak back against simplistic reductions about blackness in US culture. Part and parcel of this capaciousness is Black rock's frequent embrace of technical virtuosity.

That is, for writers like Tate, Black rock tends to—needs to—perform those multiple styles better than other artists operating in just one.[6] Building on precedents from Bad Brains to Living Colour, Screaming Headless Torsos to the Roots, today, younger artists like Anjimile, Arlo Parks, Bartees Strange, Blackstarkids, Christelle Bofale, NNAMDÏ, Vagabon—who often come from and reflect a broad African diaspora—are filtering Mahon's Black rock aesthetic through more contemporary sounds; but there is a core idea that remains intact.

Mahon and Tate have both written about the critical social functions that this kind of Black rock performs, its self-evident virtuosity a powerful manifestation of Black excellence even in the face of resistance, its genre-spanning appetite aimed squarely at essentialist cultural assumptions that don't see blackness as appropriate for certain sounds and have some investment in keeping people in their respective places. From jazz and improvised music to the radical genre-smashing that birthed hip hop, the virtuosity and polystylism central to Black rock aesthetics are informed by the unbroken history of Black experimentalism in this country. Additionally, as George E. Lewis (2008) has written about the Association for the Advancement of Creative Musicians (AACM), a further function of being prolific across multiple genre spaces is the ability to resist being pigeonholed, pinned down, or dissected in the context of a critical apparatus with an investment in doing so, threatened by what it cannot contain.

Following this last point, I want to discuss this kind of Black rock through the idea of *kaleidoscopic opacity*: frustrating the glare of the spotlight not by hiding from it but by flourishing in spite of it, kaleidoscopic opacity guards against both critical dismissal and critical reduction by performing blisteringly, undeniably well, and across multiple styles. In this way, kaleidoscopic opacity is related to the same kind of genre promiscuity I discussed in relation to Mitski and SASAMI, in particular, and could well be a modality of expression common to and emerging from experiences of (queer) diasporic subjectivities. I introduce it in this chapter in order to note the longer history of purposeful obfuscation as a technique and explicit political posture on the part of African American musicians, from the very earliest days of what W. E. B. Du Bois called the "sorrow songs" straight through to the present.

6. "For as long as I can remember every conceptual breakthrough in Black music has been accompanied by a new superhuman evolution in technique and virtuosity of some kind. . . . I don't think this has ever been a virtuosity for virtuosity's sake thing but a virtuosity of expressive necessity—to say everything that demanded to be spoken about Black consciousness in any given era when the social space allowed Black bodies, minds, spirits was otherwise infinitely more circumscribed" (Tate 2012, 21).

In *Queer Times, Black Futures*, Kara Keeling takes up Édouard Glissant's notion of opacity in regard to film and cinematic imagery—but also music: "Glissant argues it is important for marginalized groups to 'insist' upon remaining opaque to the terms, languages, and logics of dominant groups . . . Within this context, 'unaccountability' marks a refusal to be bound to dominant standards of measure, recognition, and evaluation" (Keeling 2019, 46). If this impulse to reticence under the glare of the white press resonates with the present discussion, there are nevertheless multiple ways of throwing critics off the trail. One method for remaining inscrutable is to hide or obscure—another is to proliferate. Kaleidoscopic opacity does not darken the lens through which dominant society attempts to view Black art, but instead explodes it in refracted color. Moving in multiple directions at once—and beautifully—kaleidoscopic opacity frustrates any attempt to reduce, classify, bracket, or contain. It is too many things at once for that kind of imposition.

Where NNAMDÏ performs virtuosity, technical capacity, and visionary capaciousness within one album or even one track, Vagabon has explored different genres in two distinct records, taking time to build worlds. Aware of her project and her power, "Tamko describes *Vagabon* as a flex: she plays many of the instruments you hear on it, and she learned the digital audio software Logic Pro so she could produce it almost entirely on her own (she is the sole producer credited on all but one song)" (Gathright 2019). As to the stylistic departure, "Tamko describes the shift in sound as a 'rejection of being pigeonholed'" (Gathright 2019), saying, "I guess what I'm trying to say is that this album is me doing whatever the f*** [*sic*] I want because I can do whatever I want, you know?" (Tamko, quoted in Gathright 2019).

This insistence, and the opacity it produces, marks out a difference between Black rock aesthetics and postmodern/postgenre discourse. It's true that Black rock musicians are not the only ones mashing or bridging genre spaces; in fact, in some ways, this is more than anything an imperative in contemporary pop music, a reflection of the value that has been placed on both "omnivorous consumption" in the poptimist era (Peterson and Kern 1996; James 2017) as well as vibes-based appeals to genre transcendence. For contemporary postgenre discourse, genre labels have become passé in the same way that identity politics has—we are *better than* genre, in other words (which of course does not stop us from policing it when its boundaries are understood to be inappropriately transgressed).[7] But we need to understand those discourses as financialized fictions, just as we need to understand the

7. I am not so subtly invoking Lil Nas X here, and the removal of "Old Town Road" from the *Billboard* country charts. For more, see Hansen 2022, Molanphy 2023, and Royster 2022.

stylistic stretching long performed by Black rock aesthetics as a distinct intervention into those same profit-seeking modes. Just because postgenre discourse has become a kind of cultural norm does not mean that we should understand what Vagabon and NNAMDÏ are doing as analogous with an artist like Justin Bieber; in using multiple genres, styles, and associations within their work, artists like Vagabon and NNAMDÏ don't reflect the contemporary state of genre-less taste hierarchies as much as they assert a place for themselves in whatever tradition, pointing out the historical fact that the work of Black musicians has all along informed even ostensibly "white" popular music genres.

This maneuvering works because genre remains powerful, if more difficult to discern. For one thing, as Robin James has shown, artists of color get interpreted differently when they transgress genre spaces than when white performers do (2017). For another, and by extension, the discourse about postgenre popular music treats diversity in contemporary pop as desirable in the same way that "postracial" neoliberalism does: instrumentalizing (profitable, attractive, nonthreatening) identity discourse for its own purposes, "postgenre" discourse claims to be above arbitrary musical distinctions (and by extension, arbitrary identity positions) while implicitly operating from invisible center of whiteness. In this sense, diversity is incorporated selectively and on the terms of the mainstream liberal viewpoint. As James provocatively puts it, claims on behalf of contemporary pop music's postgenre status are tantamount to claims of a "postracial" US society: false, firstly, but also profitable for those in a position to benefit. Finally, James has more recently turned attention to the ways in which algorithmic modes of organizing sound—though ostensibly divorced from outdated genre distinctions—nevertheless continue to produce predictable inequalities insofar as they map themselves onto affective states, emotions, or moods (rendered legible via algorithmically generated playlists) that mirror normative power dynamics and assumptions in our culture (James 2024c). Ultimately, then, genre isn't disappearing as much as it is being repurposed; where categorization previously functioned as a gatekeeping mechanism, today it is more likely to be performatively overcome in pursuit of a different means of biopolitical regulation, the "mood/vibe/affect" vector that more closely aligns with the ways in which music has been financialized (James 2024c).

We need to understand the stylistic stretching long performed by Black rock aesthetics as distinct from this kind of postgenre discourse. Instead, I am claiming that artists like Vagabon evince Black rock aesthetics in order to articulate a critique of white supremacy by demonstrating how much significance we still attach to genre—albeit selectively—and then by transgressing those boundaries anyway. Indeed, Tamko implicitly rejects the idea that genres don't mean anything anymore—aren't any longer associated with ostensibly outdated identity positions—insofar as she leverages those genres precisely in order to comment on listener expectations. In other words, in order to confuse and frustrate mainstream readings of Black music, it still has to be a *surprise* to that same mainstream when Black artists stretch, perhaps especially (and ironically) when that stretching involves the rock genre. In order for their critique (Black musicians belong in every genre, Black musicians can do "whatever the fuck [they] want") to work—for it to be necessary to articulate in the first place—it has to be understood that some genres are gatekept as white, that we don't actually live in a postracial/postgenre world. The argument doesn't work if you think we've already arrived at a postgenre world, in which every multigenre work is simply postmodern methodology. Race, gender, nationality, and other identity markers are as tightly sutured to genre constructions as they've ever been—even as genres themselves are shifting and contingent cultural formations. Presented with the terms of these formations, artists like Vagabon refuse to stay in their lanes, or more to the point, rightly claim inheritance on behalf of all of them.

Every Woman

The "thesis" of 2019's *Vagabon* is the track "Every Woman," whose video shows Tamko alone in the woods, living inside of a clear plastic bubble. Though the too-familiar imagery of isolation depicted here might strike us as eerily prescient of the COVID-19 pandemic, there is quite clearly no crisis that has driven Tamko's character in the woods in this 2019 video; instead she seems calm, more at home than anything, moving serenely through a series of domestic activities—drying clothes, studying, making fire. On the video's release Tamko published a statement explaining:

> It's an ode to all those who feel different and who actively search and fight for space. When I was approached by Cameroonian filmmaker Lino Asana, I was really, really excited to work with an artist from my country. There was this immediate understanding of one another. So many scenes of this video feel reminiscent of my early life in Cameroon, the chores I would do as a kid, the way we lived simply and humbly. The bubble displayed in this video represents an invitation to find yourself in this world. (Tamko, quoted in Yoo 2019)

Figure 15. Vagabon, "Every Woman," screenshot from the video

In this quote, "those who feel different" don't have space readily available to them, don't have ready-made places or genres of activity that could help compose a space within which to thrive; instead, they have to "fight for space" by making it themselves. Here, Tamko implies that this kind of space-making has been made easier through collaboration in general, but also specifically with an artist who is also from Cameroon, an artist who perceives the world in the same way and who practices the same kind of place-making that Tamko does.

To recognize the "otherness" of oneself in relation to "the world" requires understanding how that world is defined by one dominant modality of being, how it is organized according to the needs and perspectives of a presumed straight-white-male inhabitant. Tamko has to find a space in the wilderness because there is no place for someone like her in the "real world," built as it is around the sensibilities of that minority so violently aware of its waning significance. "All the women I meet are tired," Tamko sings, indirectly but absolutely calling this world into relief, a world that renders men into things simultaneously incapable and demanding. Because of the very inadequacy of normative masculinity, women are required to pick up the slack, to make the world run. The critique here takes place so deftly that listeners who aren't on a wavelength might miss it altogether. On the other hand, those who understand need not be told. It is this latter group who allows Tamko to ultimately conclude that she is "not alone," even when on her own. There is, however inapparent it might seem in daily life or else a protective bubble, nevertheless a community in common.

While Tamko's statement on the video makes its politics clear enough, the imagery also resonates with several precedents across Black aesthetics and Afrofuturist discourses, specifically. Building on Saidiya Hartman's reading of the "nonevent of emancipation" as the state's insistence on "keeping blackness outside and in the field," Sarah Jane Cervenak and J. Kameron Carter write that "blackness remains outdoors even when brought indoors, even when brought into (settler) home ownership, into self-possession" because "having a home and some semblance of domestic life never really meant/means unencroachable citizenship" (2017, 47).[8] Likewise, for Keeling, this feeling of "homelessness at home" is an abyssal emergence occasioned by the "apocalyptic catastrophe" of the Middle Passage, persisting in new forms. "We are forged in its wake," she writes, improvising in the always already post-apocalyptic world that Afrofuturism has long theorized and disavowed.[9]

From the jump, then, Tamko's positioning herself in the forest is notable for the ways that it situates her within longer discourses about Black ontology and history. But pushing further, the clear plastic bubble specifically reaches outward, connecting to other works as a matter of shelter, habitat, or refuge. For example, resonant with Tamko's bubble as well as Afrofuturist critiques of the apocalypse are Kapwani Kiwanga's *Vivarium* installations, which I saw in Toronto's Museum of Contemporary Art in 2023. Consisting of clear, inflatable plastic, "each of the bulbous forms appears to have grown in symbiosis with a plant in mind, and they are fragile in and of themselves, governed by their own condition of being reliant on the air they contain" (MOCA Toronto 2023b). Beyond resonating with Tamko's enclosure, Kiwanga's vivariums are part of a series of projects that think through indigenous knowledge practices in ways that reconfigure lost understanding of the earth as a kind of Afrofuturist technology.

Not unlike Sun Ra, around whom Kiwanga produced the forty-three-minute *Sun Ra Repatriation Project* in 2009, Kiwanga has presented herself as "a galactic anthropologist from the year 2278" with a particular expertise in "earth civilizations" and "forgotten Earth-Star complexes in terrestrial memory" (in Steingo 2017, 4). Building on Afrofuturist traditions, Kiwanga connects visions of the future with unfulfilled promises (literally and figuratively) of the past:[10] "In the past, intercultural exchange was common

8. With thanks to Lauren M. Cramer for directing me to this work.

9. In this Keeling also brings to mind Christina Sharpe's "wake work" (2016), which theorizes the cataclysm of the Middle Passage as a singularity out of which we have not emerged.

10. Likewise, "That Sun Ra arrives in Oakland, California, in 1967 as a gift from the ancestors suggests that he appears to fulfill the terms of a long-ago dream, perhaps to redeem the freedom dreams of the ancestors—dreams of futures past" (Keeling 2019, 61).

Figure 16. Kapwani Kiwanga, "Vivarium: Apomixis," 2023 (foreground) "Vivarium: Adventitious," 2023, (background), PVC transparent, steel, color and MDF, installation view in *Remediation* at MOCA Toronto (courtesy the artist, Galerie Poggi, Paris, Galerie Tanja Wagner, Berlin, and Goodman Gallery, Cape Town, Johannesburg and London; © ADAGP, Paris / SOCAN, Montreal 2022; photo by Laura Findlay), https://www.gallerieswest.ca/magazine/stories/kapwani-kiwanga/

between planet Earth and various star systems" she said of *The Deep Space Scrolls* project in 2015, while also clarifying that the remnants of such systems can still be found in deep space (in Steingo 2017, 4). Her *Vivarium* sculptures thus echo the recovery of lost forms of knowledge—Black and Indigenous epistemologies assailed by settler colonialism—foregrounding plant cultivation as both futuristic technology and meditation on the ways in which "botany has long held a relationship to both exploitation and acts of resistance and how plant life has and may intervene in the rejuvenation of contaminated environments" (MOCA Toronto 2023a). Resisting what Stefano Harney and Fred Moten (2021) call "the first theft" of "rightful ownership" (13) over the earth—in other words, "global improvement, worldly usufruct" (15)—Kiwanga's inflatable vivariums, situated in an exhibition full of verdant green, remain empty. Therefore, "rather than controlling an archived specimen for human consumption, these are forward or future looking projections of what a vivarium may one day become; one where the plant is surrounded by a protective environment that it has the possibility to use as a structure for growth and support, rather than being enclosed, captured, and encased" (MOCA Toronto 2023b). The work of the *Vivarium* is, in other words, speculative, an opening of indeterminate outcome. In the same way that Tamko and the women about whom she sings rest from their labor, Kiwanga's empty infrastructures gesture towards the not-yet-here, the interstitial potentiality of queer futurity. As Keeling formulates, "the challenge in these speculative fictions is to create another world by spreading things and phenomena, including ideas and modes of embodiment and living, which are not recuperated into the familiar ones undergirding property, ownership, dispossession, white supremacy, and misogyny, as well as their attendant modes of propriety" (Keeling 2019, 68–69).

In service of this challenge, might Tamko and Kiwanga's enclosures open up the possibility of Black, queer, and feminist futures? "Might the limbo be an undisclosed iteration of that glistening transience itself, the 'fleeting character' of an other freedom?" (Cervenak and Carter 2017, 50). In opening space for such possibilities, Vagabon reaches out from the Big Feelings universe, expanding its remit while connecting with other nodes in the variegated constellation of Black experimentalisms and, in so doing, pointing a way forward. That this happens in community evinces the aspirations of an indie rock scene using disappointment to "furnish grounds for affective solidarity" (Marcus 2023, 13), refusing, in other words, the unbearable present, aware of its own inadequacy, earnestly reaching for another world by means both big and small, every day.

Outro

On March 31, 2023, the indie supergroup boygenius released an album long anticipated by fans of the kind discussed throughout this book. Five years earlier, Julien Baker, Phoebe Bridgers, and Lucy Dacus—whose individual careers in music were already accelerating—released a six-track EP after a brief period of mutual enchantment. "It was not *like* falling in love," Bridgers later clarified. "It *was* falling in love" (quoted in Zhang 2023). Expecting to record one track and leaving the studio with six, the EP seemed to represent potential that the band themselves weren't quite prepared to deal with.

Before *The Record* finally dropped, the music press started buzzing. Whereas many of the artists discussed in this book have established careers below a certain threshold of mainstream visibility (however one might define it), a series of major profiles was starting to make the situation feel as if it would be different for boygenius—that this would be something bigger, culturally, than a pristine indie record. Among these, *Rolling Stone*'s January feature stood out. Titled "How boygenius Became the World's Most Exciting Supergroup" (Martoccio 2023), the extensive profile was notable in part for how its accompanying photoshoot explicitly recreated Nirvana's iconic 1994 cover for the same magazine. By '94, Nirvana had already become overburdened by what the band represented in the cultural landscape: a new movement in rock history, uniquely reflective of the situation faced by an entire generation of Americans. To place boygenius in a similar posture therefore does more than allow them to continue commenting on the history of the rock canon (which it does, which they have); it also makes a statement about where the genre is going, particularly after a more than decade-long period in which rock has *not* been America's popular music genre.

Though the music of boygenius fits squarely in the aesthetic universe of Big Feelings artists, what sets their sound apart is the way that their coequal singing and songwriting makes unmistakably clear the collaborative, community-oriented approach central to so many working in this space. Many tracks on *The Record* soar as a result of the entwining of the three musicians' voices, and this kind of robust harmonization is a core feature of their songwriting. This is perhaps most clearly audible in the opening "Without You Without Them," a fully a capella prelude built from a thick texture of commingled voices. But as Carl Wilson noted in his *Slate* review, even in songs with a clear lead, that singer is just as likely to be singing someone else's lyrics as their own, as the distribution of writing labor is also a heavy mix of all three voices (Wilson 2023b). "Lifting each other up [is] how we create," Bridgers says in *Rolling Stone*. "We all get to be the lead. We all get the high of each other being in the front, which is so sick and has been the ethos of this band since day one" (Martoccio 2023).

This ethos is also demonstrated visually, for example, in the lyrics booklet, where each musician's handwriting indicates who was responsible for which lines. *The Record*'s cover meanwhile equalizes the bandmembers by on the one hand disembodying them, representing each musician with one of their arms alone; on the other hand, the group's deep and intimate relationships with one another are evoked in the arrangement of those arms, which in their reaching upward evoke the Three of Cups, a tarot card about community and sisterhood, a card that references both the liberating feeling of being able to let go of the world when immersed in friendship, as well as the kind of deep self-knowledge that can each come from so knowing another.[1] The tarot references, the sapphic love songs, the paradoxical tension of an anthem like "Not Strong Enough"—which feels as empowering as it does heartbreaking—collectively sound everything that Big Feelings aspires to name. It is an expression of queer community and the kind of mutual admiration that can make a mess out of categories of feeling, keeping us instead in the liminal place between platonic and romantic love, where both categories feel inadequate to the always-deferred opening that animates our desire. To my ear, what the music captures more than anything is the constitutive emptiness that attends any deep experience with those closest to us—any epic dinner party, getaway weekend, or aimless afternoon—the kind of unresolvedness or incompleteness that makes us feel that we are still missing something, even when together, which is nothing other than the animating desire to see those same people again, already, a preemptive missing. "Love, politics, suffering" (*Pitchfork* 2023)—as well as joy, friendship, desire, exploration, uncertainty, existential dread—*The Record* swells with an entire world of sentiments, per-

1. Indicative of the central importance of friendship to this band, I hear the Three of Cups in lines like "I remember who I am when I'm with you," from the fourth track, "True Blue." Additionally, it is relevant that Baker, Bridgers, and Dacus have matching band tattoos, two as of this writing, one of which is another interpretation of the Three of Cups iconography.

spectives, and feelings. But this record's queerness manifests perhaps most of all in its performance of the fragile, earth-shaking magic that can happen when you find your people, some other precious few who seem to vibrate on your frequency, and in the context of a world that convinced you that you were alone. *The Record* is about the difficulty of holding onto this feeling, the life situations that engender it, and the world-making change that it can produce. In a culture that makes no space for friendship, how can we hold onto it, even when it feels too overwhelming to understand? This is what makes fierce friendship radical, and part of how it can resound as a queer praxis by virtue of its context.

Nearly immediately after winning Grammy Awards for "best alternative album," "best rock performance," and "best rock song" in 2024, boygenius announced an indefinite hiatus. There is something symbolic in this, for me, because this is the only band I can think of to have achieved such mainstream success in the past decade with the kinds of explicitly indie rock sounds that have not been, across that same time period, very popular. While we can take the band at their word in terms of the reasoning, it also strikes me as something of a statement for them to disband after touring the one album responsible for their sudden ascent, asking us to interrogate why we seemed to cling so tightly to their example. In hindsight, it is almost as if they were trying to save us from witnessing their special kind of indie music become something other than what it had been: among other things, a moment in time.

The primary purpose of this book has been to take seriously an important moment in indie rock and the musical/social issues that matter for both its practitioners and its listeners. In offering this account, my first goal has been to do some justice to the communities who care about this music. Secondarily, I hope that *Big Feelings* has raised concepts, scholarship, and arguments that help to think through the complex entanglements between sound and social life, and which may have introduced readers to new material along the way. As I have said throughout, I imagine this work, ideally, as both generative and humble, resisting grand claims about either my own formulations or else the significance of the music. It's true that I hear the women and queer musicians at the forefront of contemporary indie rock challenging and changing what rock music is and sounds like, what it means and what it can do (and for whom). But at the same time—and as these artists are themselves aware—they are doing so in a long lineage of queer and feminist predecessors, who have continued to innovate in the genre, even if unnoticed. What's different about this particular moment, it seems to me, is that rock music is not the dominant force in popular music that it once was, that it has returned to its subcultural roots in part by virtue of the sheer dominance of other genres, from hip hop to country. By contrast, the closest rock music has come to the top of the charts in the past decade or so has been as a kind of reference or affect selectively deployed by major pop stars like Olivia Rodrigo ("Good 4 U"), Willow Smith ("Transparent Soul"), SZA ("F2F"), or Childish Gambino ("Lithonia"). This is to say both that rock music has not been the popular music genre of the past two decades (plus), and also that it remains a potent cultural force that can be tapped in a culture that at least ostensibly prizes omnivorous musical taste.

If genre characteristics still signify powerful ideas about self, identity, community, and value, it has been some time since guitar rock's connotations have spoken for the broadest coalition of the listening public. From this perspective, it may be rock's very irrelevance to the zeitgeist that has allowed for the current, thriving indie scene: beneath a certain threshold of popularity, the upside of indie bands' struggles to coordinate ever more aspects of their own careers has been the relatively autonomous space they have had—in the press, in broader media discourse—to explore, reformulate, and push indie music as they have seen fit. In marked contrast to the media environment in the '90s and 2000s, these innovations have happened largely outside the glare of a scrutinizing, patriarchal gaze; in an era when mainstream conversations around (post/popular) feminism and popular music have focused squarely on epochal figures like Beyoncé and Taylor Swift—dynamics unfortunately exacerbated by the near total collapse of alternative outlets for music journalism (of which *Pitchfork*'s downfall is only the latest example)—indie artists have been left largely to their own devices, which they have quietly used to remake the genre.

And yet, it is also true that a select number of these artists have risen out of their initial DIY contexts, playing larger venues, charting, and otherwise achieving mainstream markers of iconic music industry success. In 2022, for example, Mitski's *Laurel Hell* was the best-selling album in the United States during the week of its release, and hit number five on the *Billboard* 200, the first top-ten for an album from the label Dead Oceans. That same year, Mitski was nominated for an Academy Award for cowriting "This Is a Life," a key musical moment in the Oscar-winning film *Everything Everywhere All at Once*. Japanese Breakfast's mainstream breakout happened a year earlier, with the near simultaneous release of her critically acclaimed memoir, *Crying in H Mart*, and her third studio album, *Jubilee*, also widely praised. Based on a *New Yorker* essay with the same title, Zauner's memoir debuted at number two on the *New York Times* bestseller list, has continued to sell at high levels, and is currently being adapted into a film. For its part, *Jubilee* was nominated for four Grammy Awards, hit number fifty-six on the *Billboard* 200 list, and appeared on the list of "Top 50 Albums of 2021" at *Paste*, *NPR*, *Pitchfork*, *Rolling Stone*, *Slant*, *Stereogum*, *The Guardian*, and *Uproxx*, among others.

This kind of mainstream visibility raises questions about whether or not and to what extent the themes this book has traced might change when such bands become more tightly imbricated with the larger music industry, the record labels, venue behemoths, and other corporations responsible for the stratified and exploitative music industry landscape. This is a pertinent concern, especially given the degree to which performances of intimacy are a central component of indie's affective sense-construction: in other words, whether or not fans will be able to experience the kinds of almost private, close-knit community experiences that can happen at indie shows when artists like Mitski are selling out the Central Park SummerStage remains to be seen. But even if they can, experience and scholarship alike suggest that their experiences of mediated intimacy will differ in such larger venues (Stiegler and Campbell 2023). In a similar way, such newfound popularity puts pressure on the indie rock (sub)genre I've been concerned with theorizing in this book: when Big Feelings goes mainstream, does it also fall apart? It may well be the case, particularly if we read into the fact that Japanese Breakfast and Mitski have both found their new popularity through sounds that have moved away from overt indie rock characteristics. This is not to suggest that they have become in some way less "authentic" but only that their mainstream success and their shifts away from rock music have coincided, perhaps not coincidentally. As these artists continue to explore new creative paths, will listeners' relationships with this music correspondingly change?

Insofar as Big Feelings constitutes a semi-coherent phenomenon that emerged from a particular conjuncture in underground music, it seems in some ways inevitable that mainstream exposure would change how the music functions and resonates in our culture, as has been the case with most appropriations of independent music by dominant industry forces throughout music history. And yet, the music's social function may well remain intact: even as mainstream popularity introduces complications around who this music is for, the politics of Big Feelings have always been less about changing the world and more finding a way to live within it. It is not a nihilistic politics, but it also isn't revolutionary; it aims for the kind of recognition that listeners never see in global politics, and it treats the capacity to live with simple dignity as utopian, considering. This kind of recognition—the capacity to make listeners feel seen and heard—can certainly survive the transformations that follow fame.

Beyond the affective intervention I've called "Big Feelings," where indie rock goes from here remains a speculation: while the glare of the media's gaze complicates the aesthetic and political questions sketched out in this book, those questions are ones that will ultimately be answered by the listeners, searching in collectivity for sounds that affirm their existence. In any case and wherever this music goes, what will surely continue is the organization of people intolerant of the present around sounds that propose alternative futures, worlds of softness and care, of deep bonds and fabulous glamor, militant resistance and a refined sense for the magic of the quotidian. Anything but apathetic, Big Feelings musicians today pursue these utopian politics in nuanced, multifaceted ways—including music as just one mode of engagement, a juxtapolitical means of forming communities, and finding joy, of sustaining beauty amid the calamity of now.

Appendix A

The Bands

Below, I include an incomplete list of bands that I've encountered and which I hear as producing a Big Feelings affect throughout at least one record in their oeuvre. A series of Venn diagrams might be helpful for thinking about each band, but for the sake of space I will limit myself here to listing the bands that I hear as most squarely occupying a Big Feelings position, as well as the groups that share most qualities while taking a different approach with one or another category. This list, surely too short, is also reflected in the Big Feelings playlist (see appendix C) and includes:

Alice Phoebe Lou; All Dogs; Alvvays; Bachelor; beabadoobee; Beach Bunny; Big Thief; Black Belt Eagle Scout; Blondshell; boygenius; Broken Social Scene; Bully; Christelle Bofale; Daffo; Diet Cig; Fazerdaze; Francis of Delirium; Frankie Cosmos; Free Cake for Every Creature; Girlpool; GOON; Great Grandpa; Gum Country; Hana Vu; Hello Mary; Hiding Places, Hop Along; illuminati hotties; Indigo De Souza; Japanese Breakfast; Jay Som; Juliet Ivy; Julien Baker; Kate Davis; Lady Lamb; Land of Talk; Lucy Dacus; Lomelda; Mannequin Pussy; Mei Semones, Mitski; Momma; MUNA; Palehound; Phoebe Bridgers; Pictoria Vark, Pity Sex; P.S. Eliot; Remember Sports; Retirement Party; Rosie Tucker; SASAMI; Slow Pulp; Snail Mail; Soccer Mommy; Tanukichan; the Beths; the Ophelias; Title Fight; Trophy Wife; Vagabon, Van Dale; Waxahatchee; Wednesday; Wet Leg; Why Bonnie; Wolf Alice; Wye Oak; and Yuck.

Appendix B

(Some) Songs with the Big Feelings Progression

Alice Phoebe Lou: "Lover / / Over the Moon"
Anna Burch: "Can't Sleep"
Black Belt Eagle Scout: "Scorpio Moon"
Blueboy: "Clearer"
Broken Social Scene: "Cause=Time"
Fazerdaze: "Last to Sleep"; "Little Uneasy"; "Bedroom Talks"
Diet Cig: "Broken Body"; "Stare into the Sun"
Hana Vu: "Hammer"; "Alone"
i hate mirrors: "it hurts, now that you're gone"
Indigo De Souza: "Real Pain"
Jesus and the Mary Chain: "Just Like Honey"
Land of Talk: "This Time"
Mannequin Pussy: "I Don't Know You"
Phoebe Bridgers: "Kyoto"
Pity Sex: "Wappen Beggars"
Snail Mail: "Heatwave"
Soccer Mommy: "Cool"; "Royal Screw Up"; "Henry"
Vagabon: "The Embers"
Yuck: "Milkshake"; "Stutter"

Appendix C

A Note on the Playlists

As a part of this project, I've compiled two Big Feelings playlists, found at the following links:

1. https://open.spotify.com/playlist/3TtxcU7k3R64UIEUed4wn1?si=f02821537981498b
2. https://open.spotify.com/playlist/0JBqhOO0JSof8hOShuMc0m?si=f6b64d68623c46ef

Of these, the second requires more explanation.

At the risk of making it impractical to listen to, I've made the second playlist extensive for two reasons: first, I want it to be somewhat representative of the concept, which requires a lot of music. Taken together, it should help to orient listeners toward the sound this book is dedicated to unpacking. Second, the playlist is large because I hope that no matter how you come to this music—whether seasoned listener or recent fan—there will be something new for you. Although I have in select places taken care to order the tracks, because of its size, I would ultimately recommend that the whole thing be engaged on shuffle.

It should also be noted that not all of the music here fits into the "core" Big Feelings concept; as with the book itself, I felt it important to at least gesture at some of the history informing Big Feelings, some of the bands that sound important influences, or who share certain features while departing in other key ways from the principle aesthetic. In general, bands that are significant to the concept of Big Feelings get more tracks than bands who feel ancillary or tangential.

The first playlist is much more straightforward, and comprises only tracks that are explicitly discussed in the book. This list finds its truest expression when burned to disk or copied to cassette, shared earnestly and worn within an inch of its life. Alas, I fear the requisite knowledge may be lost to time, a tragedy made all the more so for how good the music is.

Finally, please note the absence of two of my favorite Pumpkins songs: "Here's to the Atom Bomb" (the *Judas Ø* version, not the one from *Machina II*), and one of my top-fives, the aching, lo-fi romance, "Slow Dawn." These are currently unavailable on Spotify, which I begrudgingly chose for its expediency. I do encourage you to seek them out otherwise.

Appendix D

Interview Methodology and Respondent Information

The ethnographic process engaged for this book is neither comprehensive nor objective, but rather reflects certain biases and tendencies that I feel ultimately aided in my understanding (but which are therefore important to clarify). I identified respondents for this project in one of two ways, either by reaching out to them directly via Instagram direct message (DM), or else by finding myself in relevant social situations wherein I surveyed folks in order to locate fans of this music. While it was easy enough to find fans of contemporary indie bands across my everyday encounters, the Instagram group was important in order to make at least some attempt to reach outside my personal sphere.

I decided to message folks on Instagram who commented directly on a given musician's Instagram post, showing appreciation or support. I further selected for accounts that seemed active, and were not private. Finally, I tried, but did not make systematic attempts, to message a diverse group of folks, based solely on what visual cues were available via their own posts. When I reached out, I invited them to share their thoughts about the music they love. The majority of accounts I messaged did not respond. But those who did expressed enthusiasm for the overall project, and an eagerness to speak with me about their favorite bands. From these messages, I set up Zoom or phone calls, asking interviewees a series of questions about who they are, why they gravitate toward the kind of music described in this book, and how they understand it, both musically and in terms of their own social lives.

The second group of respondents I found in more organic ways, through conversations with friends, colleagues, and students who either expressed eagerness to speak with me, or else volunteered the names of friends, roommates, and partners who were known to be fans of the music. Before giving a conference paper on this topic, or before teaching about indie rock in class, I would for example display a list of Big Feelings bands and suggest that anyone in the group who loved this music and wanted to talk with me about it might want to get in touch for a book that I was writing. We then set up Zoom or in-person meetings in the same way as the first group. Given that there was no incentive to sit down for an interview—as well as the fact that I work in academia—it is unsurprising that my respondent pool skews toward musicians, students, and other creative professionals who already tend to engage with the music on their own.

An additional note about interviewing my students: in all cases, when I spoke with my own students, it was strictly on a volunteer basis, based on their preestablished interest in the musicians I wanted to ask about. While I occasionally surveyed larger groups of students about their reactions to simple questions, all extended conversations were conducted outside of class time, and in a context that was established in advance as entirely divorced from their studies in my courses. I asked for and received consent from these students to be recorded and to have their responses represented in my academic work. Though all these students invited me to use their full names, I have chosen to keep their surnames anonymous to provide an extra degree of distance, which I feel is appropriate (if perhaps unnecessary).

Finally, I incorporate into this book sentiments gleaned from more atmospheric, less formal conversations many more people, folks I spoke with conversationally (at shows, in coffee shops, and so on) and who have helped inform my overall impressions of the indie rock scene from 2019 to 2024. Beyond these ongoing conversations, I conducted formal conversations with fifteen people, ranging from 20 minutes to 1.5 hours. Twelve of these respondents are white, two are Black, and one is Asian American. Eight respondents volunteered that they identify as members of the queer community, though it is possible that more identify as queer and did not choose to share that information. Two identified as neurodivergent, where two volunteered that they are medicated for anxiety and/or depression. Ten described a more generalized range of anxiety disorders. Six respondents were in their early twenties, one in his late forties, and six are otherwise between the ages of twenty-five and thirty-five. Eleven respondents work or have worked extensively in the arts, whether professionally or as students. I spoke with three undergraduate students and four graduate students, two STEM-field researchers, and one speech language pathology student.

When I asked for this kind of identifying demographic information, I did so in a general and informal way, so respondents only volunteered selective information based on what felt comfortable and relevant to them. Therefore,

I don't have complete or specific demographic information for each respondent, nor do I feel that it was important to do so. I present what I have again only to confirm my general sense that this small pool was largely representative of the kinds of Big Feelings fan communities I have encountered throughout the course of this project, whether in conference talks or at shows. Predominantly but not exclusively white, queer, college-educated, progressive, young, and involved in the arts, this group represents what I believe is a productive bias, demonstrating important trends across the fan communities who listen to this music. As I hope this book demonstrates, the investments and worldly orientations of such fans have been fleshed out in sharp and nuanced ways by each of these participants, to whom I am immensely grateful.

References

Abdurraqib, Hanif. 2024. *There's Always This Year: On Basketball and Ascension*. Penguin Random House.

Ahmed, Sara. 2006. *Queer Phenomenology: Orientations, Objects, Others*. Duke University Press.

Ahmed, Sara. 2013. "Making Feminist Points." *feministkilljoys*, September 11. https://feministkilljoys.com/2013/09/11/making-feminist-points/

Ahmed, Sara. 2014. *The Cultural Politics of Emotion*. 2nd ed. Edinburgh University Press.

Ahmed, Sara. 2017. *Living a Feminist Life*. Duke University Press.

Alcántara, Ann-Marie. 2024. "Everyone's Talking About Ohio. It Has Nothing to Do with Ohio." *Wall Street Journal*, August 21. https://www.wsj.com/lifestyle/ohio-slang-meme-gen-alpha-8c69a9e6

Alderton, Zoe. 2018. *The Aesthetics of Self-Harm: The Visual Rhetoric of Online Self-Harm Communities*. Routledge.

Anderson, Sini, dir. 2013. *The Punk Singer*. IFC Films.

Anderson, Stacey. 2022. "Mitski Doesn't Owe You Any Answers." *ELLE*, February 4. https://www.elle.com/culture/music/a38983880/mitski-asian-american-identity-essay/

Azerrad, Michael. 2001. *Our Band Could Be Your Life: Scenes from the American Indie Underground, 1981–1991*. Little, Brown.

Bachelor. 2021. "Doomin' Sun." Track 10 on *Doomin' Sun*. Polyvinyl Record Co.

Ballance, Laura, John Cook, and Mac McCaughan. 2009. *Our Noise: The Story of Merge Records, the Indie Label that Got Big and Stayed Small*. Algonquin Books.

Banet-Weiser, Sarah. 2018. *Empowered: Popular Feminism and Popular Misogyny*. Duke University Press.

Bannister, Matthew. 2006. *White Boys, White Noise: Masculinities and 1980s Indie Guitar Rock*. Routledge.

Bargetz, Brigitte. 2015. "The Distribution of Emotions: Affective Politics of Emancipation." *Hypatia* 30 (3): 580–96.

Baumgarten, Mark. 2012. *Love Rock Revolution: K Records and the Rise of Independent Music*. Sasquatch Books.

Beaumont-Thomas, Ben. 2022. "Mitski, the US's Best Young Songwriter: 'I'm a Black

Hole Where People Dump Their Feelings.'" *The Guardian*, February 4. https://www.theguardian.com/music/2022/feb/04/mitski-us-best-young-songwriter-im-a-black-hole-where-people-dump-feelings

Becker, Julia C., Lea Hartwich, and S. Alexander Haslam. 2021. "Neoliberalism Can Reduce Well-Being by Promoting a Sense of Social Disconnection, Competition, and Loneliness." *British Journal of Social Psychology* 60 (3): 947–65.

Bell, Sadie. 2022. "A Starter Kit for Getting into the Indie-Rock Favorite Mitski." *thrillist*, February 4. https://www.thrillist.com/entertainment/nation/best-mitski-songs-albums

Bennett, Andy. 2008. "'Things They Do Look Awful Cool': Ageing Rock Icons and Contemporary Youth Audiences." *Leisure/Loisir* 32 (2): 259–78.

Benshoff, Harry M. 1997. *Monsters in the Closet: Homosexuality and the Horror Film.* Manchester University Press.

Berlant, Lauren. 1998. "Intimacy: A Special Issue." *Critical Inquiry* 24 (2): 281–88.

Berlant, Lauren. 2000. "The Subject of True Feeling: Pain, Privacy, and Politics." In *Transformations: Thinking Through Feminism*, edited by Sara Ahmed, Jane Kilby, Celia Lury, Maureen McNeil, and Beverly Skeggs. Routledge.

Berlant, Lauren. 2008. *The Female Complaint: The Unfinished Business of Sentimentality in American Culture*. Duke University Press.

Berlant, Lauren. 2011. "Public Feelings Salon with Lauren Berlant." Barnard Center for Research on Women, May 10. YouTube video, https://www.youtube.com/watch?v=rlOeWTa_M0U

Berlant, Lauren. 2022. *On the Inconvenience of Other People*. Duke University Press.

Berman, Stuart. 2009. *This Book Is Broken: A Broken Social Scene Story*. House of Anansi Press.

Bernard, Zoë. 2024. "It Shouldn't Be So Hard to Live Near Your Friends." *Vox*, July 23. https://www.vox.com/even-better/354903/it-shouldnt-be-so-hard-to-live-near-your-friends

Bethune, Sophie. 2019. "Gen Z More Likely to Report Mental Health Concerns." *Monitor on Psychology* 50 (1): 20.

Bevan, David. 2008. Review of *Some Are Lakes*, by Land of Talk. *Pitchfork*, October 1. https://pitchfork.com/reviews/albums/12235-some-are-lakes/

Blistein, Jon. 2022. "Sasami's Heavy Metal for Soft Souls." *Rolling Stone*, January 14. https://www.rollingstone.com/music/music-features/sasami-squeeze-artist-you-need-to-know-1281087/.

Bikini Kill. 1991. "Riot Grrrl Manifesto." In *Bikini Kill Zine 2*.

Bimm, Morgan. 2022. "Girl Music of the Indie Rock Persuasion: Amplifying Indie Through 2000s Girl Culture." PhD Dissertation, York University.

Boak, Sara. 2015. "Mother Revolution: Representations of the Maternal Body in the Work of Tori Amos." *Popular Music* 34 (2): 296–311.

Born, Georgina. 2005. "On Musical Mediation: Ontology, Technology, and Creativity." *Twentieth-Century Music* 2 (1): 7–36.

Born, Georgina, and Andrew Barry. 2018. "Music, Mediation Theories, and Actor-Network Theory." *Contemporary Music Review* 37 (5–6): 443–87.

boygenius. 2023. "Without You Without Them." Track 1 on *The Record*. Interscope.

Brintnall, Kent L. 2007. "Re-Building Sodom and Gomorrah: the Monstrosity of Queer Desire in the Horror Film." *Culture and Religion* 5 (2): 145–60.

Broken Social Scene. 2002. "Almost Crimes." Track 4 on *You Forgot It in People*. Arts and Crafts.

Brooks, Daphne A. 2021. *Liner Notes for the Revolution: The Intellectual Life of Black Feminist Sound*. Belknap Press.

Brown, Shelina. 2014. "Scream from the Heart: Yoko Ono's Rock and Roll Revolution." In *Countercultures and Popular Music*, edited by Sheila Whiteley and Jedediah Sklower. Ashgate.

Brown, Shelina. 2018. "Yoko Ono's Experimental Vocality as Matrixial Borderspace: Theorizing Yoko Ono's Extended Vocal Technique and Her Contributions to the Development of Underground and Popular Vocal Repertoires, 1968–Present." PhD Dissertation, University of California, Los Angeles.

Brown, Shelina. 2023. "Two Nights at the Hollywood Bowl: Yoko Ono Revivalism and Asian American Women's Visibility in the Post-Pandemic Era." Paper presented at the International Association for the Study of Popular Music conference, June 27 (Minneapolis).

Brown, Wendy. 2019. *In the Ruins of Neoliberalism: The Rise of Antidemocratic Politics in the West*. Columbia University Press.

Browne, David, Jon Dolan, Jon Freeman, et al. 2022. "100 Best Debut Albums of All Time." *Rolling Stone*, July 1. https://www.rollingstone.com/music/music-lists/100-best-debut-albums-of-all-time-143608/

C., Beth. 2023. Interview with the author, October 30.

Capetola, Christine. 2020. "'Gimme a Beat!': Janet Jackson, Hyperaurality, and Affective Feminism." *Journal of Popular Music Studies* 32 (4): 95–117.

Caramanica, Jon. 2017. "Women Dominating Rock: There's More to the Conversation." *New York Times Popcast*, September 11. https://www.nytimes.com/2017/09/11/arts/music/popcast-women-rock-bands.html

Caramanica, Jon. 2022. "Mitski, In and Out of the Spotlight." *New York Times Popcast*, February 16. https://www.nytimes.com/2022/02/16/arts/music/popcast-mitski.html

Carson, Anne. 1995. *Glass, Irony, and God*. New Directions.

Cateforis, Theo. 2022. "Soft/Loud." American Musicological Society Lecture Series at the Rock and Roll Hall of Fame, December 15. Video available at https://education-44.wistia.com/medias/r3384z2h24

Cateforis, Theo, and Elena Humphreys. 1997. "Constructing Communities and Identities: Riot Grrrl New York City." In *The Music of Multicultural America: Performance, Identity, and Community in the United States*, edited by Kip Lornell and Anne K. Rasmussen. University Press of Mississippi.

Cavanagh, David. 2024. *The Creation Records Story: My Magpie Eyes Are Hungry for the Prize*. 2nd ed. Faber and Faber.

Centers for Disease Control and Prevention. 2023a. "CDC report shows concerning increases in sadness and exposure to violence among teen girls and LGBQ+ youth," *NCHHSTP Newsroom*, archived February 22, 2024, at https://web.archive.org/web/20240222130931/https://www.cdc.gov/nchhstp/newsroom/fact-sheets/healthy-youth/sadness-and-violence-among-teen-girls-and-LGBQ-youth-factsheet.html

Centers for Disease Control and Prevention. 2023b. "Mental Health." *CDC*, archived February 14, 2024, at https://web.archive.org/web/20240214084055/https://www.cdc.gov/healthyyouth/mental-health/index.htm

Cervenak, Sarah Jane, and J. Kameron Carter. 2017. "Untitled and Outdoors: Thinking with Saidiya Hartman." *Women and Performance: A Journal of Feminist Theory* 27 (1): 45–55.

Chatterjee, Rhitu. 2023. "The Mental Health of Teen Girls and LGBTQ+ Teens Has Worsened Since 2011." *NPR*, February 13. https://www.npr.org/2023/02/13/1156610138/the-mental-health-of-teen-girls-and-lgbtq-teens-has-worsened-since-2011

Christgau, Georgia. 1995. "The Girls Can't Help It." In *Rock She Wrote: Women Write About Rock, Pop, and Rap*, edited by Evelyn McDonnell and Ann Powers. Plexus. Originally published in *The Village Voice*, October 30, 1978.

Ciccone, Vanessa. 2020. "'Vulnerable' Resilience: The Politics of Vulnerability as a Self-Improvement Discourse." *Feminist Media Studies* 20 (8): 1315–18.

Clein, Emmeline. 2020. "The Smartest Women I Know Are All Dissociating." *Buzzfeed News*, November 20. https://www.buzzfeednews.com/article/emmelineclein/dissociation-feminism-women-fleabag-twitter

Clement, Brett. 2020. "Convention and Invention in Harmonic and Melodic Theories for Rock Music." In *The Bloomsbury Handbook of Rock Music Research*, edited by Allan Moore and Paul Carr. Bloomsbury.

Coates, Norma. 1997. "(R)evolution Now? Rock and the Political Potential of Gender." In *Sexing the Groove: Popular Music and Gender*, edited by Sheila Whiteley. Routledge.

Coates, Norma. 1998. "Can't We Just Talk About Music: Rock and Gender on the Internet." In *Mapping the Beat: Popular Music and Contemporary Theory*, edited by Thomas Swiss, John Sloop, and Andrew Herman. Blackwell.

Coates, Norma. 2003. "Teenyboppers, Groupies, and Other Grotesques: Girls and Women and Rock Culture in the 1960s and early 1970s." *Journal of Popular Music Studies* 15 (1): 65–94.

Cobain, Kurt. 1992. Liner Notes to *Incesticide,* by Nirvana. DGC Records.

Cohen, Cathy J. 1997. "Punks, Bulldaggers, and Welfare Queens: The Radical Potential of Queer Politics?" *GLQ: A Journal of Lesbian and Gay Studies* 3 (4): 437–65.

Cohen, Cathy J. 2019. "The Radical Potential of Queer? Twenty Years Later." *GLQ: A Journal of Lesbian and Gay Studies* 25 (1): 140–44.

Cohen, Sara. 1997. "Men Making a Scene: Rock Music and the Production of Gender." In *Sexing the Groove: Popular Music and Gender*, edited by Sheila Whiteley. Routledge.

Cornish, Audie, Connor Donevan, and Cyrena Touros. 2020. "Soccer Mommy on 'Color Theory': 'I Want To Keep Growing Until I Hit the Ceiling.'" *NPR*, March 5. https://www.npr.org/2020/03/05/808956494/soccer-mommy-on-color-theory-i-want-to-keep-growing-until-i-hit-the-ceiling

Coscarelli, Joe. 2017. "Rock's Not Dead, It's Ruled By Women: The Roundtable Conversation." *New York Times*, September 1. https://www.nytimes.com/2017/09/01/arts/music/rock-bands-women.html

Coscarelli, Joe, Caryn Ganz, Jon Caramanica, and John Pareles. 2017. "Women Are Making the Best Rock Today. Here Are the Bands That Prove It." *New York Times*, September 5. https://www.nytimes.com/interactive/2017/09/05/arts/music/25-women-making-best-rock-music-today.html

Creed, Barbara. 1993. *The Monstrous Feminine: Film, Feminism, Psychoanalysis*. Routledge.

Crenshaw, Kimberlé Williams, Luke Charles Harris, Daniel Martinez HoSang, and

George Lipsitz, eds. 2019. *Seeing Race Again: Countering Colorblindness Across the Disciplines*. University of California Press.

Cusumano, Katherine. 2017. "Girl of the Moment: Laetitia Tamko, AKA Vagabon, Has This Indie Rock Star Thing Under Control." *W*, February 22. https://www.wmagazine.com/story/laetitia-tamko-vagabon-musician-infinite-worlds-the-embers

Cvetkovich, Ann. 2003. *An Archive of Feelings: Trauma, Sexuality, and Lesbian Public Cultures*. Duke University Press.

Cvetkovich, Ann. 2012. *Depression: A Public Feeling*. Duke University Press.

Dahlman, Ian. 2009. "'A Big Beautiful Mess': Collectivity, Capitalism, Arts & Crafts, and Broken Social Scene." Master's Thesis, Ryerson and York University.

Davies, Helen. 2001. "All Rock and Roll Is Homosocial: Representations of Women in the British Rock Music Press." *Popular Music* 20 (3): 301–19.

Davis, Angela Y. 1998. *Blues Legacies and Black Feminism: Gertrude "Ma" Rainey, Bessie Smith, and Billie Holiday*. Vintage Books.

Dawkins, Lucy, dir. 2015. *My Secret World: The Story of Sarah Records*. Yes Please Productions.

de Boise, Sam. 2014. "Cheer Up Emo Kid: Rethinking the 'Crisis of Masculinity' in Emo." *Popular Music* 33 (2): 225–42.

de Clercq, Trevor. 2017. "Embracing Ambiguity in the Analysis of Form in Pop/Rock Music, 1982–1991." *Music Theory Online* 23 (3). https://mtosmt.org/issues/mto.17.23.3/mto.17.23.3.de_clercq.html

de Clercq, Trevor. 2019. "The Harmonic-Bass Divorce in Rock." *Music Theory Spectrum* 41 (2): 271–84.

de Clercq, Trevor. 2021. "The Logic of Six-Based Minor for Harmonic Analyses of Popular Music." *Music Theory Online* 27 (4). https://mtosmt.org/issues/mto.21.27.4/mto.21.27.4.de_clercq.html

De Souza, Indigo. 2021. "Hold U." Track 8 on *Any Shape You Take*. Saddle Creek Records.

DiPiero, Dan. 2022. *Contingent Encounters: Improvisation in Music and Everyday Life*. University of Michigan Press.

DiPiero, Dan. 2023. "'I Wanna Be That Cool': Soccer Mommy's Big Feelings." *Journal of Popular Music Studies* 35 (2): 39–65.

Doktor, Stephanie. 2024. "On the Failure of White Feminism: When PJ Harvey and Björk Covered the Rolling Stones' 'Satisfaction.'" *Journal of the American Musicological Society* 77 (1): 103–62.

Dolan, Emily I. 2010. "'. . . This Little Ukulele Tells the Truth': Indie Pop and Kitsch Authenticity." *Popular Music* 29 (3): 457–69.

Doll, Christopher. 2017. *Hearing Harmony: Toward a Tonal Theory for the Rock Era*. University of Michigan Press.

Dresch, Donna. 1995. "Chainsaw." In *Rock She Wrote: Women Write About Rock, Pop, and Rap*, edited by Evelyn McDonnell and Ann Powers. Originally published in *Jigsaw*, winter 1989.

Du Bois, W. E. B. 1999. *The Souls of Black Folk*, originally published 1903. W. W. Norton.

Duggan, Lisa. 2011/2012. "Beyond Marriage: Democracy, Equality, and Kinship for a New Century." *The Scholar and Feminist Online* nos. 10.1–10.2 (Fall/Spring). https://sfonline.barnard.edu/beyond-marriage-democracy-equality-and-kinship-for-a-new-century/

Dumas, Raechel. 2018. *The Monstrous-Feminine in Contemporary Japanese Popular Culture*. Palgrave Macmillan.

Dunn, Kevin, and May Summer Farnsworth. 2012. "'We ARE the Revolution': Riot Grrrl Press, Girl Empowerment, and DIY Self-Publishing." *Women's Studies* 42 (2): 136–57.

Eastaugh, David. 2019. "Sarah Records Special with Michael White," show notes. *C86 Podcast*, November 5. https://www.c86show.org/e/sarah-records-special-with-michael-white/

Eastaugh, David. 2022. "Miki Berenyi-Lush & Piroshka." *C86 Podcast*, September 11. https://www.c86show.org/e/miki-berenyi-lush-piroshka/

Eidsheim, Nina Sun. 2015. *Sensing Sound: Singing and Listening as Vibrational Practice*. Duke University Press.

Ervin, Keona K., Terrion Williamson, Crystal Moten, Erik McDuffie, and Ashley Howard. 2023. "Black Midwestern Solidarities." Conference Roundtable at the American Studies Association (Montréal).

Factora, James. 2019. "This Musician's 80s-Inspired Indie Rock Is Quietly Revolutionary." *them*, August 23. https://www.them.us/story/jay-som-anak-ko-interview

Factora, James. 2024. "A Terrifying 300 Anti-LGBTQ+ Bills Have Already Been Introduced in 2024." *them*, January 19. https://www.them.us/story/300-anti-lgbtq-bills-state-legislatures-aclu

Ferguson, Sarah. 2012. "Kurt Cobain and the Politics of Damage." In *The Rock History Reader*, 2nd ed., edited by Theo Cateforis. Routledge.

F., Deanna. 2022. Interview with the author, September 20.

F., Sarah. 2022. Interview with the author, October 11.

Finn, Rachel. 2019. "Standing in the Way of Control." *Line of Best Fit*, October 10. https://www.thelineofbestfit.com/features/interviews/vagabon-reinventon-interview-2019

Fisher, Laura. 2013. "Minor Feelings." *New Inquiry*, July 1. https://thenewinquiry.com/minor-feelings/

Fisher, Mark. 2009. *Capitalist Realism: Is There No Alternative?* Zero Books.

Foucault, Michel. 1997. "Friendship as a Way of Life." In *Ethics: Subjectivity and Truth*, edited by Paul Rabinow. New Press.

Fonarow, Wendy. 2006. *Empire of Dirt: The Aesthetics and Rituals of British Indie Music*. Wesleyan University Press.

Fournier, Karen. 2015. *The Words and Music of Alanis Morissette*. Praeger.

Frith, Simon, and Angela McRobbie. 1990. "Rock and Sexuality." In *On Record: Rock, Pop, and the Written Word*, edited by Simon Frith and Andrew Goodwin. Routledge.

G., Dan. 2022. Interview with the author. October 11.

Gaar, Gillian G. 2002. *She's a Rebel: The History of Women in Rock and Roll*. Seal Press.

Gale, Emily. 2023. "How Olivia Rodrigo Produced a Powerful Teen Girl Album." *Raidió Teilifís Éireann*, October 5. https://www.rte.ie/brainstorm/2023/1002/1408480-olivia-rodrigo-guts-album-teenage-girls-music/

Garrison, Ednie Kaeh. 2000. "U.S. Feminism-Grrrl Style! Youth (Sub)Cultures and the Technologics of the Third Wave." *Feminist Studies* 26 (1): 141–70.

Gathright, Jenny. 2017. "Vagabon's *Infinite Worlds* Meditates On The Politics Of Space." *NPR*, February 16. https://www.npr.org/2017/02/16/515241684/first-listen-vagabon-infinite-worlds

Gathright, Jenny. 2019. "'There Will Be No Darkness': Laetitia Tamko On The Making Of *Vagabon*." *NPR*, October 15. https://www.npr.org/2019/10/15/757514260/stream-laetitia-tamko-on-the-making-of-vagabon

Geffen, Sasha. 2020. *Glitter Up the Dark: How Pop Music Broke the Binary*. University of Texas Press.

Gill, Rosalind, and Shani Orgad. 2018. "The Amazing Bounce-Backable Woman: Resilience and the Psychological Turn in Neoliberalism." *Sociological Research Online* 23 (2): 477–95.

Godin, Geneviève. 2022. "Monstrous Things: Horror, Othering, and the Anthropocene." *Post-Medieval Archaeology* 56 (2): 116–26.

Goh, Ronald. 2020. "Beabadoobee On Her Biggest Influences, the Iconic 90s, and Growing Up." *Popspoken*, September 22. https://popspoken.com/music/2020/09/beabadoobee-on-her-biggest-influences-the-iconic-90s-and-growing-up

Goldfine, Jael. 2017. "Sad Girls, Bad Girls: 'Sadgirl' Indie Rock Cultures of Public Feeling as Alternative to Girl Power." Honors thesis, Cornell University.

Goldfine, Jael. 2019. "The Rise of the Vulnerable Heroine." *Paper*, April 3. https://www.papermag.com/vulnerable-heroine-kesha-lady-gaga-beyonce-2633185821.html#rebelltitem2

Goodman, William. 2017. "Pavement's *Slanted and Enchanted* Turns 25: Why the Smart-Ass, Slacker Masterpiece Is the Definitive Indie Rock Album." *Billboard*, April 20. https://www.billboard.com/music/rock/pavement-slanted-and-enchanted-album-indie-masterpiece-7767802/

Gopinath, Gayatri. 2018. *Unruly Visions: The Aesthetic Practices of Queer Diaspora*. Duke University press.

Gottlieb, Joanne, and Gayle Wald. 1994. "Smells Like Teen Spirit: Riot Grrrls, Revolution, and Women in Independent Rock." In *Microphone Fiends: Youth Music, Youth Culture*, edited by Andrew Ross and Tricia Rose. Routledge.

Grajeda, Tony. 2002. "The 'Feminization' of Rock." In *Rock over the Edge: Transformations in Popular Music Culture*, edited by Roger Beebe, Denise Fulbrook, and Ben Saunders. Duke University Press.

Great Grandpa. 2019. "Human Condition." Track 9 on *Four of Arrows*. Double Double Whammy.

Grover, Stacy Jane. 2023. *Tar Hollow Trans: Essays*. University Press of Kentucky.

H., Sam. 2023. Interview with the author. November 20.

Haddon, Mimi. 2020. *What Is Post-Punk?: Genre and Identity in Avant-Garde Popular Music, 1977–82*. University of Michigan Press.

Hakimian, Rob. 2019. "Vagabon Interview: 'The Reason That I Want to Hold Space in the Music Industry Is So That Other People Like Me Can Follow.'" *Saved by Old Times*. Originally published on *The 405*, October 21. https://savedbyoldtimes.com/features/2019/10/21/vagabon-interview-the-reason-that-i-want-to-hold-space-in-the-music-industry-is-so-that-other-people-like-me-can-follow

Hamori, Kate. 2023. "'It's Brutal Out Here': Adolescence, Betrayal, and Vulnerability in Olivia Rodrigo's *SOUR*." *American Music Perspectives* 2 (2): 198–207.

Hansen, Kai Arne. 2022. *Pop Masculinities: The Politics of Gender in Twenty-First Century Popular Music*. Oxford University Press.

Harney, Stefano, and Fred Moten. 2021. *All Incomplete*. Minor Compositions.

Hartzman, Karly. 2022. Liner notes for *Mowing the Leaves Instead of Piling 'em Up*, by

Wednesday. Bandcamp, March 11. https://wednesdayband.bandcamp.com/album/mowing-the-leaves-instead-of-piling-em-up

Harvilla, Rob. 2023. *60 Songs That Explain the '90s*. Hachette.

Hayes, Jerika O'Connor. 2023. "Sad Girl Music as Complaint Collective: Joanna Newsom's *Have One on Me* and Mitski's *Puberty 2*." Master's thesis, University of Cincinnati.

Hesmondhalgh, David. 1999. "Indie: The Institutional Politics and Aesthetics of a Popular Music Genre." *Cultural Studies* 13 (1): 34–61.

Hibbett, Ryan. 2005. "What Is Indie Rock?" *Popular Music and Society* 28 (1): 55–77.

Hiwatt, Susan. 1971. "Cock Rock." In *Twenty Minute Fandangos and Forever Changes: A Rock Bazaar*, edited by Jonathan Eisen. Random House.

Hofman, Ana. 2020. "The Romance with Affect: Sonic Politics in a Time of Political Exhaustion." *Culture, Theory and Critique* 61 (2–3): 303–18.

Hogan, Marc. 2007. Review of *Applause Cheer Boo Hiss* EP, by Land of Talk. *Pitchfork*, March 28. https://pitchfork.com/reviews/albums/10029-applause-cheer-boo-hiss-ep/

Holmes, Jessica. 2023. "Billie Eilish and the Feminist Aesthetics of Depression: White Femininity, Generation Z, and Whisper Singing." *Journal of the American Musicological Society* 76 (3): 785–829.

hooks, bell. 2002. *Communion: The Female Search for Love*. HarperCollins.

Hopper, Jessica. 2021. "Emo: Where the Girls Aren't." In *The First Collection of Criticism by a Living Female Rock Critic*, revised and expanded ed., 257–64. Farrar, Straus and Giroux. Originally published In *Punk Planet* #56, July 2003.

Horowitz, Juliana Menasce, and Nikki Graf. 2019. "Most U.S. Teens See Anxiety and Depression as a Major Problem Among Their Peers." *Pew Research Center*, February 20. https://www.pewresearch.org/social-trends/2019/02/20/most-u-s-teens-see-anxiety-and-depression-as-a-major-problem-among-their-peers/

Houston, Taylor Martin. 2012. "The Homosocial Construction of Alternative Masculinities: Men in Indie Rock Bands." *Journal of Men's Studies* 20 (2): 158–75.

HRC Staff. 2023. "Ohio House Passes Multiple Anti-LGBTQ+ Bills; Human Rights Campaign Condemns Passage & Urges Against Senate Passage." Human Rights Campaign, June 22. https://www.hrc.org/press-releases/ohio-house-passes-multiple-anti-lgbtq-bills-human-rights-campaign-condemns-passage-urges-against-senate-passage

Huang, Vivian L. 2018. "Inscrutably, Actually: Hospitality, Parasitism, and the Silent Work of Yoko Ono and Laurel Nakadate." *Women and Performance: A Journal of Feminist Theory* 28 (3): 187–203.

Huang, Vivian L., and Summer Kim Lee. 2020. "Contingency Plans: An Introduction." *Women and Performance: A Journal of Feminist Theory* 30 (1): 1–19.

@indigofaraway. 2022. "Stop sleepwalking through it all," Instagram post, November 3. https://www.instagram.com/p/Ckg5dyOvxjv/?img_index=3

Iyer, Vijay. 2002. "Embodied Mind, Situated Cognition, and Expressive Microtiming in African-American Music." *Music Perception: An Interdisciplinary Journal* 19 (3): 387–414.

Jacques, Alison. 2001. "You Can Run But You Can't Hide: The Incorporation of Riot Grrrl into Mainstream Culture." *Canadian Women's Studies* 20/21 (4): 46–50.

Jaggar, Alison M. 1989. "Love and Knowledge: Emotion in Feminist Epistemology." *Inquiry* 32 (2): 151–76.

Jagota, Vrinda. 2018. "How Taylor Swift Inspired Soccer Mommy's Emotional Indie-Pop," *Paper*, July 6. https://www.papermag.com/soccer-mommy#rebelltitem20

James, Robin. 2015. *Resilience and Melancholy: Pop Music, Feminism, Neoliberalism*. Zero Books.

James, Robin. 2017. "Is the Post- in Post-Identity the Post- in Post-Genre?" *Popular Music* 36 (1): 21–36.

James, Robin. 2018. "Poptimism and Popular Feminism." *Sounding Out!*, September 17. https://soundstudiesblog.com/2018/09/17/poptimism-and-popular-feminism/

James, Robin. 2020. "Music and Feminism in the 21st Century." *Music Research Annual*, no. 1: 1–25.

James, Robin. 2023. *The Future of Rock and Roll: 97X WOXY and the Fight for True Independence*. University of North Carolina Press.

James, Robin. 2024a. "Antonoffied Pop Vs Brat & The Stakes of Elite Musical Taste in Pop's Girlboss Era." *It's Her Factory*, August 18. https://www.its-her-factory.com/2024/08/antoniffied-pop-vs-brat-the-stakes-of-elite-musical-taste-in-pops-girlboss-era/.

James, Robin. 2024b. "Introduction to *GOOD VIBES ONLY*." *It's Her Factory*, August 23. https://www.its-her-factory.com/2024/08/introduction-to-good-vibes-only/

James, Robin. 2024c. "Musical Genre Is Not Disappearing." *It's Her Factory*, January 16. https://www.its-her-factory.com/2024/01/musical-genre-is-not-disappearing/

James-Wilson, Matthew. 2020. "What It's Like to Be Black in Indie Music." *Pitchfork*, September 28. https://pitchfork.com/features/article/what-its-like-to-be-black-in-indie-music/

Jewell, Katherine Rye. 2023. *Live from the Underground: A History of College Radio*. University of North Carolina Press.

@john.roseboro. 2023. "No more cool people 🤢🙅♀🧊❄️/Only warm people 😊🙆♀❤️🔥." Instagram post, October 16. https://www.instagram.com/p/Cyd5-rMuxNY/

Jolie, Raechel Anne. 2020. *Rust Belt Femme*. Belt Publishing.

Jolie, Raechel Anne. 2024. "Girl Culture Panic and the Failures of Feminism." *radical love letters*, January 9. https://raechelannejolie.substack.com/p/girl-culture-panic-and-the-failures

Kasambala, Natty Bakhita. 2017. "Introducing Vagabon: 'This is who I am. My music is what I'm offering.'" *gal-dem*, archived July 22, 2024, at https://https://web.archive.org/web/20240722113615/https://gal-dem.com/introducing-vagabon-i-music-im-offering/

Kearney, Mary Celeste. 1997. "The Missing Links: Riot Grrrl–Feminism–Lesbian Culture." In *Sexing the Groove: Popular Music and Gender*, edited by Sheila Whiteley. Routledge.

Kearney, Mary Celeste. 2017. *Gender and Rock*. Oxford University Press.

Keeling, Kara. 2019. *Queer Times, Black Futures*. New York University Press.

Keenan, Elizabeth K., and Lisa Darms. 2013. "Safe Space: The Riot Grrrl Collection." *Archivaria*, vol. 76 (Fall): 55–74.

Khanna, Vish. 2023. "Land of Talk." *Kreative Control* podcast, October 10. http://vishkhanna.com/2023/10/10/ep-808-land-of-talk/

Kopcienski, Jacob A. 2023. "Sounding Queer Appalachia." PhD dissertation, Ohio State University.

Kornbluh, Anna. 2024. *Immediacy: Or, The Style of Too Late Capitalism*. Verso.

Kristeva, Julia. 1982. *Powers of Horror: An Essay on Abjection*. Translated by Leon S. Roudiez. Columbia University Press.

@ladylambjams. 2021. "I am beside myself to wake up to this article today in @gomagazineny by @samrosefromthedead." Instagram post, October 21. https://www.instagram.com/p/CVTIS-9FxaC/?hl=en

L., Alyssa. 2022. Interview with the author. October 11.

L., Stephen. 2022. Interview with the author. September 15.

Lee, Summer Kim. 2019. "Staying In: Mitski, Ocean Vuong, and Asian American Asociality." *Social Text* 37 (1): 27–50.

Lee, Summer Kim. 2020. "Asian Americanist Critique and Listening Practices of Contemporary Popular Music." In *The Oxford Encyclopedia of Asian American Literature and Culture*, edited by Josephine Lee. Oxford University Press.

Lewis, George E. 2008. *A Power Stronger Than Itself: The AACM and American Experimental Music*. University of Chicago Press.

Lifter, Rachel. 2019. *Fashioning Indie: Popular Fashion, Music, and Gender*. Bloomsbury.

Lindau, Elizabeth Ann. 2016. "'Mother Superior': Maternity and Creativity in the Work of Yoko Ono." *Women and Music: A Journal of Gender and Culture*, no. 20: 57–76.

Liu, Runchao. 2019. "Visions of China: Avant-Orientalism, Art Rock, and Conflicted Otherness." *Cinéma & Cie* 19 (33): 107–20.

Liu, Runchao. 2021. "Sounding Orientalism: Radical Sounds and Affects of Asian American Women Who Rock." PhD Dissertation, University of Minnesota–Twin Cities.

Lorde, Audre. 1984. *Sister Outsider: Essays and Speeches*. Crossing Press.

Lordi, Emily. 2013. *Black Resonance: Iconic Women Singers and African American Literature*. Rutgers University Press.

Lordi, Emily. 2020. *The Meaning of Soul: Black Music and Resilience Since the 1960s*. Duke University Press.

Lustig, Caitlin, and Hong-An Wu. 2022. "Tarot as a Technology of Care." *Interactions* 29 (4): 24–29.

M., Destiny. 2023. Interview with the author, November 16.

M., Katie. 2022. Interview with the author, September 30.

Mahon, Maureen. 2004. *Right to Rock: The Black Rock Coalition and the Cultural Politics of Race*. Duke University Press.

Mahon, Maureen. 2020. *Black Diamond Queens: African American Women and Rock and Roll*. Duke University Press.

Maiden, Beth. 2019. Foreword to *Queering the Tarot*, by Cassandra Snow. Weiser Books.

Manalansan IV, Martin F., Chantal Nadeau, Richard T. Rodríguez, and Siobhan B. Somerville. 2014. "Queering the Middle: Race, Region, and a Queer Midwest." *GLQ: A Journal of Lesbian and Gay Studies* 20 (1–2): 1–12.

Marcus, Sara. 2010. *Girls to the Front: The True Story of the Riot Grrrl Revolution*. Harper Perennial.

Marcus, Sara. 2023. *Political Disappointment: A Cultural History from Reconstruction to the AIDS Crisis*. Harvard University Press.

Martoccio, Angie. 2023. "How boygenius Became the World's Most Exciting Supergroup." *Rolling Stone*, January 19. https://www.rollingstone.com/music/music-featu

res/boygenius-julien-baker-phoebe-bridgers-lucy-dacus-the-record-interview-1234660514/

Massumi, Brian. 2002. *Parables for the Virtual: Movement, Affect, Sensation*. Duke University Press.

Massumi, Brian. 2015. *Politics of Affect*. Polity Press.

Masters, Jeffrey. 2020. "Chani Nicholas Explains Why Queer People Love Astrology." *Advocate*, January 7. https://www.advocate.com/women/2020/1/07/chani-nicholas-explains-why-queer-people-love-astrology

McCammon, Sarah, and Candice Wang. 2022. "Sasami Finds Catharsis in Nu-Metal on Her New Album *Squeeze*." *NPR*, February 27. https://npr.org/2022/02/27/1083303620/sasami-finds-catharsis-in-nu-metal-on-her-new-album-squeeze

McClary, Susan. 1991. *Feminine Endings: Music, Gender, and Sexuality*. University of Minnesota Press.

McDonnell, Evelyn. 1997. "Rebel Grrrls." In *Trouble Girls: The "Rolling Stone" Book of Women in Rock*, edited by Barbara O'Dair. Random House.

McDonnell, Evelyn, and Ann Powers, eds. 1995. *Rock She Wrote: Women Write About Rock, Pop, and Rap*. Plexus.

McKinney, Kelsey. 2018. "Celebrating a Year of Women in Music." *Village Voice*, March 8. https://www.villagevoice.com/2018/03/08/celebrating-a-year-of-women-in-music/

McMenamin, Lexi. 2023. "The Infinite Gay Joy of boygenius." *them*, March 23. https://www.them.us/story/boygenius-the-record-profile-phoebe-bridgers-lucy-dacus-julien-baker.

McRobbie, Angela. 2009. *The Aftermath of Feminism: Gender, Culture, and Social Change*. SAGE Publications.

@mei_semones. Instagram Account. https://www.instagram.com/mei_semones/

MOCA Toronto. 2023a. "Kapwani Kiwanga: *Remediation*." Museum of Contemporary Art, Toronto. February 24–July 23. https://moca.ca/exhibitions/kapwani-kiwanga-2023/

MOCA Toronto. 2023b. Wall text for Kapwani Kiwanga, *Remediation*. February 24—July 23.

Molanphy, Chris. 2023. *Old Town Road*. Duke University Press.

Momii, Toru. 2021. "Music Analysis and the Politics of Knowledge Production: Interculturality in the Music of Honjoh Hidejirō, Miyata Mayumi, and Mitski." PhD Dissertation, Columbia University.

Morris, Bonnie. 2015. "Olivia Records: The Production of a Movement." *Journal of Lesbian Studies* 19 (3): 290–304.

Moss, Emma-Lee. 2016. "Mitski: 'Why Is It So Hard to Understand That I'm in Control?'" *The Guardian*, June 20. http://theguardian.com/music/2016/jun/20/lo-fi-solo-rocker-mitski-new-album-puberty-2

Muñoz, José Esteban. 2009. *Cruising Utopia: The Then and Now of Queer Futurity*. New York University Press.

Napolin, Julie Beth. 2020. *The Fact of Resonance: Modernist Acoustics and Narrative Form*. Fordham University Press.

Nguyen, Mimi Thi. 2012. "Riot Grrrl, Race, and Revival." *Women and Performance: A Journal of Feminist Theory* 22 (2/3): 173–96.

Nico. 2024. "A Queer History of Blue Eyeshadow, Pop Culture's Time-Honored Symbolic Hue." *Autostraddle*, August 8. https://www.autostraddle.com/queer-history-of-blue-eyeshadow/

NNAMDÏ. 2022. "Live at Lincoln Hall." *Audiotree STAGED*. YouTube video, https://www.youtube.com/watch?v=3LsNtNQDjjI

NNAMDÏ. 2023. "Sudafed." Track 15 on *Please Have a Seat (Deluxe)*. Sooper Records.

O'Connor, Sarah. 2018. "Millennials Poorer Than Previous Generations, Data Show." *Financial Times*, February 23. https://www.ft.com/content/81343d9e-187b-11e8-9e9c-25c814761640

Oliver, Kelly. 2020. "Shame, Depression, and Social Melancholy." *Sophia* 59 (1): 31–38.

Ophelias. 2023. Interview with the author, March 28.

Orgad, Shani, and Rosalind Gill. 2022. *Confidence Culture*. Duke University Press.

Osborn, Brad. 2020. "The Subdominant Tritone in Film and Television Music." *Current Musicology*, no. 107 (Fall): 62–92.

Panepinto, Samantha. 2021. "Longing, Love, Learning: Queer Desire and the Music of Lady Lamb." *GoMag*, October 21. http://gomag.com/article/longing-love-learning-queer-desire-the-music-of-lady-lamb/

Paynter, Eleanor. 2024. *Emergency in Transit: Witnessing Migration in the Colonial Present*. University of California Press.

Pelly, Jenn. 2017. *The Raincoats*. 33 1/3. Bloomsbury Academic.

Peppet, Spencer. 2024. "Shared Language: Niche Internet Subcultures and Making Friends." *Double Virgo* substack, February 3. https://spencerpeppet.substack.com/p/shared-language

Peters, Sean. In Process. "Life in Plastic (It's Fantastic): The Significance of the Cassette Tape to Punk Rock in Four Stories." PhD dissertation, Cornell University.

Petersen, Anne Helen. 2020. *Can't Even: How Millennials Became the Burnout Generation*. Mariner Books.

Peterson, Richard A., and Rodger M. Kern. 1996. "Changing Highbrow Taste: From Snob to Omnivore." *American Sociological Review* 61 (5): 900–907.

Petras, Kim. 2019. *Turn Off the Light*. BunHead.

Phillips, Amy. 2003. "Golden Shower of Hits: You Forgot It in People/The Smell of Our Own." *Village Voice*, August 31. https://www.villagevoice.com/golden-shower-of-hits/

Phillips-Hutton, Ariana. 2018. "Private Words, Public Emotions: Performing Confession in Indie Music." *Popular Music* 37 (3): 329–50.

Picchi, Aimee. 2018. "Millennials Are Much Poorer Than Their Parents." *CBS News*, November 30. https://www.cbsnews.com/news/millennials-are-much-poorer-than-their-parents-data-show/

Pitchfork. 2023. "Supergroup Therapy With Boygenius' Phoebe Bridgers, Lucy Dacus, and Julien Baker." March 30. https://pitchfork.com/features/podcast/supergroup-therapy-with-boygenius-phoebe-bridgers-julien-baker-and-lucy-dacus/

Pollard, Alexandra. 2015. "Why Are Only Women Described as 'Confessional' Singer-Songwriters?" *The Guardian*, April 9. https://www.theguardian.com/music/2015/apr/09/why-are-only-women-described-as-confessional-singer-songwriters

Powers, Ann. 2015. "You've Got a Home: June Millington's Lifelong Journey in Rock." *NPR*, November 19. https://www.npr.org/sections/therecord/2015/11/19/456581427/youve-got-a-home-june-millingtons-lifelong-journey-in-rock

Powers, Ann. 2019. "Billie Eilish Is the Weird Achiever of the Year." *NPR*, December 10.

https://npr.org/2019/12/10/786451710/billie-eilish-is-the-class-of-2019s-weird-achiever

Price, Margaret. 2015. "The Bodymind Problem and the Possibilities of Pain." *Hypatia* 30 (1): 268–84.

Propst, Paula Danielle. 2017. "Sonic Feminism: Intentionality, Empathy, and Emotions at Rock and Roll Camps." PhD dissertation, University of California Riverside.

Rancière, Jacques. 1999. *Disagreement: Politics And Philosophy*. Translated by Julie Rose. University of Minnesota Press.

Rancière, Jacques. 2004. *The Politics of Aesthetics*. Translated by Gabriel Rockhill. Bloomsbury.

Reynolds, Simon. 2009. "Younger Than Yesterday: Indie-Pop's Cult of Innocence." In *Bring the Noise: 20 Years of Writing about Hip Rock and Hip-Hop*. Faber and Faber Limited. Originally published in *Melody Maker*, June 28, 1986.

Reynolds, Simon. 1989. "Against Health and Efficiency: Independent Music in the 1980s." In *Zoot Suits and Second-Hand Dresses: An Anthology of Fashion and Music*, edited by Angela McRobbie. Macmillan.

Richardson, Mark. 2022. "Soccer Mommy Hits the Perfect Balance: Thanks to Producer Daniel Lopatin, the Easy Melodicism of Sophie Allison's Emotive Rock Acquires New Dynamism." *Wall Street Journal*, June 19. https://www.wsj.com/articles/soccer-mommy-hits-the-perfect-balance-sometimes-forever-soccer-mommy-sophie-allison-clean-color-theory-daniel-lopatin-11655504040

Rockeman, Olivia, and Catarina Saraiva. 2021. "Millennials Are Running Out of Time to Build Wealth." *Bloomberg*, June 3. https://www.bloomberg.com/features/2021-millennials-are-running-out-of-time/

Robinson, Dylan, and Patrick Nickleson. 2023. "The Feeling of Knowing Music." In *The Affect Theory Reader 2: Worldings, Tensions, Futures*, 273–92. Duke University Press.

Roy, Elodie Amandine. 2014. "Perfect Pop Story: Sarah Records (1987–1995)." In *Litpop: Writing and Popular Music*, edited by Rachel Carroll and Adam Hansen. Ashgate Publishing.

Royster, Francesca. 2022. *Black Country Music: Listening for Revolutions*. University of Texas Press.

Ruland, Jim. 2022. *Corporate Rock Sucks: The Rise and Fall of SST Records*. Hachette.

Rytlewski, Evan. 2022. Review of *90 in November*, by Why Bonnie. *Pitchfork*, August 23. https://pitchfork.com/reviews/albums/why-bonnie-90-in-november/

Sahim, Sarah. 2015. "The Unbearable Whiteness of Indie." *Pitchfork*, March 25. https://pitchfork.com/thepitch/710-the-unbearable-whiteness-of-indie/

Sanneh, Kelefa. 2004. "The Rap Against Rockism." *New York Times*, October 31.

Schilt, Kristen. 2003. "'A Little Too Ironic': The Appropriation and Packaging of Riot Grrrl Politics by Mainstream Female Musicians." *Popular Music and Society* 26 (1): 5–16.

Scholl, Elysia. 2022. "Bad Bad Hats, The Ophelias at McMenamins Mission Theater." *McMenamin's Blog*, May 31. https://blog.mcmenamins.com/music-review-bad-bad-hats-the-ophelias-mcmenamins-mission-theater-5-25-2022/

Schwartz, Andi. 2020. "Soft Femme Theory: Femme Internet Aesthetics and the Politics of 'Softness.'" *Social Media + Society* 6 (4): 1–10.

Schwartz, Andi. 2024. "'Any Cosmo Girl Would've Known': Collaboration, Feminine Knowledge, and Femme Theory in *Legally Blonde*." *Sexualities* 27 (8): 1430–44.

Schwartz, Casey. 2022. "The Age of Distracti-pression." *New York Times*, July 9. https://www.nytimes.com/2022/07/09/style/medication-depression-anxiety-adhd.html

Seigworth, Gregory J., and Melissa Gregg. 2010. "An Inventory of Shimmers." In *The Affect Theory Reader*, edited by Melissa Gregg and Gregory J. Seigworth. Duke University Press.

Seigworth, Gregory J. and Carolyn Pedwell. 2023. "Introduction: A Shimmer of Inventories." In The Affect Theory Reader 2, edited by Gregory J. Seigworth and Carolyn Pedwell. Duke University Press.

Sellers, John. 2008. *Perfect from Now On: How Indie Rock Saved My Life*. Simon & Schuster.

Shank, Barry. 2014. *The Political Force of Musical Beauty*. Duke University Press.

Sharpe, Christina. 2016. *In the Wake: On Blackness and Being*. Duke University Press.

Sheedy, Sydney. 2022. "Folk Survivals, Spurned Witches, and Thwarted Inheritance, or, What Makes the Occult Queer?" *Arc: The Journal of the School of Religious Studies, McGill University*, no. 50: 1–42.

Sheth, Aarohi. 2023. "How Tarot Helped Me See Myself Beyond the Gender Binary." *them*, July 27. https://www.them.us/story/tarot-helped-me-see-myself-beyond-gender-binary-personal-essay

Shumway, David. 2014. "The Singer-Songwriter and the Confessional Persona." In *Rock Star: The Making of Musical Icons from Elvis to Springsteen*. Johns Hopkins University Press.

Siegfried, Kate. 2019. "Feeling Collective: The Queer Politics of Affect in the Riot Grrrl Movement." *Women's Studies in Communication* 42 (1): 21–38.

Smith, Chris. 2009. "Smells Like Teen Spirit, 1991–2008." In *101 Albums That Changed Popular Music*. Oxford University Press.

Smith, Thomas. 2019. "The Big Read–Beabadoobee: 'I want to live in the '90s!'" *NME*, October 25. https://www.nme.com/big-reads/the-big-read-beabadoobee-interview-space-cadet-dirty-hit-2561006

Snapes, Laura. 2021. "Big Feelings and Nowhere to Go: How Gen Z Reinvented the Power Ballad." *The Guardian*, February 19. https://www.theguardian.com/music/2021/feb/19/olivia-rodrigo-drivers-license-gen-z-reinvented-the-power-ballad

Soccer Mommy. 2022. "Still." Track 11 on *Sometimes Forever*. Loma Vista.

Song, Sandra. 2018. "Don't Call Mitski 'Emotional.'" *Nylon*, August 13. https://www.nylon.com/articles/mitski-be-the-cowboy-interview

Spicer, Mark. 2017. "Fragile, Emergent, and Absent Tonics in Pop and Rock Songs." *Music Theory Online* 23 (2). https://mtosmt.org/ojs/index.php/mto/article/view/342

Spielmann, Katherine, ed. 2020. *Now Is The Time to Invent!: Reports from the Indie Rock Revolution, 1986–2000*. Verse Chorus Press.

Spiers, Emily. 2015. "'Killing Ourselves Is Not Subversive': Riot Grrrl from Zine to Screen and the Commodification of Female Transgression." *Women: A Cultural Review* 26 (1/2): 1–21.

Steingo, Gavin. 2017. "Kapwani Kiwanga's Alien Speculations." *Images Re-vues*, no. 14: 1–20.

Stewart, Kathleen. 2007. *Ordinary Affects*. Duke University Press.

Stiegler, Zack, and Todd Campbell. 2023. *Musical Intimacy: Construction, Connection, and Engagement*. Bloomsbury Academic.

Stone, Aug. 2022. "The Horrors of Britpop: An Interview with Heavenly." *The Quietus*, November 29. https://thequietus.com/interviews/heavenly-band-interview/

Stover, Chris. 2017. "Affect and Improvising Bodies." *Perspectives of New Music* 55 (2): 5–66.

Strong, Catherine. 2011. *Grunge: Music and Memory*. Routledge.

Stryker, Susan. 2024. *When Monsters Speak: A Susan Stryker Reader*, edited by McKenzie Wark. Duke University Press.

Sunrise Movement. 2021. "We Are Sunrise." Twitter video, March 5. https://twitter.com/sunrisemvmt/status/1367901589718073347

Sweeney, Joey. 2007. "Indie Pop Goes Twee." In *The Rock History Reader*, edited by Theo Cateforis. Routledge.

Tamanna, Yusuf. 2019. "LGBTQI+ POC POV." *Notion*, February 1. https://notion.online/lgbtqi-poc-pov/

Tanner, Lindsey. 2023. "CDC Data Shows U.S. Teen Girls 'In Crisis' with Unprecedented Rise in Suicidal Behavior." *PBS News Hour*, February 13. https://www.pbs.org/newshour/health/cdc-data-shows-u-s-teen-girls-in-crisis-with-unprecedented-rise-in-suicidal-behavior

Tasker, Yvonne, and Diane Negra, eds. *Interrogating Postfeminism: Gender and the Politics of Popular Culture*. Duke University Press, 2007.

Tassell, Nige. 2022. *Whatever Happened to the C86 Kids?* Nine Eight Books.

Tate, Greg. 2012. "Black Rockers vs. Blackies Who Rock, or The Difference Between Race and Music." In *Pop When the World Falls Apart: Music in the Shadow of Doubt*, edited by Eric Weisbard. Duke University Press.

Taylor, Jodie. 2012. *Playing it Queer: Popular Music, Identity, and World-Making*. Peter Lang.

Taylor, Neil. 2020. *C86 and All That: The Creation of Indie in Difficult Times*. Inkmonkey Editions.

Temperley, David. 2007. "The melodic-harmonic 'divorce' in rock." Popular Music 26 (2): 323–42.

Temperley, David. 2018. *The Musical Language of Rock*. Oxford University Press.

Temperley, David, and Trevor de Clercq. 2013. "Statistical Analysis of Harmony and Melody in Rock Music." *Journal of New Music Research* 42 (3): 187–204.

Thelandersson, Fredrika. 2023. *21st Century Media and Female Mental Health: Profitable Vulnerability and Sad Girl Culture*. Palgrave Macmillan.

Thilesen, Tonje. 2021. "Bachelor (Jay Som and Palehound) Release Another Bangin' Ode for Queer Desire." *Flood Magazine*, March 24. https://floodmagazine.com/86195/watch-bachelor-stay-in-the-car/

Thompson, Marie. 2017. *Beyond Unwanted Sound: Noise, Affect, and Aesthetic Moralism*. Bloomsbury Academic.

Thompson, Marie, and Ian Biddle. 2013. "Introduction: Somewhere Between the Signifying and the Sublime." In *Sound, Music, Affect: Theorizing Sonic Experience*, edited by Marie Thompson and Ian Biddle. Bloomsbury Press.

Tongson, Karen. 2006. "Tickle Me Emo: Lesbian Balladeering, Straight-Boy Emo, and the Politics of Affect." In *Queering the Popular Pitch*, edited by Sheila Whiteley and Jennifer Rycenga. Routledge.

Tongson, Karen. 2011. *Relocations: Queer Suburban Imaginaries*. New York University Press.

Vallese, Joe, ed. 2022. *It Came From the Closet: Queer Reflections on Horror*. Feminist Press at the City University of New York.

Velasquez, Juan. 2021. "Jay Som and Palehound's New Band Bachelor Is All About Queer Friendship." *them*, May 27. https://www.them.us/story/bachelor-jay-som-palehound-doomin-sun-interview.

Vesey, Alyxandra. 2018. "Playing in the Closet: Female Rock Musicians, Fashion, and Citational Feminism." In *Emergent Feminisms*, edited by Jessalynn Keller and Maureen E. Ryan. Routledge.

Vesey, Alyxandra. 2021. "Selling Sonic Girlhood: Feminizing Indie Rock through Music Supervision on MTV's *Awkward*." *JCMS: Journal of Cinema and Media Studies* 60 (5): 217–42.

Vu, Hana. 2024. Romanticism. Ghostly International.

Waksman, Steve. 2009. *This Ain't the Summer of Love: Conflict and Crossover in Heavy Metal and Punk*. University of California Press.

Wald, Gayle. 1998. "Just a Girl? Rock Music, Feminism, and the Cultural Construction of Female Youth." *Signs* 23 (3): 585–610.

Ward, Jane. 2020. *The Tragedy of Heterosexuality*. New York University Press.

Warfield, Liam, Walter Crasshole, and Yony Leyser. 2021. *Queercore: How to Punk a Revolution: An Oral History*. PM Press.

White, Michael. 2016. *Popkiss: The Life and Afterlife of Sarah Records*. Bloomsbury.

Williamson, Terrion L., ed. 2020. *Black in the Middle: An Anthology of the Black Midwest*. Belt Publishing.

Wills, Dominic. 2001. Liner notes to *Ciao! Best of Lush*. 4AD. https://www.lightfromadeadstar.org/Biographies/Index.htm

Wilson, Carl. 2023a. "*Daisy Jones & the Six* Wasn't Only Inspired by Fleetwood Mac." *Slate*, March 29. https://slate.com/culture/2023/03/daisy-jones-six-fleetwood-mac-broken-social-scene.html

Wilson, Carl. 2023b. "The New Album from Rock's Greatest Supergroup Shows It Finding a Style All Its Own." *Slate*, March 30. https://slate.com/culture/2023/03/boygenius-record-phoebe-bridgers-album-review.html

Wong, Mandy-Suzanne, and Nina Sun Eidsheim. 2016. "Corregidora: Corporeal Archaeology, Embodied Memory, Improvisation." In *Negotiated Moments: Improvisation, Sound, and Subjectivity*, edited by Gillian Siddall and Ellen Waterman. Duke University Press.

Yao, Xine. 2021. "The Craft: QTBIPOC Tarot in Mariko Tamaki and Jillian Tamaki's *Skim*." In *Q & A: Voices from Queer Asian North America*, edited by Martin Manalansan, Alice Y. Hom, and Kale Bantigue Fajardo. Temple University Press.

Yoo, Noah. 2019. "Vagabon Shares New Song 'Every Woman': Watch the Video." *Pitchfork*, October 14. https://pitchfork.com/news/vagabon-shares-new-song-every-woman-watch-the-video/

Zeisler, Andi. 2017. *We Were Feminists Once: From Riot Grrrl to CoverGirl®, the Buying and Selling of a Political Movement*. Public Affairs.

Zhang, Cat. 2023. Review of *The Record*, by boygenius. *Pitchfork*, March 31. https://pitchfork.com/reviews/albums/boygenius-the-record/

Zhang, Jenny. 2017. "Mitski: The Cleanest Death." *Yours Truly*, archived January 30, 2017, at https://web.archive.org/web/20170130095110/http://yourstru.ly/stories/mitski

Zoladz, Lindsay, 2020. "Songs for Feeling Your Feelings: Soccer Mommy Writes Through Her Life on *Color Theory*." *The Cut*, February 27. https://www.thecut.com/2020/02/encounter-with-musician-soccer-mommy.html

Zoladz, Lindsay. 2022. "Mitski Is More Than TikTok." *New York Times Magazine*, March 13. https://www.nytimes.com/interactive/2022/03/11/magazine/mitski.html

Index